D1526643

The Meaning of Life: Religious, Philosophical, Transhumanist, and Scientific Perspectives is the first book to summarize the writings of the important contemporary theologians, philosophers, and scientists on the question of the meaning of life. In addition the book deals with the relevance of death for the question of meaning, as well the importance that the potential scientific elimination of death will have for humanity's concern regarding meaning. Finally the book considers the question of the meaning of life in the context of cosmic evolution and deep time, offering in the end an answer to the question of whether life is or is not ultimately meaningful.

John G. Messerly PhD, currently lectures in the philosophy department at Seattle University. He taught previously at St. Louis University and The University of Texas at Austin. His is the author of *Piaget's Concepetion of Evolution* and numerous peer-reviewed articles. He lives in Seattle, Washington with his wife of 32 years.

The Meaning of Life:
Religious, Philosophical, Transhumanist, and Scientific Perspectives

John G. Messerly

Durant & Russell Publishers

Cover Photo – Skyline Divide near Mt. Baker, Washington State. USA

Copyright © 2012 John G. Messerly Ph.D.

All rights reserved.

ISBN: 0988822415
ISBN-13: 978-0988822412

DEDICATION

For my children—John Benjamin, Katie Jane, Anne Marie,
and Joshua Harrison—that you may live forever
in a good, beautiful, and meaningful world;

And for Jane … that together we may somehow join them.

The Wine of Life keeps oozing drop by drop,
The Leaves of Life keep falling one by one.
Ah, make the most of what we may yet spend,
Before we too into the dust descend...

Oh threats of Hell and Hopes of Paradise!
One thing at least is certain—This Life flies;
One thing is certain and the rest is Lies;
The Flower that once has blown for ever dies.

The rising Moon that looks for us again—
How oft hereafter will she wax and wane
How oft hereafter rising look for us
Through this same garden - for one of us in vain!

~ Omar Khayyam 1120 C.E. (from *The Rubaiyat*)

Contents

INTRODUCTION – THE PROBLEM OF LIFE

Imagine a number of men in chains, all under sentence of death, some of whom are each day butchered in the sight of the others; those remaining see their own condition in that of their fellows, and looking at each other with grief and despair await their turn. This is an image of the human condition.
~ Blaise Pascal

*We are not at one. We have no instincts
like those of migratory birds. Useless, and late,
we force ourselves onto the wind,
and find no welcome from ponds where we alight.
We comprehend flowering and fading simultaneously.*
~ Rainer Marie Rilke

When I consider the brief span of my life, swallowed up in the eternity before and after, the little space which I fill, and even can see, engulfed in the infinite immensity of spaces of which I am ignorant, and which know me not, I am frightened, and am astonished at being here rather than there; for there is no reason why here rather than there, now rather than then.
~ Blaise Pascal

Life can only be understood backwards, but it must be lived forwards.
~ Soren Kierkegaard

*Insignificant mortals, who are as leaves are,
and now flourish and grow warm with life,
and feed on what the ground gives,
but then again fade away and are dead.*
~ Homer

*A precipice in front of you, and wolves behind you,
in your rear; that is life.*
~ Latin Proverb

1

Life is hard. It includes physical pain, mental anguish, war, hatred, anxiety, disappointment, and death. Life's problems are so significant that humans try desperately to alleviate and avoid them. But mere words cannot convey the depth and intensity of the suffering in human life. Consider that persons are starving, imprisoned, tortured, and suffering unimaginably as you read this; that our emotional, moral, physical, and intellectual lives are limited by our genes and environments; that our creative potential is wasted because of unfulfilling or degrading work, unjust incarceration, unimaginable poverty, and limited time; and that our loved ones suffer and die—as do we. Contemplate the horrors of history when life was often so insufferable that death was welcomed. What kind of life is this that nothingness is often preferable? There is, as Unamuno said, a "tragic sense of life." This idea haunts the intellectually honest and emotionally sensitive individual. Life sometimes seems not worth the trouble.

Of course the above does not describe all of human life or history. There is love, friendship, honor, knowledge, play, beauty, pleasure, creative work, and a thousand other things that make life, at least sometimes, worthwhile, and at other times pure bliss. There are parents caring for their children, people building homes, artists creating beauty, musicians making music, scientists accumulating knowledge, philosophers seeking meaning, and children playing games. There are mountains, oceans, trees, sky and flowers; there is art, science, literature, and music; there is Rembrandt, Darwin, Shakespeare, and Beethoven. Life sometimes seems too good for words.

Now assuming that we are lucky enough to be born without any of a thousand physical or mental maladies, or into bondage, famine, or war, the first problems we confront are how to feed, clothe, and shelter ourselves. Initially we have no choice but to rely on others to meet our basic needs, but as we mature we are increasingly forced to fulfill these needs on our own. In fact most human effort, both historically and presently, expends itself attempting to meet these basic needs. The structure of a society may aid us in satisfying our needs to differing extents, but no society fulfills them completely, and many erect impediments that make living well nearly impossible. We often fail to meet our basic needs through no fault of our own.

But even if we are born healthy and into a relatively stable environment, even if all our basic needs are met, we still face difficulties. We seek health and vitality, friends and mates, pleasure and happiness. Our desires appear unlimited. And presuming that we fulfill these desires, we still face pressing philosophical concerns: What is real? What can we know? What should we do? What can we hope for? And, most importantly, what is the meaning of life in a world that contains so much suffering and death? This is the central philosophical question of human life. Fortune may shine upon us but we ultimately suffer and perish, raising the question of the point of it all. If all our hopes, plans, longings, and loves ultimately vanish, then what does it all mean? Our question is not just academic; it penetrates to the core of the human existence.

Given the gravity of our query, we propose a thorough investigation into the question of the meaning of life. We will look carefully at the ideas of those who have thought deeply about the question, allowing our own ideas to slowly emerge. In the process we will follow the truth wherever it leads, never cheating like the youths that Kierkegaard described: "There are many people who reach their conclusions about life like schoolboys: they cheat their master by copying the answer out of a book without having worked the sum out for themselves." We want to work out the answers for ourselves—so that the answers will be our own. Unsure of whether any answers will be forthcoming, we must hope that Rainer Marie Rilke was right when he said: "Live your questions now, and perhaps even without knowing it, you will live along some distant day into your answers." If we do not cheat, and if loving the questions leads to at least provisional answers, then with Francis Bacon we will be able to proudly claim: "Thus have I made as it were a small globe of the intellectual world, as truly and faithfully as I could discover."

May 2012, Seattle, Washington

CHAPTER 1 – UNDERSTANDING THE QUESTION OF THE MEANING OF LIFE

To be, or not to be: that is the question:
Whether 'tis nobler in the mind to suffer
The slings and arrows of outrageous fortune,
Or to take arms against a sea of troubles,
And by opposing end them?
~ William Shakespeare

We are such stuff
As dreams are made on, and our little life
Is rounded with a sleep...
~ William Shakespeare

All my life I struggled to stretch my mind to the breaking
point, until it began to creak, in order to create a great
thought which might be able to give a new meaning to life, a
new meaning to death, and to console mankind.
~ Nikos Kazantzakis

1. The Importance of the Question

Albert Camus opens his essay "The Myth of Sisyphus" with these haunting lines: "There is but one truly serious philosophical problem, and that is suicide. Judging whether life is or is not worth living amounts to answering the fundamental question of philosophy."[1] Karl Jaspers wrote: "The question of the value and meaning of existence is unlike any other question: man does not seem to become really serious until he faces it."[2] Victor Frankl said: "man's search for meaning is the primary motivation of his life" and "... concern about a meaning of life is the truest expression of the state of being human."[3] The contemporary philosopher Robert Solomon considered the question of life's meaning to be "the ultimate question of philosophy."[4] While major philosophers in the Western tradition have had much to say about the goal or final end of a human life, most have not—until the twentieth century—specifically addressed the question of life's meaning, and many have avoided it altogether.

4

In the Western world this lack of concern with the question of the meaning of life was in large part due to the domination of the Christian worldview. During the long period from about the 5th through the 18th century, the question of life's meaning was not especially problematic, since the answer was obvious. That answer was, roughly, that the meaning of life was to know, love, and serve god in this life, and to be with him forever in heaven. According to this view all the suffering of the world would be redeemed in the afterlife so that the sorrows of the world could be seen to have been worth it in the end, when we are united with god. However, with the decline of the influence of this worldview in subsequent centuries, the question of the meaning of life became a more pressing one, as we see beginning with nineteenth century thinkers such as Nietzsche and Schopenhauer. In the twentieth century the question took on a new urgency and western philosophers have increasingly written on the subject. Thus, with the exception of Schopenhauer, our text will concentrate exclusively on twentieth and twenty-first century thinkers.

My own view is that the question of life's meaning is the most important philosophical question, and possibly the most important question of any kind. This is not to say that it should be the only thing one thinks about, or that noble things cannot be done or happy lives cannot be lived without thinking about it. In fact one can think too much about it and, in the worst cases, compulsive analysis may lead to or manifest mental illness. Socrates claimed that "the unexamined life is not worth living," but the over-examined life is certainly not worth living either. Life may simply be too short to spend too much of one's life thinking about life. (The Latin translation of Aristotle reads: "primum vivere deinde philosophare," "First live, later philosophize.") Many persons in all walks of life have lived good and happy lives without thinking deeply about meaning, or without answering the question even if they have thought much about it. In short, philosophers should not overestimate the importance of their ruminations.

Still, such an important question demands some reflection. Without a tentative answer to the question there seems to be no ultimate justification for any action, or even a reason to be at all. To put it somewhat differently: What is the point of living, if you don't know the point of living? Why do anything, if you don't know why you should do anything? You might answer that you live because you have a will to live or a self-preservation instinct; but that merely explains why you *do* go on, it does not justify why you *should* go on. Of course you can certainly remain alive without thinking about these questions, and circumstances force many people to spend their lives trying to survive, leaving little time for philosophical contemplation. But for those with sufficient leisure time, for those that have their basic needs met, do they not have some obligation to think about the meaning of their lives, and by extension the meaning of life in general? Might not such thinking improve their lives and benefit others? If so, then thinking about the question of meaning is certainly worthwhile. For the moment, we will assume it is.

2. What Do We Mean by Life?

What does the word *life* refer to in the question, "what is the meaning of life?" It may be interpreted in multiple ways:

1. What is the meaning of the smallest entities imaginable?
2. What is the meaning of my individual life; what is my purpose?
3. What is the meaning of all human life; of humans generally?
4. What is the meaning of all life; of all living things?
5. What is the meaning of all that exists; of all space and time?
6. What is the meaning of everything that is or could possibly be?

Thus when we ask about life we may have in mind something small and particular, something large and universal, or anything in between. We may wonder about the meaning of the sub-atomic particles that constitute us; of the unimaginably large universe of which we are a part; or even of an infinite number of universes that may intersect our own. But for most people such issues are tangential to their main concern. When they ask about the meaning of life, they want to know the meaning of their individual lives or the meaning of the cosmos as a whole. And these questions are connected. Questions about our individual lives: "Why am I here?"

"What is my purpose?" "Why should I go on?" are related to questions about the universe: "Why does it exist?" "Does it have a purpose?" "What does it all mean?" To fully understand our question we will need to understand this connection.

We may construe this connection in a number of ways. On the one hand, individual lives may be meaningful as part of a meaningful universe; or individual lives may be meaningful even though the universe is meaningless. On the other hand, individual lives may be meaningless even though the universe is meaningful; or both individual lives and the universe may be meaningless. The important point is that there is a connection between the meaning, or lack of it, of an individual life and the meaning, or lack of it, of the cosmos. So although our question may not be perfectly clear, we will assume that *when most people ask the meaning of life question, they are asking about the meaning of their individual life in the context of everything that is.* And this is how we understand the question.

3. What Do We Mean by *Meaning*?

What then do we mean by *meaning*? A simple way to understand the meaning of any word is to consider synonyms. For meaning, we might substitute importance, point, significance, value, worth, or purpose for meaning. The use of synonyms is somewhat imprecise but it largely how we grasp any concept. If I am right about this, then defining the meaning of the word meaning is no more problematic than defining other words used in philosophical discourse. Applying this method, the question of the meaning of life asks for the importance, point, significance, value, worth or purpose of my individual life in the context of all that is.

However, we should go beyond merely appealing to synonyms, and try to specifically determine whether the word meaning is being properly applied in this context. If the word meaning does not properly apply to life, then the question is unintelligible or meaningless. After all, there are questions which appear meaningful but which are not such as: "how high is up?" or "what is the biggest number?" or "how much does red weigh?" Perhaps the question of the meaning of life is like this. Maybe meaning does not apply properly to life at all, anymore than weight applies to color.

Some philosophers have made precisely this claim, arguing that words or symbols have meaning because of what they refer to, but that life does not refer to anything but itself. For example, the word cat means the animal, and a stop sign means stop because they refer to cats and stop signs. They draw their meaning primarily from the conventions of a language or system of signs, and the intention of the speaker. But what does life specifically refer to? It does not seem to refer in this way, and thus does not have meaning in this way.

Yet there are other ways we use the word meaning. For example, we say that smoke means fire, certain spots mean measles, or that punching someone often means you are angry with them. In these cases the word *mean* refers to our drawing a conclusion or casual inference. We see smoke, spots, or punching, and we infer fire, measles, or anger. So unlike words and signs— which draw their meaning *exclusively* from human conventions— casual relationships have meaning that is in some sense independent of human conventions or intentions. (Following Paul Grice, we might say that words and signs have non-natural meaning, whereas casual inferences have natural meaning.)

The example of punching someone is particularly revelatory, since life, like punching, is an activity. If nose punching has meaning—it means that someone is angry—then the activity of one's life can mean that one values knowledge, self-improvement, power, riches, physical pleasure, improving the human condition, etc. When we view activities—punching or human lives—we try to infer the meaning of them from what we see, hear, feel, and think. So the word meaning does properly apply to life in the same way it applies properly to other activities. *Your life is an activity which means that you value or believe, or do not value or believe, that something is worthwhile.* By observing a life we can try to determine what it means—at least to the person living it.

4. What is the Meaning of the Entire Question?

We could then ask a bigger question: what is the meaning of valuing knowledge or riches or pleasure? Your life may reveal that you value them, that they have meaning to you, but what is the value or meaning of your life from a universal perspective? *What does a life mean, not only to the person living it, but from an eternal point of view?* And this is the other part of what we mean when we ask the meaning of life question. We want to know what our lives mean both from the inside, and from the outside.

But even this does not quite capture the full meaning of our question. For we have so far stressed our activity in the world as the manifestation of what life means to us. Yet we are interested not only in what we do, and what the universe does—activities—but in what we and the universe cannot do. We are in many ways impotent; we cannot effect the position of the planets, or alter the fact of universal entropy. We have no control over the initial conditions in which we were born, the physical forces that act on us, or the entire history of the universe which molded and constrains us. Moreover, the universe appears indifferent to us; it does not answer our prayers, or protect us from asteroids or aging. In fact, this is the source of much angst in the modern mind; that the universe is perhaps hostile to us or, at the very least, indifferent to us. It does not seem to care about us, and we are at its mercy.

Since we are in many respects powerless in the face of universal forces, and the universe appears indifferent to our concerns, the meaning we give our life through activities and projects may not be enough to give it meaning. We may want to write a great book or fall in love, but we may not live long enough to do either—through no fault of our own. Thus life may be rendered meaningless regardless of what we do because of our limitations and universal indifference. In asking the meaning of life question then, we want to know the meaning of all activity and non-activity alike, of all that happens and does not happen, of everything. The question, which may be the biggest we can ask, can be stated thus: *what does our individual life mean in the context of all actual, possible, and conceivable things taken in their totality?*

When the question is put like this, we see that it is enormous and probably unanswerable short of omniscience. Perhaps then we will need to reformulate our question somewhat to ultimately make sense of it. But even as posed it is not a meaningless question simply because it is large; and something has gone wrong with philosophy if it reaches that conclusion.

5. Is It Possible to Answer the Question?

Since our question appears so huge and complex—we might say it is the ultimate why question—it raises the question of whether we can answer it at all. I think we can, assuming we make explicit what we mean by answering our question. We cannot expect mathematical or scientific precision. If our expectations are too high, if we expect precision from our answers, we are bound to be disappointed.[5] However, we need not conclude from this that we can know nothing of our subject. From the fact that one cannot know something with certainty or with a great precision, it does not follow that one cannot know anything at all.

Of course, the radical epistemological skeptic makes exactly this claim—we cannot know anything—but there is no knockdown philosophical argument that necessitates that conclusion. In the absence of such an argument, we assume that rational inquiry will be useful in our pursuit of an answer. Reason has proven itself to be a powerful instrument with which to understand ourselves and our world, and there is no a priori reason to think it will not be helpful in our search for the meaning of life. Given our proviso, that we can only expect limited precision from our answer, we now consider what answers to our question might look like.

6. A Taxonomy of Possible Answers

Answers to the question of the meaning of life fall into one of three categories:

1. Negative (nihilistic) answers—life is meaningless;
    a. Affirmation—it is good that life is meaningless;
    b. Acceptance—it is not good that life is meaningless;

2. Agnostic (skeptical) answers—we don't know if life is meaningful;
    a. The question is unintelligible;
    b. The question is intelligible, but unanswerable;

3. Positive answers—life is meaningful;
 a. Supernatural (theistic) answers—meaning from transcendent gods;
 b. Natural (non-theistic) answers—meaning created/discovered in natural world;
  i. meaning is objective—discovered or found by individuals;
  ii. meaning is subjective—created or invented by individuals.

Think of these responses on a continuum:

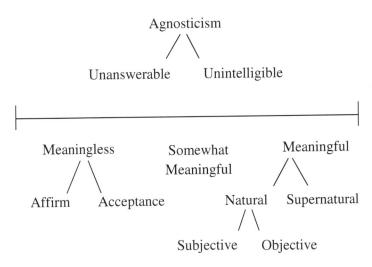

We should note first that agnosticism is placed above the continuum because it is a meta-view. Agnostics are not halfway between the two ends of the continuum; they do not think life is partly meaningful and partly meaningless. Instead they argue that the issue cannot be resolved either because the question makes no sense or, if it does make sense, cannot be answered, or, if it can be answered, we have no way of knowing whether that answer is correct.

Also note that these divisions are not exclusive or exhaustive but guidelines to the plethora of views one might hold. Thus many philosophers' views do not fall clearly within a given label. For example, agnostics may hold that the question is basically unintelligible, yet claim that a few positive things can be said, or that the question is mostly, but not completely, unanswerable. And naturalists typically hold that there are both objective and subjective components to meaning.

This latter distinction between objective and subjective naturalists is particularly hard to draw. If philosophers emphasize subjective values that are dependent on individuals as the source of meaning, we categorize them as subjective naturalists. If they emphasize objective values that are independent of people as the source of meaning, we categorize them as objective naturalists. But many thinkers will blur this line arguing that we both create our own meaning, and discover it in objectively good things. The primary distinction between the two is that those I call objectivists tend to defend the idea of objective value whereas the subjectivists do not. At any rate, categorizing responses helps situate particular views within a broader context, although the specifics of various views must speak for themselves.

7. Meaning of Life Answers and Other Philosophical Views

It may be helpful in understanding specific views if we note at the outset how answers to meaning of life questions are extensions of other views in philosophy. Thus:

Negative answers – These are extensions of metaphysical, epistemological, and moral *nihilism*. If one argues that nothing ultimately matters—not reality, knowledge or morality—then one is probably committed to nihilism regarding the meaning of life. This view can be further divided between those who positively affirm that life is meaningless, and those who begrudgingly accept life's meaninglessness.

Agnostic answers – These are extensions of metaphysical, epistemological, and moral *skepticism*. If one is skeptical of our ability to ask or answer pertinent questions in metaphysics, epistemology, or ethics, then one is likely to be skeptical of our ability to ask or answer questions about the meaning of life.

Positive answers (theistic) – These are extensions of metaphysical, epistemological, and moral *supernaturalism*. If one holds there to be a supernatural basis for metaphysical, epistemological, and moral truth, then one is probably committed to a supernatural basis for meaning.

Positive answers (non-theistic) – These are extensions of metaphysical, epistemological, and moral *naturalism*. If one holds there to be only natural metaphysical, epistemological, and moral truth, then one is surely committed to a naturalistic view of meaning. This view can be further subdivided between objectivists, who think you primarily discover value and meaning in the natural world; and subjectivists, who think you primarily create your own value and meaning in an otherwise meaningless cosmos.

This connection between metaphysical, epistemological, ethical issues, and questions of meaning should be self-evident. It is easy to see that the question "is meaning objective or subjective?" is similar to the questions: "is reality objective or subjective?" or "is truth subjective or objective?" or "is value subjective or objective?" Again the question "what is meaningful?" is similar to the questions "what is real?" or "what is true?" or "what is good?" Thus we find striking parallels between answers to the question of meaning, and answers to other basic philosophical questions.

Such parallels suggest that answers to the meaning of life question must await answers to these other philosophical issues. Unless we know which metaphysical, epistemological or ethical view is correct, how can we know which view of the meaning of life is best? So the problem with choosing between our various answers—nihilism, skepticism, supernaturalism, and naturalism— is that they are parts of differing philosophies of life or world views. And if our view of the meaning of life follows from our world view, then our question becomes: how do we choose between world views? So now we have come full circle. Answers to the meaning of life question depend on our choosing a world view—a metaphysical, epistemological, ethical system. In that case, we could dispense with the meaning of life question entirely and investigate the philosophical world views upon which our view of meaning rests. Then, after determining whether say ethical objectivism or relativism is better supported by reason, our view of the meaning of life would inexorably follow.

But we should not draw this conclusion too hastily. It is not certain that our view of meaning follows from our world view, even if we have one. Furthermore, the process may work in reverse; perhaps our view of meaning comes first, and then leads us to our world view. Yes, it will be difficult to answer questions of meaning first, but it is difficult to answer other important philosophical questions as well. Our question may be no harder to answer than the philosophical questions to which philosophers devote great effort. If efforts to investigate other complex philosophical questions are worthwhile, then so is this investigation. In fact, an analysis of the question of meaning may tell us something important about what is real, what we can know, and what we should value. Thus there is no a priori reason to postpone our pursuit.

8. Objective and Subjective Meanings of Life

To further illuminate the question of the meaning of life, consider the possible relationships between objective and subjective meaning. There are four. It might be that there is: 1) neither objective nor subjective meaning; 2) both objective and subjective meaning; 3) objective meaning but no subjective meaning; 4) subjective meaning but no objective meaning. All nihilists hold view 1; all theists and some non-theists hold view 2, and either may also hold view 3 (Individuals may have not believed or acted in a way conducive to attaining subjective meaning); and the remaining non-theists hold view 4. Agnostics do not know which of these views hold, or if any of them make sense.

Thus there is only one group that holds that meaning is completely subjective—subjective non-theists—all others on our continuum hold that life is objectively something. (Although one could claim that the subjectivists hold *objectively* that meaning is subjective.) Nihilists hold that it is objectively meaningless, agnostics that it is objectively unanswerable or unintelligible, theists and some non-theists that it is, or at least can be, objectively meaningful. Subjectivists differ from nihilists in their belief that life can be subjectively meaningful despite objective meaninglessness.

9. Do Our Attitudes or Personalities Determine Our Answers?

An emphasis on the subjectivity of meaning suggests another idea—that our attitudes or emotions influence our view of meaning at least as much as philosophical considerations, with those attitudes themselves becoming part of one's view of the meaning of life. For example, an agnostic regarding the meaning of life might react optimistically or pessimistically to their skepticism. Nihilists might respond to meaninglessness with irony, fear, defiance, regret, sadness, resignation, or affirmation. A supernaturalist believes that the gods give life meaning, yet may resent this, wishing the gods spent more time minding their own business; or a non-theist may rejoice in their belief that meaning is totally subjective, feeling now free of external constraint. Your personality probably determines and influences your view of the meaning of life as much as philosophical positions or world views. This is not to say that one's attitude changes anything objectively, merely that a subjective attitudinal response is an important component of one's views about meaning—so much so that the attitude may be indistinguishable from the stated philosophical position.

Perhaps these emotional responses or attitudes transcend all our rational analysis, leading to anything from deep satisfaction to despair. In that case our analysis is hardly neutral, but thoroughly infused by deep emotions, prejudices, desires, and feelings. Our philosophy may simply reflect our personality, all philosophy may indeed be autobiography, as a number of philosophers have suggested. In any case, it is probably impossible to separate our reason and emotion from each other. In fact, recent research suggests emotions play an important part in our reasoning.[6] Thus we may believe that life has meaning because we cannot live if we think otherwise; or perhaps we deem life meaningless because we think that will impress existential intellectuals. Who knows the full reasons why we believe what we do?

Yet there is some evidence that abstract reasoning and our emotional responses are separate, and lead to different results when applied to philosophical issues. For instance, consider the "trolley problem," where a runaway train approaches a fork in the track with one person tied to the track on one side, and five persons tied to a track on the other. People are more likely to recommend flipping a switch diverting a train to kill one person rather than five, than they are to recommend pushing a single individual in the train's path to divert it—even though the outcome of the actions is the same in both cases. The typical explanation of this discrepancy, supported by some scientific evidence, is that flipping the switch is a more neutral action that elicits a cognitive response whereas pushing the person elicits a more emotional response.[7]

We just do not know—and scientific investigation has not yet demonstrated fully—how our brain fuses its rational and emotional components to make philosophical decisions, assuming that such a model is even an accurate description of brains; we just do not know how our brains evaluate these issues. It could be that abstract reasoning leads to certain conclusions concerning meaning, but that strong emotional responses resist those conclusions; or it could be that conclusions are arrived at after some dual rational-emotional brain does its evaluating. We cannot be sure. Given this uncertainty as to the role reasons, feelings, and attitudes play in the evaluative process, we should be skeptical of our own philosophical conclusions, remembering that we may be prejudiced or mistaken. But this does not mean our attitudes or emotions are irrelevant; it would hardly be rational to dismiss them. In the end, if we really want to know what is true, we should continually reevaluate all of our tentative conclusions, even though this does not guarantee success. We should remain fallibilists.

10. Do We Ask Because We Are Sick, Decadent, or Unhappy?

Yet, contrary to all we have said so far, Freud may have been right when he claimed: "The moment a man questions the meaning of life, he is sick ..."[8] There is no doubt that the question arises more often when things go badly, than when they go well, but surely the question can arise at any time. What if the question arises all the time? What if one asks it compulsively, and finds that doing so ruins one's enjoyment of life? Such an individual might be obsessive-compulsive in a clinical sense, but compulsively thinking about such an important question is not *necessarily* detrimental to mental health, or a sign of, mental illness. One might enjoy constantly thinking about the question in the same way that others enjoy regularly playing golf or the piano. While the connection between psychological illness and the posing of meaning questions requires further research, we will assume that Freud is wrong, that merely asking the question does not show you are mentally ill. For all we know posing deep questions is a marker of psychological health, the truest expression of humanity as Victor Frankl suggested.

It is also true that the worlds wealthy have more leisure time to ask the question. Might there not be something decadent about the world's most favored posing it, especially when so many others barely survive? Is there not something disingenuous when the well-fed muse over the worthiness of their lives? It is plausible that the *people* posing the question are decadent or disingenuous, but that does not mean the *question* is worthless or trivial. Maybe the well off should be more thankful for their gifts, but that hardly shows there is something wrong with asking the question. For all we know some good might come from their contemplation—maybe the philosophically contemplative will become more generous as a result of it! Thinking does often lead to acting. While psychological states like illness or self-indulgence could motivate the inquiry, we assert that our motivations are sincere, and anticipate that our findings will be beneficial. Often the truths derived from theoretical considerations accrue to all; let us hope that is so in this case.

Finally, in connection with psychological attitudes, we might briefly mention happiness. If we were happy, would we still wonder about the meaning of life? And if not, does that mean that happiness is the meaning of life? We probably do think less about meaning when we are happy, but even then meaning questions may arise. For example, we may be disturbed by the thought that our happiness will not last forever. A number of the thinkers we discuss will address the relationship between meaning and happiness, but we can say a few things at the outset. First, it may be that happiness is the meaning of life. If one is happy, lives well, has a good life, what more meaning could one want? Aristotle thought this way, although it is not clear that he thought the happy life and the meaningful one were coextensive. However, most philosophers do *not* think that happiness and meaning are synonymous, even though both are usually thought of as goods.[9] Here is why.

It seems easy enough to imagine a life being happy without it being meaningful. One could be happy connected to a futuristic happiness machine or torturing children all day, but we would probably hesitate to call such lives meaningful. Alternatively, one's life might be very meaningful but unhappy, as when engaged in doing one's duty or some altruistic activity. If happiness is not the same as meaning then perhaps the moral life is the meaningful life. But that does not seem right either, inasmuch as lives can be meaningful without reference to morality—by engaging in productive work or even in trivial things that we enjoy. Of course it could be that happiness or morality adds to meaning. Perhaps a life is more meaningful than it otherwise would be if it were also happy or moral. But this does not mean that happiness, morality and meaning are the same. Meaning is typically thought to be a sui generis good.

To summarize what we have said so far: our question is important, meaningful, potentially answerable, similar to other philosophical questions, not necessarily symptomatic of mental illness, decadence, or unhappiness, and not obviously the same as happiness or morality. Given such considerations there is not sufficient reason to abandon our study. Since answering our question involves drawing reasonable inferences about the world, we now ask some further questions: 1) what facts about ourselves are relevant to our analysis? 2) why would any facts be relevant to meaning? And 3) what facts about the cosmos are relevant to our analysis? We will consider each in turn.

11. The Fact of Our Death

What facts about us are relevant to our analysis? The obvious answer is that every fact about ourselves is at least somewhat relevant, but we will focus on one of them. Of all the issues that haunt talk of meaning, none is more prominent than death. This is the fact above all others which causes many to doubt life's meaning. It is not surprising that Tolstoy's Ivan Ilyich is consumed on his deathbed with the meaninglessness of his life, or that death figures so prominently in the world's literature about the meaning of life. Consider these haunting lines from James Baldwin:

> Life is tragic simply because the earth turns and the sun inexorably rises and sets, and one day, for each of us, the sun will go down for the last, last time. Perhaps the whole root of our trouble, the human trouble, is that we will sacrifice all the beauty of our lives, will imprison ourselves in totems, taboos, crosses, blood sacrifices, steeples, mosques, races, armies, flags, nations, in order to deny the fact of death, which is the only fact we have.[10]

There is something about these two topics, death and meaning, that binds them. The thought of oblivion or annihilation arouses even the non-philosophical among us. Specifying what it is about one's death that should or should not undermine meaning will be the subject of a number of the thinkers we will consider in subsequent chapters. For the moment we can say a few things.

First, there are multiple views of death. Death is variously said to:

1. render life meaningless;
2. detract somewhat from life's meaning;
3. add somewhat to life's meaning; or
4. be *the* thing that renders life meaningful.

Death may be thought of as bad because life is good or as a welcomed end to a miserable, painful existence. Death has always been inevitable, but increasingly the idea that science will eventually conquer death has taken root—achieved through some combination of future technologies like nanotechnology, genetic engineering, artificial intelligence, and robotics.

Some think the possibility of technological immortality renders human life meaningless, others that life can only attain its full meaning if death is overcome. But whatever view one takes, there is no way around thinking about death in conjunction with thinking about the meaning of life. Life, meaning, and death are bound together in our analysis. If we had three arms or six fingers, nothing much in our analysis of the meaning of life would change; but if we did not die our analysis would be radically different. If all our concerns with annihilation vanished, a good part of what seems to undermine meaning would disappear. To understand the issue of the meaning of life, we must think about death.

12. Facts and Meaning

Turning to our second question: *Why would any facts be relevant to meaning?* I contend that the relationship between facts and meaning has not been properly explored. We said before that we would try to infer the meaning of life from living and our observations of the cosmos. Such inferences depend obviously on the facts about ourselves and the world as best we can determine them, mindful that what we consider the facts and the conclusions we draw from them are always provisional. This should be obvious. Still, modern philosophers have been hesitant to draw philosophical conclusions, most notably about values, on the basis of facts. Beginning in the early twentieth century philosophers began charging those who drew such conclusions with committing the naturalistic fallacy—the fallacy of inferring what ought to be the case from what is the case. For example, it may be a fact that humans *are* innately aggressive, but nothing follows from that about whether they *should* be. Perhaps we should go along with our natures; perhaps we ought to try to overcome them. We cannot thus derive values from facts—assuming the naturalistic fallacy is valid.

While it is generally agreed that a straightforward deduction of values does not follow from facts, the facts seem relevant. From that fact that we are human we may not be able to infer exactly what we ought to do, but on that basis we can infer that some things are good for us—that we ought to pursue food, clothing, shelter, health, knowledge, and friendship, for example. We also assume that some things are bad for us and ought not to be pursued—pain, starvation, ignorance, loneliness and the like. If we were angels, we would not need food; if we were rocks, we would not need friends. Certain facts about us determine, at least to some extent, what is valuable to us. The fact that we have brains encased in skulls that can be pierced by projectiles does not by itself tell us that shooting someone is immoral—the facts do not lead inexorably to the value—but if the facts were different, if projectiles hitting our skulls made us feel good, then the moral prohibition against shooting projectiles at our skulls would disappear. This shows that while facts about our nature do not tell us everything that is good for us, they certainly tell us *something* about it.

Now consider meaning. All sorts of facts are relevant to meaning, as the effect the rise of modern science on questions of meaning makes evident. When the facts changed—when we became convinced that natural selection rather than the gods designed us—our confidence in meaning was shaken. Something about these new facts seemed relevant to meaning. If the fact is that aliens raise us for food, this has quite different implications for the meaning of our lives than if they made us to enjoy infinite bliss with them. The point is not to argue over which of these claims is true, but to point out that facts make a difference in our assessment of meaning, just like they do in our assessment of value. Whether I am an angel, a modified monkey, or live in a computer simulation matters when I assess what I value or whether my life has meaning. This should be nearly self-evident. Thus there can be no deep discussion of the meaning of life unless we possess some truths about ourselves and the universe.

13. Scientific Facts and Meaning

Turning to our third question, *what facts about the cosmos are relevant to our analysis?* The answer is that all of the facts, all the truths of modern science are at least somewhat relevant to considerations of meaning. But why? We have just argued that facts are relevant to meaning, but what it is specifically about scientific facts that make them especially germane? We said in our opening section that the decline of influence the Christian worldview in the West was the catalyst for the meaning of life question taking on a new significance. And what precipitated that decline? While there were certainly many factors, the rise of modern science was a prominent one. The removal of humans from the physical center of their universe with the rise of helio-centrism, and their further demotion as the center of biological creation with the rise of evolutionism undermined much of what had previously given life meaning—specifically, the view that humans were central in the creation and design of reality. In contrast, modern science advances a radically different world view whose foundation is an unimaginably large body of overwhelming evidence, one which continually grows and deepens the original insights of cosmology, biology and other sciences. One ignorant of such ideas has no chance to construct a realistic worldview.

For our purposes then, we must take into account the truths of modern science. One simply cannot have a coherent picture of what the world is like without knowing something of modern science because *science is the only cognitive authority in the world today.* Yes, there are an infinite number of things that science has yet to discover, there may be truths that science cannot by its nature uncover, and there may be other means by which to tease truth from reality than the scientific method. Furthermore, science is not dogmatic, and no matter how well confirmed its theories they are always provisional—open to change in light of new evidence. Nonetheless, we insist that the well established truths of science must be a starting point for our inquiry, as theoretical musings are no substitute for hard-won empirical evidence. Science consists of an immeasurable amount of knowledge—which is daily confirmed by the wonders of the technology it spawns. We simply must begin with the best knowledge of ourselves and our world that we have— the knowledge provided by modern science.[11]

But, as the body of scientific knowledge is vast, which parts of it are most relevant to our inquiry? The problem is that the scientific areas most relevant to our inquiry—anthropology, psychology, sociology, and history—are the least precise of the sciences; and those least relevant to our question—mathematics, physics, and chemistry—are the most precise. On the one hand, we are very certain that $E=MC^2$ or that water is H_2O, but those facts are not of much use in our investigation. On the other hand, we are not sure how to be happy, how to find meaning, or how we decide, even though those facts are quite relevant. It seems then that human sciences, as well as ethics, philosophy and theology are the most relevant to our discussion. But if we say this we are back where we started, trying to choose between world views and philosophies. If a science is to help us in our search for meaning, it must be both precise and germane to our question. Thus we ask: are there areas of science, particularly of the natural sciences, that are both precise and relevant to our inquiry?

I think cosmology and biology would be those sciences. Both are precise and both have important things to say about the meaning of life. Cosmology, broadly conceived as referring to the current state of the universe as well as to it origin and fate, is obviously applicable to our concerns. Biology is also most important; it is the science that tells us what human nature is. Given the particular importance to our inquiry of the origin, evolution, and fate of the cosmos, I suggest we focus on what science tells us about these issues to see the importance of scientific knowledge to our inquiry. Surely what we know, and do not know, about these issue is significant to our pursuit.

14. The Origin, Evolution, and Fate of the Universe

Our universe began about 13.73 billion years ago. (That humans have discovered this fact with such great precision is itself a testimony to the power of science. It is truly an astonishing discovery if you stop to think about it, and we are the first living people who have known this.) Cosmology is very speculative as to what happened before then but competing ideas include that: 1) the universe emerged from nothingness, space and time were created in the big bang and thus there was no space or time *before* the big bang; 2) the universe resulted from the movement or collision of membranes (branes), as in string theory; 3) the universe goes through endless self-sustaining cycles where, in some models, the universe expands, contracts, and then bounces back again; and 4) that the universe grew from the death of a previous universe. The last three proposals all argue that the Big Bang was part of a much larger and older universe, or multiverse if you will, and thus not the literal beginning.

Although the details of these and other competing models go beyond the scope of our inquiry, suffice it to say that none of them, or any other variants likely to be proposed, have any place in them for supernatural gods nor do they say anything about meaning. The universe is indeed mysterious, but gods apparently will not play a role in explaining it.[12] Furthermore, scientific cosmogonies have generally replaced the religious cosmogonies that preceded them, at least among the scientifically literate. The main differences between the two types of cosmogonies are first, that the scientific accounts are supported by good reasons and evidence, and second, that there is no obvious place in scientific accounts for meaning, as there was in religious creation myths. It is not surprising then that so many are threatened by a scientific worldview. Even if we are uncertain which if any of the scientific cosmogonies is true, the damage has been done; what we now know of the origin of the universe undermines our previous certainty about meaning.

When we turn to the future of the cosmos the issue is also highly speculative. The most likely scenarios based on present evidence are that the universe will: 1) reverse its expansion and end in a *big crunch*; 2) expand indefinitely, exhausting all its heat and energy ending in a *big freeze*; 3) eventually be torn apart in a *big rip*; 4) oscillate, contract, and then expand again from another big bang, the *big bounce*; or 5) never end, since there are an infinite number of universes or *multiverses*. (There are other versions of this basic story.) Needless to say, in none of these scenarios do the gods play a role nor do any of them appear especially conducive to meaning. As was the case with the origin of the universe, the important point is that there are alternative scenarios concerning the fate of the universe that were inconceivable to our ancestors, and these alternatives are not obviously comforting. The mere knowledge of these alternatives undermines our certainty about the meaning of our lives.

However, it should be admitted that science is highly speculative on such matters; these are defeasible scientific claims. Nonetheless, I would not bet against the ability of science to eventually unravel these great secrets, as the march of scientific knowledge is inexorable, and no positing of a "god of the gaps" is likely to help.[13] Until then, the good news is that views such as the multiverse theory at least give us reason to reject universal death. If universal death was assured, the case against meaning might be overwhelming, but since it is not we may have a window of meaning left open to us. The bad news is that none of the scientific theories look obviously conducive to objective meaning. To be fair, we probably don't know enough about these highly speculative areas of science to draw strong conclusions about meaning, except to say again that scientific theories about the origin and fate of the cosmos undermine the previous certainty people had regarding these issues.

In between the beginning and end of the cosmos is its evolution. If you think of this inconceivably long period of time it is easy to understand that things must evolve—they change over time. From 13.73 billion years to today there is a long story of cosmic evolution, the outline of which we know in great detail. The important point for our purposes is that human beings, an incredibly late arrival on the cosmic scene, were forged through genetic mutations and environmental selection. *This is beyond any reasonable doubt; anyone who tells you differently is either scientifically illiterate or deceiving you.*[14] Ernst Mayr, widely considered the twentieth century's most eminent evolutionary biologist, and sometimes called the Darwin of the twentieth century, put it this way: "Evolution, as such, is no longer a theory for the modern author. It is as much of a fact as that the earth revolves around the sun." He added: "Every modern discussion of

24

man's future, the population explosion, the struggle for existence, the purpose of man and the universe, and man's place in nature rests on Darwin."

In short, there is simply no way to understand anything about ourselves without understanding evolution—not our bodies, our behaviors, or our beliefs. This is why biology is so crucial to making sense of the human condition; it is *the* science that makes the study of human nature potentially precise.[15] This does not mean that knowledge of evolution tells us everything about the meaning of life, but that *the process of evolution is the indispensible consideration for any serious discussion of the meaning of human life.*

In our limited space we cannot discuss all of the implications of evolutionary biology for understanding human life and nature. Suffice it to say that the evolutionary paradigm has been gradually extended by various thinkers since Darwin to apply, not only to our bodies, but to the evolution of minds and behaviors. When we move the application of the evolutionary paradigm from body to mind we find ourselves dealing with the mind-body problem and evolutionary epistemology; when we move the paradigm from mind to behavior, we are in the realm of the fact-value problem and evolutionary ethics. Possibly we will find in the course of our study that we can apply an evolutionary model to meaning as well. *Meaning may be something that evolves as the species and ultimately the cosmos evolve.*

The importance of evolution for our understanding of meaning extends obviously then from biological to cultural evolution. The future that comes about as a result of cultural evolution may itself be the purpose of life; where we are going, more so than were we came from, may provide meaning. Could it be that the process by which we go from the past to the present is itself an unfolding of meaning? We will consider these ideas in more detail in a later chapter.

15. Universal Death and Meaninglessness

Notice that the possible stories of the origin, evolution and end of our universe present a picture that is not at first glance comforting for human beings. When we look at the facts dispassionately, there does not seem to be room for objective meaning. If all began without purpose, proceeded without design and ultimately ends, then what room is there for meaning? Universal death is the ultimate extension of our own deaths. While we may be able to reconcile ourselves with our own deaths, finding meaning in the legacy of the work or children that we leave, if all ultimately dies, if eventually there is nothing, then what meaning can things have? And that is why the possibility that there is some way to escape universal death, that things are in some way eternal, is so uplifting. Without that proviso, there may simply be no way for there to be meaning.

A way to grasp some of these ideas is through a thought experiment. Imagine that there was a previous or parallel universe where living beings once lived, labored, loved, suffered, and died. But now that world is extinct, and nothing about it remains in any fashion. Now we can say that these now unperceived and non-existing worlds mattered or had meaning to the individuals living in them, but how do they matter to us? How do they matter or have meaning from a universal perspective? What really is the difference between something gone forever that left no trace, and something that never existed?

Of course we could reply that former worlds have some minimal effect on our universe, but it is hard to see how such a small effect, if real, could give their lives universal significance. And if all of reality vanishes in the future, then the same applies to us; it will not matter that we have been. So again we see how crucial the fate of the universe is for meaning. A number of the thinkers we discuss will consider this issue and various ways around the problem. But the point should be clear. Knowledge about the universe is relevant to our discussion of the meaning of our lives, that knowledge comes from science, and the picture is not obviously positive, especially given the various scenarios of universal death. Scientific understanding reinforces the view that the meaning of life is, at the very least, problematic.

16. Conclusion

We conclude our opening chapter by affirming that our question is important, meaningful, and potentially answerable. We are mindful that our attitudes and other subjective components play a large role in the conclusions we draw, but reject the view that those who raise the question are necessarily sick or unhappy. We further conclude that the reality of our own death, as well as the nature and evolution of everything, is crucial to our concerns. And nothing that modern science has learned about the universe is obviously conducive to ultimate meaning. Nonetheless, despite the enormity and complexity of both our question and possible answers to it, we hope that we further thinking might shed light on our subject. Thus, we proceed with alacrity.

CHAPTER 2 – SUPERNATURALISTS: RELIGIOUS ANSWERS

Nietzsche taught me to distrust every optimistic theory. I knew that man's womanish heart has constant need of consolation, a need to which that super-shrewd sophist the mind is constantly ready to minister. I began to feel that every religion which promises to fulfill human desires is simply a refuge for the timid, and unworthy of a true man. ... We ought, therefore, to choose the most hopeless of world views, and if by chance we are deceiving ourselves and hope does exist, so much the better. At all events, in this way man's soul will not be humiliated, and neither God nor the devil will ever be able to ridicule it by saying that it became intoxicated like a hashish-smoker and fashioned an imaginary paradise out of naiveté and cowardice— in order to cover the abyss. The faith most devoid of hope seemed to me not the truest, perhaps, but surely the most valorous. I considered the metaphysical hope alluring bait which true men do not condescend to nibble. I wanted whatever was most difficult, in other words most worthy of man, of the man who does not whine, entreat, or go about begging.
~ Nikos Kazantzakis

I am myself a dissenter from all known religions, and I hope that every kind of religious belief will die out. Religion is based ... mainly on fear ... fear of the mysterious, fear of defeat, fear of death. Fear is the parent of cruelty, and therefore it is no wonder if cruelty and religion have gone hand in hand. My own view of religion is that of Lucretius. I regard it as a disease born of fear and as a source of untold misery to the human race.
~ Bertrand Russell

Man prefers to believe what he prefers to be true.
~ Francis Bacon

Nothing is so firmly believed as what we least know.
~ Montaigne

Any activity pursued in behalf of an ideal end against obstacles and in spite of threats of personal loss because of conviction of its general and enduring value is religious in quality. Many a person, inquirer, artist, philanthropist, citizen, men and women in the humblest walks of life, have achieved, without presumption and without display, such unification of themselves and of their relations to the conditions of existence. It remains to extend their spirit and inspiration to ever wider numbers. If I have said anything about religions and religion that seems harsh, I have said those things because of a firm belief that the claim on the part of religions to possess a monopoly of ideals and of the supernatural means by which alone, it is alleged, they can be furthered, stands in the way of the realization of distinctively religious values inherent in natural experience.
~ John Dewey

It is, I think, an error to believe that there is any need of religion to make life seem worth living...I know several young people who have been reared entirely without thought of churches, of formal theology, or any other aspect of religion, who have learned ethics not as a divine commandment but as a matter of social convenience. They seem to me quite as happy, quite as filled with purpose and with eagerness about life as any one trained to pass all his troubles on to the Lord, or the Lord's local agent, the pastor.
~ Sinclair Lewis

If God made the world I could not be that God, for the misery of the world would break my heart.
~ Arthur Schopenhauer

Morally, a philosopher who uses his professional competence for anything except a disinterested search for truth is guilty of a kind of treachery.
~ Bertrand Russell

1. Religious Answers

A straightforward and emotionally appealing response to the problem of life's meaning is that of the religions. Although they vary widely in terms of their beliefs, generally they attempt to solve the main problems of life—of evil, suffering, death and meaning—by appealing to a god or gods. Religions typically argue that suffering is meaningful or will be remedied, that our needs for justice will be satisfied, and that death will be overcome either in an afterlife, or by escaping the wheel of birth and rebirth, or by some other supernatural scenario.

We begin with a caveat. It is impossible to discuss adequately the wide variety of religious expressions and experiences in the space allotted me—there are about 38,000 denominations of Christianity alone in the world today.[1]

No doubt other religions are varied as well. Differences between denominations are themselves so vast that it is hard to recognize them as the same religion. What does St. Augustine's rejection of biblical literalism or the subtle theology of St. Thomas Aquinas have in common with modern Biblical fundamentalism? How similar is Shankara's absolute non-dualistic Vedanta to the beliefs of a typical Hindu? The answer is, in both cases, not much. Moreover, if you also consider that individuals within denominations have different understandings of their faiths, one could plausibly claim that there are as many types of religious beliefs as there are religious believers! Such considerations make an exhaustive discussion of religious answers to the meaning of life impossible.

Other questions arise too. What is religion? Is Buddhism a religion? Is Christianity? Is science motivated by religious impulses? Is any search for truth ultimately religious in its nature? Soren Kierkegaard, probably the most important Christian theologian of the 19th century, did not think that calling yourself a Christian, attending church, or ascribing to dogmas made you a Christian. So what does make you a Christian, Muslim, or Hindu? The answer is that we really don't know. Given these considerations—that religion is varied, multifaceted, and hard to define—it is obvious that religions answer the question in multiple ways. Thus we propose to look at a few sample religious answers to our question that will serve as exemplars of a religious approach.

2. Leo Tolstoy: A Crisis of Meaning and a Leap of Faith

Leo Tolstoy (1828–1910) was a Russian writer widely regarded as among the greatest of novelists. His masterpieces War and Peace and Anna Karenina represent some of the best realistic fiction ever penned. He also was known for his literal interpretation of the teachings of Jesus, particularly those of the Sermon on the Mount, and he later became a pacifist and Christian anarchist. His ideas of non-violent resistance influenced Mahatma Gandhi and Martin Luther King. Near the end of his life, he finally rejected his wealth and privilege and became a wandering ascetic, dying in a train station shortly thereafter. The following summary is from a short work entitled: "A Confession" written in 1882, and first published in 1884. Tolstoy was one of the first thinkers to pose the problem of life's meaning in a modern way.

Tolstoy says he wrote to make money, take care of his family, and to forget questions about the meaning of life. But later—when seized with questions about the meaning of life and death—he came to regard his literary work as a waste of time. Without an answer to questions of meaning, he was incapable of doing anything. Despite fame, fortune, and family, he wanted to kill himself; being born, he said, was a stupid trick that was played on him. "Sooner or later there would come diseases and death…all my affairs…would sooner or later be forgotten, and I myself would not exist. So why should I worry about all these things."[2] Life was represented for Tolstoy by an Eastern parable where a man hangs onto a branch inside of a well, with a dragon at the bottom, a beast at the top, and the mice eating the branch to which he clings. There is no way out and the pleasures of life—honey on the branch—are ruined by our inevitable death. Everything leads to the truth: "And the truth is death."[3] The recognition of death and the meaninglessness of life ruin the joy of life.

The sciences provide some knowledge but this type of knowledge does not give comfort, and the kind of knowledge which would give comfort—knowledge about the meaning of life—does not exist. One is left with the realization that all is incomprehensible. Tolstoy suggests that the feeling of meaninglessness comes more often to the learned than to the simple people. Thus he began to look to the working class for answers, individuals who both ask and answer the question of the meaning of life. He notes that they did not derive meaning from pleasure, since they had so little of it, and yet they thought suicide to be a great evil. It seemed then that the meaning of life was not found in any rational, intellectual knowledge but rather "in an irrational knowledge. This irrational knowledge was faith..."[4] Tolstoy says he must choose between reason, from which it follows that there is no meaning, and faith, which entails rejecting reason. What follows is that if reason leads to the conclusion that nothing makes sense, then the rational is actually irrational. And if irrationality leads to meaning, then irrationality is really rational—presuming that one wants meaning rather than truth.

Tolstoy essentially argued that rational, scientific knowledge only gives you the facts; it only relates the finite to the finite, it does not relate a finite life to anything infinite. So that "no matter how irrational and monstrous the answers might be that faith gave, they had this advantage that they introduced into each answer the relation of the finite to the infinite, without which there could be no answer."[5] Only by accepting irrational things—the central tenets of Christianity—could one find an answer to the meaning of life. So one must have faith, but what is faith? For Tolstoy "faith was the knowledge of the meaning of human life...Faith is the power of life. If a man lives he believes in something."[6] And he found this faith, not in the wealthy or the intellectuals, but in the poor and uneducated. The meaning given to the simple life by simple people … that was the meaning Tolstoy accepted. Meaning is found in a simple life and religious faith.

Summary – Questions about the meaning of life are crucial, but our rational science cannot answer these questions. Thus we must adopt a non-rational solution; we must accept the non-rational faith of the simple person. Ironically, this non-rational faith is rational, since it provides a way to live.

3. Antony Flew: Tolstoy and the Meaning of Life

Antony Garrard Newton Flew (1923 – 2010) was a British philosopher. Belonging to the analytic and evidentialist schools of thought, he was notable for his works on the philosophy of religion and outspoken atheism. Flew taught at the universities of Oxford, Aberdeen, Keele and Reading, and at York University in Toronto. In a 1963 essay titled "Tolstoi and the Meaning of Life," Flew reconstructs Tolstoy's argument as follows:

1. if all ends in death then life is meaningless;
2. all ends in death;
3. thus life is meaningless.
4. if life is meaningless then there are no desires that are reasonable to fulfill
5. thus there are no desires that are reasonable to fulfill.

Flew denies that the fact of death necessitates the conclusion that life is meaningless; he also denies that for something to matter it must go on forever. One could even argue the opposite, that it is our mortality that gives life its meaning. Flew distinguishes the fact of suffering and death from the evaluative conclusion Tolstoy draws from them—that life is pointless and meaningless. He did not have to draw this conclusion. Tolstoy also assumed the simple people knew something he did not, since they did not suffer from his condition. But he did not have to draw this conclusion either. The fact that simple people do not suffer from despair does not mean they possess knowledge of the meaning of life—maybe they just do not respond to life like Tolstoy does. Moreover, the fact that the peasants were not troubled by life like Tolstoy says nothing about whether their beliefs were true.

However, none of this counts against Tolstoy if we interpret him not as expounding any dogma, but rather as recommending a way to live. Tolstoy preached a way of life not connected with the discovery of a mystic truth. Instead he advocated a religion that can be reduced to ethics and psychology. He found a solution to his condition, not in answers to his questions, but in a religious therapy for his symptoms that is itself devoid of cognitive content. Tolstoy found his answer in faith.

Summary – Tolstoy found the solution to the problem of meaning in his faith.

4. David Swenson: God as the Underlying Unity

David Swenson (1876-1940) was a Kierkegaard Scholar who taught at the University of Minnesota in the 1920s and 1930s. In his article, "The Dignity of Human Life," published in 1949, he argued that humans live not only in the present, as non-human animals do, but in the past and future. This concern for past and future is distinctively human, and connects them with the eternal.

To prepare themselves to live in the present, the young need to be trained to contribute to life, to learn the specialized skills that will help them and others. But they need something else—they need "a view of life."[7] This is not acquired through formal education but is a product of self-knowledge and subjective conviction: "a view of life is the reply a person gives to the question that life asks of him."[8] Essentially, this view of life is that which will give one's life meaning, worth, and dignity.

Swenson notes that all persons desire happiness, so much so that those who are unhappy have "failed to realize [their] humanity."[9] But for thinking beings happiness is not a pleasant momentary enjoyment of the present, but something much deeper. Complete happiness requires that life be infused with "a sense of meaning, reason, and worth."[10] A view of life therefore should answer the following: "What is that happiness which is also a genuine and lasting good?"[11] Aristotle believed that happiness consists in possessing certain really good things that most people desire—creative work, good food, friends, music, aesthetic enjoyment, wealth, freedom, etc.

However, Swenson notes a number of problems with this approach. First, this leaves us with so many desires that we are torn by different impulses, and we do not find the peace that comes from devotion to a single end. Second, we are a captive of desires which themselves depend on an external world over which we do not have control. So if we do not fulfill our desires we may fall into despair. Third, most of these things are not intrinsically valuable. Some, like health and beauty are relative; others, like money and power are only good if one knows how to use them.

A final reason to reject the Aristotelian approach is that some people are way ahead in the race for these goods, as they have been bestowed with talent or circumstances that most of us lack.

Swenson believes this inequality should be deeply troubling to any sympathetic human being, arguing that he cannot enjoy happiness that others cannot have. That which gives life meaning must be inclusive; it must be something to which all have access. It must be something absolute that underlies life and may be found by all who seek it. "The possibility of making this discovery … is … the fundamental meaning of life, the source of its dignity and worth."[12] With this discovery comes true happiness.

These considerations lead Swenson to ethics and then duty which "is the eternal in man."[13] In ethical considerations we discover the infinite worth of the individual; essentially, we find the eternal in human beings. Nevertheless, humans cannot create their own meaning, since they are derivative of the gods, but they can discover meaning by surrendering to the will of the gods. Swenson knows this message may fall on deaf ears, especially of the young. Youth are idealistic and quixotic; the mature are realistic and sensible. But all must accept that we are equally human; this is the moral realization that lends dignity and meaning to our lives.

Summary - Human beings need a view of life in order to find meaning and happiness in life. Swenson rejects the view that meaning and happiness consist of acquiring any number of good things, primarily because this makes them dependent upon particular circumstances. Instead the meaning of life must be something that underlies life and that all can attain. God is this underlying unity in which one can find meaning and happiness.

5. Louis Pojman: Religion Gives Meaning to Life

Louis Pojman (1935-2005) was an American philosopher and ordained minister who received a D. Phil from Oxford University and a PhD from Union Seminary. He was a particularly prolific author of numerous philosophy texts and anthologies used at many universities in the United States.

In his 2002 essay "Religion Gives Meaning to Life," he argued that if classical theism is true then:

1. "We have a satisfying explanation of the origins and sustenance of the universe."[14] Furthermore, if theism is true, then the universe cares about us, the problem of evil

is answered, and the universe is imbued by its creator with meaning. In contrast, the naturalist view starts and ends without value and meaning. From such despair comes further despair.

2. "Theism holds that the universe is suffused with goodness, that good will win out over evil."[15] We have help in the battle of good over evil, and justice over injustice, which gives us the confidence to carry on the fight. We know that good will ultimately triumph. In contrast, in a meaningless universe, nothing matters.

3. "God loves and cares for us."[16] Our gratitude for this love motivates us to live moral lives. In contrast, secularism does not recognize this cosmic love and does not produce moral saints. "From a secular point of view, morality is not only stupid, it is antilife, for it gives up the only thing we have, our little ego in an impersonal, indifferent world."[17]

4. "Theists have an answer to the question, "Why be Moral?"[18] Since god loves you and justice is guaranteed, you will get what you deserve. Thus you have a reason to be moral; doing good deeds is in your self-interest. In contrast, a non-theist has a hard time answering this question since it is so tempting to be an egoist.

5. "Cosmic Justice reigns in the universe."[19] There is moral merit and no moral luck. You will be judged as you deserve to be.

6. "All persons are of equal worth."[20] This follows from being created in the image of god. In contrast, secularism has no justification for this belief, since it is obvious that individuals are not created equal without the god hypothesis. Why should the superior not then dominate the inferior?

7. "Grace and forgiveness—a happy ending for all."[21] We can be forgiven by divine power.

8. "There is life after death."[22] We will all live forever in a blissful state.

Given the above, and given that we are just as free in a theistic world, "it seems clear that the world of the theist is far better and more satisfying to us than one in which God does not exist."[23] Of course, as Pojman admits, the problem is that we don't know if theism is true. He responds that unless one thinks that theism is almost certainly false, one might as well live as if it is true, since it is superior to the alternatives. "It is good to gamble on God. Religion gives us a purpose to life and a basis for morality that is too valuable to dismiss lightly. It is a heritage that we may use to build a better civilization and one which we neglect at our own peril."[24]

Summary – Theism is superior to non-theism in many ways, especially in its ability to provide meaning for life. Thus, unless one is virtually certain theism is false, one might as well live as if it is true. Betting that there is a god is advantageous to the individual.

6. Reinhold Niebuhr: The Self and Its Search for Ultimate Meaning

Karl Paul Reinhold Niebuhr (1892 – 1971) was an American theologian and commentator on public and political affairs. Niebuhr was the archetypal American intellectual of the Cold War, and one of the best-known theologians of the time. His views dismayed both religious conservatives and religious liberals alike.

In "The Self and Its Search for Ultimate Meaning" (1955) Niebuhr argues that the religious inclination derives from "the freedom of the self over its rational faculties." [25] This freedom rejects certain solutions to the problem of the meaning of life—going beyond mere considerations of causation—to discern a creative mystery at the heart of existence. Our attempt to penetrate to the heart of the ultimate mystery invites three basic responses.

The first response posits the self as the most significant, as the ultimate mystery and source of meaning; either the individual or collective self. Niebuhr maintains that this is idolatry that either disproportionately elevates the self or debases it by reducing it to a collective. The second response is what Aldous Huxley called "The Perennial Philosophy."[26] Here the meaning of life and ultimate mystery are found in the underlying unity between self and all being. But even this approach is limited by the finitude of living beings.

The third response finds meaning and mystery in the personality of a god. Niebuhr admits that the notion of the personality of a god is problematic, but so is the idea of personality generally. God judges humans harshly, as too pretentious and prideful; but the severity of a god's judgment is assuaged by the god's mercy. It is only this third alternative that recognizes the discontinuity of self and the ultimate reality that makes faith indispensable. In contrast, the first response is futile—we cannot create our own meaning— and the second is pretentious—introspection reveals we are not identical with ultimate reality. Therefore the third alternative is best, above all because it does not explain the self away as does naturalism or mysticism.

In the end we must have faith in the mystery of "a power and a love beyond our comprehension..."[27] He admits that "there is no way of making this faith or this hope "rational" by analyzing the coherences of nature and of reason."[28] Yet we do have a pragmatic justification for believing that such power exists and will ultimately satisfy us because "it answers the ultimate problems of the human self."[29] We must commit ourselves to having this faith.

Summary – The religious response which recognizes the distinction between self and a merciful god is the most satisfying response to the question of the meaning of life.

7. Philip Quinn: The Meaning of Life According to Christianity

Philip L. Quinn (1940 - 2004) was a philosopher and theologian who earned his PhD in philosophy from the University of Pittsburgh. Quinn was on the faculty of Brown University, and in 1985, he assumed a position as the John A. O'Brien Professor of Philosophy at the University of Notre Dame.

In his 1997 piece, "The Meaning of Life According to Christianity" Quinn dismissed the claim that the meaning of life question is itself meaningless. He argues that we can define two sorts of meanings that life might have: 1) *axiological meaning* (AM)—human life has AM if it has both positive intrinsic value and is on the whole valuable for the person living it ; or 2) *teleological meaning* (TM)—a human life has TM if all of the following are true: a) it contains some non-trivial, subjective, purposes; b) such purposes have positive value; and c) actions performed to achieve these purposes are done with zest. A life might have AM and not TM; it might have TM and not AM, it might have no meaning, or it might have *complete meaning*

(CM)—both positive AM and TM.

Quinn notes that we can tell narratives of human lives or of the human race which might reveal lives containing complete meaning—for Christians the narrative of the life of Jesus reveals such meaning. Quinn considers some problems with living as an imitator of Jesus, for instance, that it might lead to TM meaning but not AM meaning. Such concerns lead him to add something else for complete meaning: "survival of bodily death seems required to secure...positive complete meaning ..."[30] Turning to narrative of the entire human race, Christians have the narrative of salvation history which reveals some of god's purposes; and we can find meaning by aligning ourselves to these purposes. But what of those who do not align themselves with god's purposes? Are they condemned or does god save them? Quinn leaves the question open.

Quinn then addresses Thomas Nagel's claim that from an objective point of view our lives have little significance; a view that the Christian narrative of world history repudiates. Still, humans need remember that from god's point of view, there are other things besides humans that are important. Moreover, Christians should be humble about the meaning they derive from their narratives, as there are many narratives and many interpretations of these narratives, not to mention that other religions have reasonable things to say about the meaning of life. Thus Christians should be modest about their claim that they know life's complete meaning, even if they think Christian stories are best at providing insight. "When Christianity secures life's meanings, it should not offer Christians so much security that they acquire the arrogant tendency to see their story apart from and above all other sources of insight into life's meanings."[31]

Summary – A human life has complete meaning if and only if it: 1) has both positive intrinsic value and is on the whole valuable for the person living it; 2) contains some non-trivial, subjective, valuable purposes that are engaging for that person; and 3) we have immortal souls. From a Christian perspective the world does have complete meaning, although we cannot be certain of how it does.

8. John Cottingham: A Supernatural Conception of Meaning

John Cottingham was born in London and received his PhD from Oxford University. He is presently Professor Emeritus of Philosophy at the University of Reading and an Honorary Fellow of St John's College, Oxford. He is one of the most important proponents today of the view that life is meaningless without a god.

In his recent book, *On The Meaning of Life,* Cottingham defends a supernatural conception of meaning. He maintains that being moral is necessary for meaning in life, but denies that it is sufficient—something else is needed for a life to be counted as meaningful. Cottingham provides two reasons for thinking that a moral life is not sufficient for a meaningful life.

First, Cottingham argues that our endeavors must be successful in order to be meaningful, but that only the god of traditional theism could order reality in such a way that our efforts will truly be successful, presumably because of the existence of an afterlife where justice reigns. Second, he argues that morality must be grounded in a god who issues moral rules that are eternal and absolute, in order for our lives to really have significance. Together these two claims serve as a reply to those who would advance a naturalistic account of meaning. Our moral ends are often thwarted in this world, thus we need another world to confer full significance on our actions. In brief, morality must have an objective basis in a god for morality to really matter.

But it is not only the existence of a god and a soul as necessary to confer meaning that interests Cottingham. He also argues that *belief* in their existence is necessary in order to encourage us to engage in moral projects; that is, the promise of eternal justice and eternal life inspires us to be moral. Thus Cottingham is claiming both that life cannot be meaningful without a god or a soul, and that such beliefs themselves motivate us to be moral. How do we maintain beliefs in gods and souls in the absence of sufficient evidence? This is where the religious life comes in; it encourages the moral actions and religious beliefs that give life meaning. As Cottingham puts it:

> … because of the fragility of our human condition, we need
> more than a rational determination to orient ourselves towards
> the good. We need to be sustained by a faith in the ultimate

resilience of the good; we need to live in the light of hope. Such faith and hope, like the love that inspires both, is not established within the domain of scientifically determinate knowledge, but there is good reason to believe it is available to us through cultivating the disciplines of spirituality. Nothing in life is guaranteed, but if the path we follow is integrally linked, as good spiritual paths are, to right action and self-discovery and respect for others, then we have little to lose; and if the claims of religion are true, then we have everything to gain. For in acting as if life has meaning, we will find, thank God, that it does.32

Summary – Without a god there would be no objective moral principles and without those principles life is meaningless. Furthermore, without a god we could not achieve moral end and without doing so life is meaningless. Finally, without a belief in a god we would not be sufficiently inspired to be moral, and thereby not able to find meaning.

9. William Lane Craig: Life is Absurd Without God and Immortality

William Lane Craig (1949 -) is an American Evangelical Christian apologist known primarily for his work in the philosophy of religion. He is a critic of: evolution, atheism, metaphysical naturalism, logical positivism, postmodernism, moral relativism, Catholicism, Mormonism, Islam, homosexuality, and non-fundamentalist Christian theology. He is a fellow of the Discovery Institute, whose goal is to force public high schools in the United States to teach creationist ideas in their science classes alongside of accepted scientific theories. (As far as I know he has not advocated teaching science in religion classes.) He is currently a Research Professor of Philosophy at Talbot School of Theology, Biola University, an evangelical Christian university.

Craig's piece "The Absurdity of Life Without God"[33] argues that life is absurd without a god. The fundamental reason for this is that without a god both the individual and the entire universe will end without a proper resolution. In that case there would be no hope of escaping our fate and life would lack significance, value, or purpose.

Craig argues that there is no ultimate meaning without immortality because if everything dies it does not matter that previously the universe, the human race, or any individual had existed. Still, immortality is not enough for meaning, since an unending life could be meaningless. For full meaning we need a god, without which humans must accept the view of Beckett, Sartre, and Camus—that life is meaningless. In addition, without gods there is no objective morality and moral relativism reigns.

Craig claims that if we really think about the universe as rushing toward oblivion we should realize that there is no hope or purpose without a god. Without a god we are accidents of nature, and there is no reason or purpose for our existence. With a god there is hope; without a god there is only death and despair. The implications of atheism are strong indeed. The basic problem with an atheistic response is that one cannot live happily with such a view. Either the atheist is consistent and recognizes life is meaningless, or is inconsistent and assumes there can be meaning without gods.

All of this leads Craig to the conclusion that it is a practical impossibility to live as an atheist. Without a god life is objectively meaningless, so atheists pretend that life has meaning by saying it has subjective meaning. Without a god, there is no morality and everything is permissible, so atheists assume there is some other ground for an objective ethics. Without a god there is no immortality where justice will reign, where the wicked will be punished and the virtuous rewarded. Without a god there is no purpose in life, so atheists make up some purpose for it.

The despair of the atheistic view contrasts sharply with the Christian world view. In that view a god exists, we are eternal, and we can be with this god. Christianity thus provides the conditions for a meaningful, valuable, and purposeful life. We can thus live happily.

Summary – Life is absurd without the Christian god, but meaningful if that god exists and we are eternal.

10. Thomas V. Morris: Pascal and the Meaning of Life

Tom Morris (1952 -) is a former Professor of Philosophy at the University of Notre Dame, and founder of the Morris Institute of Human Values. His 1992 book, *Making Sense of it all: Pascal and the Meaning of Life*, puts forth the case for a Christian answer to the question of life's meaning based on the philosophy of Blaise Pascal (1623-1662).[34]

Morris begins by summarizing Tolstoy's argument, which he also finds mouthed by many of the characters in Woody Allen films: 1) Everything in the world, including my life, will end; so 2) All the consequences of my life will end; thus 3) my life and everything else is meaningless. Morris immediately wonders about the connection drawn here between finitude and meaninglessness. Immortality does not render the question of meaning irrelevant, as we can still ask the meaning of immortal lives. Thus no necessary connection between finitude and meaning should be drawn.

To understand the connection between death and meaning we need not then suppose that the absence of death implies the existence of meaning. To better understand this connection between death and meaning, Morris proposes a general thesis of meaning he calls "the endowment thesis." It states that: "something has meaning if and only if it is endowed with meaning or significance by a purposive agent or group of agents."[35] For example, consider human language. Words do not have intrinsic or essential meaning; the word water does not intrinsically mean liquid H_2O anymore than the words "aqua" or "wasser" do. Rather, words are endowed with meaning by linguistic convention, they get their meaning extrinsically. Thus meaning is derivative, it is never intrinsic.

At this point many philosophers conclude that life has subjective meaning—the subjective endowment thesis if you will— meaning that derives from activities we value and enjoy. Morris grants this argument may block one from committing suicide, but it does little else. One problem, if meaning is entirely subjective, is that we can find meaning but compulsive stamp collecting or by being the world's best torturer of innocent children. But don't the goals or purposes around which we center our lives matter? Doesn't it make some difference what activities we orient our lives around? Surely the answer to both questions is yes, and yet a subjective theory of meaning seems to have to answer no to both questions.

Another problem with the endowment thesis is that we must have control over things to endow them with meaning. Morris calls this the control thesis: "we can endow with meaning only those things over which we have the requisite control."[36] The problem is that we have little or no control over those things most significant to meaning like our birth, life, suffering, or death. And without this control we cannot, at least to a large extent, make our lives meaningful.

Morris concludes that if meaning is a matter of endowment, then either there is no objective meaning or some purposive agent, power, or plan gives our lives meaning. The failure of subjective endowment combined with the endowment thesis of meaning leads to objective endowment as the only answer. And that is why Morris says that Tolstoy turned to faith in god, and why so many characters in Woody Allen's films talk about god. Death then does not eliminate meaning, rather it is a sign of our ultimate lack of control over our lives. Thus questions about meaning lead to the search for some ultimate, objective reality to make sense out of them.

The remainder of Morris' book attempts to repudiate skepticism, explain the hiddenness of god, defend Pascal's wager, and shield Christian belief against the skeptics. In the end Morris' analysis relies on the notion of grace, that we have freely received the favor of god. "It is only by the grace of God that faith, reason, and the meaning of life can finally come together in mutual fulfillment."[37] As for the relationship between reason and faith, perhaps Pascal said it best: "the heart has its reasons which reason knows nothing of."

Summary – Meaning must be endowed. But we cannot endow our own lives with meaning because we do not have control over our lives and deaths. Meaning must therefore be endowed by an external purposive agent like a god.

11. William James: Life is Worth Living if We Have Faith

William James (1842 – 1910) was trained as a medical doctor, was one of the most important figures in the history of American philosophy, and was a pioneering psychologist. He is the brother of the novelist Henry James, and friend of numerous intellectuals including: Ralph Waldo Emerson, Charles Sanders Peirce, Bertrand Russell, Josiah Royce, Ernst Mach, John Dewey, Mark Twain, Henri Bergson and Sigmund Freud. He spent his entire academic career at Harvard. The following is a summary of an address James gave to the Harvard YMCA in 1895 entitled: "Is Life Worth Living?"

James began by noting that some answer this question with a temperamental optimism that denies the existence of evil—for example the poet Walt Whitman and philosopher Rousseau. For both of them to breathe, to walk, or to sleep is joy or felicity itself. According to James, the problem with this approach is that such moods are impermanent, and the personalities that experience them are not universal; if they were, the question of whether life is worth living would not arise. Instead most of us oscillate between joy and sadness, between ecstasy and despair, and therefore for most of us the thought that life is not worth living occasionally arises. Almost anyone in the midst of some merriment and suddenly confronted with death, disease, and suffering, would find that their unabated exuberance about life quickly dispelled.

Suicide is evidence that not all individuals are temperamentally optimistic, and many more experience despondency after philosophical reflection. If such reflection about the ultimate nature of things breeds despair, how can reflection combat that gloom? James provides a preview to his answer: "Let me say, immediately, that my final appeal is to nothing more recondite than religious faith."[38] The reason for this is that pessimism results from a religious demand that has not been satisfied. The chief source of this pessimism is our reflective grasp of the contradiction between the facts of nature and our desire to believe there is something good behind those facts. For the credulous such reflective pessimism does not surface, but for more scientific minded there are only two possible solutions to the apparent discord: 1) forgo a religious or poetic reading of reality and accept the bare facts of nature; or 2) adopt new beliefs or discover new facts to reconcile a religious reading of reality with the hard facts of science.

But what new religious beliefs might hasten this reconciliation? James claims that the essence of religious supernaturalism is the view that the natural order is part of a larger reality which in turn gives significance to our mundane existence and explains the world's riddles. These are the kinds of belief that might aid us in our search for meaning. James now presents a preview of his conclusion: "that we have a right to believe the physical order to be only a partial order; that we have a right to supplement it by an unseen spiritual order which we assume on trust ...”[39]

To those who claim that his approach is mystical or unscientific, James responds that science and the scientifically minded should not be arrogant. Science gives us a glimpse of what is real, but its knowledge is miniscule compared to the vastness of our ignorance. Agnostics admit as much but will not use their ignorance to say anything positive about the unknown, counseling us to withhold assent in matters where the evidence is inconclusive. James accepts such a view in the abstract, but neutrality cannot be maintained practically. If I refrain from believing in the supernatural, I express my refrain by acting as if the supernatural is not real; by not acting as if religion were true, one effectively acts as if it were not true. But science has no authority to deny the existence of an invisible world that gives us what the visible world does not. Science can only say what is, it cannot speak of what is not; and the agnostic prescription to proportion assent to evidence is merely a matter of taste.

The benefits of believing in an unseen spiritual world are practical and if we remove this comfort from human beings, suicidal despair may result. As for the claim that such belief is just wishful thinking, James reminds us how little we know of reality relative to omniscience. While such belief is based on the possibility of something rather than its confirmed reality, human lives and actions are always undertaken with uncertainty. If the only way off a mountain is to leap, then you must trust yourself and leap—if you hesitate too long the outcome is certain death. Although we cannot be sure of much, it is best to believe in the practical, in that which helps us live.

For James the issue of whether life is worth living is similar. You can accept a pessimistic view of life and even commit suicide—you can make something true for yourself by believing it. But suppose instead you cling to the view that there is something good beyond this world? Suppose further that your subjectivity will not yield to gloom, that you find joy in life. Have you not then made life worth living? Yes, we can make our lives worth living with our optimism. So it is our faith in an unseen world, in a religious or spiritual world, that grounds our belief in this world's worthiness. Courage means risking one's life on mere possibility, and the faithful believe in that possibility. James concludes with the following exhortation:

These, then, are my last words to you: Be not afraid of life. Believe that life is worth living, and your belief will help create the fact. The 'scientific proof' that you are right may not be clear before the day of judgment ... is reached. But the faithful fighters of this hour, or the beings that then and there will represent them, may then turn to the faint-hearted, who here decline to go on, with words like those with which Henry IV greeted the tardy Crillon after a great victory had been gained: "Hang yourself, brave Crillon! We fought at Arques, and you were not there. "[40]

Summary – We need to be optimistic and have faith in an unseen spiritual world for life to be meaningful.

12. Huston Smith: Meaning from the Generic Religious Standpoint

Huston Smith (1919 -) is one of the world's foremost scholars on world religions and his 1958 book The World's Religions is the best-selling book in its field. He has served on the faculties of Washington University in St. Louis, MIT, Syracuse, and the University of California-Berkeley.

In his article "The Meaning of Life in the World's Religions," (2000) Smith specifically addresses the question of how the generic religious standpoint supplies an answer to the question of meaning. He begins by asserting: "That life is meaningful is religion's basic posit, and the claim can be elucidated both subjectively and objectively, the difference being whether we are thinking primarily of life's meaning for us or, alternatively, trying to determine its meaning in the total scheme of things."[41] Human life is objectively meaningful because it expresses god's infinity; that is, without us god would not be god.

Smith explains this cryptic notion by saying that we are part of a great chain of being which extends down from the heavenly world to the physical world. The distinction between these two worlds is an essential element of the world's religions. We encounter the physical world with our senses aided by our technological instruments (microscopes, telescopes), and we encounter the heavenly world with our intuition, thoughts and feelings. We begin with our human traits and elevate and extend them far enough and we encounter gods. This archetype of human beings is more real than actual humans, ultimately being transpersonal and ineffable. Our purpose from god's perspective is to complete god's infinity by including us, creatures who can flesh out that infinity. And what could be more meaningful than making god, god? And if such an answer is too esoteric, one can meditate or serve god to experience meaning.

Smith now asks whether the basic posit of religion is true but he grants that there is no way to decisively resolve the query. Life and the world come to us ambiguously, so we have no conclusive ground on which to assert its meaning. Nonetheless there are some considerations that weigh in favor of religions' basic posit. They are that the phenomena of life typically present themselves as problems in hope of solutions which call for human effort and the support of others. Religion corresponds well to this with the concepts of suffering, hope, effort, and grace. Thus while the religious view cannot be shown to be true, its vision describes the phenomena of life quite well. It maps categories of reality that appear imbedded in our experience of that reality.

Summary – Religion posits that there is a meaning to life and there are good reasons to think that the religious posit is true.

13. John Hick: Religion and Cosmic Optimism

John Hick (1922 - 2012) is a world-renowned authority and an advocate of religious pluralism. He is often described as the most significant philosopher of religion in the 20th century. He has taught at Cambridge, Birmingham, Princeton, Cornell, and Claremont Graduate School, and is the author of more than twenty five books.

His article "The Religious Meaning of Life" (2000) claims that religious meaning concerns itself with the question of the nature of the universe and our part in it, as well as whether the universe is ultimately hostile, benign, or indifferent to our concerns. His hypothesis is that the great world religions are characterized by cosmic optimism. "That is to say, the meaning of life is such that we can have an ultimate trust and confidence, even in life's darkest moments of suffering and sorrow."[42]

This cosmic optimism means that our current state can be replaced by a better one and in the limitless good of nirvana, for example, meaning is found. Similar claims can be made for other great religions. The Christian gospels present the good news (the notion of eternal punishment undermines cosmic optimism but is not a biblical doctrine according to Hick), Judaism's optimism derives from the special relationship between god and his people, Islam affirms that the universe is benign and our lives will be fulfilled in paradise, and Hinduism teaches that we move toward liberation. Cosmic optimism provides the means by which various religions answer the question of life's meaning. Hick concludes:

> the meaning for us of our human life depends upon what we believe to be the nature of the universe in which we find ourselves. The great world religions teach that the process of the universe is good from our human point of view because its ultimate principle...or its governor...is benign...This is basically a very simple and indeed...obvious suggestion—though not necessarily any the worse for that.[43]

Summary – The world's religions advocate a cosmic optimism which is characterized by the belief that the universe is benign and thusly meaningful.

14. Are Religious Claims True?

The main problem with *any* of these proposed answers is that religious beliefs may be false—the gods may be imaginary. After all, there is no convincing evidence for the gods, an afterlife, or other supernatural phenomena that persuades most philosophers; in fact, much of the available evidence suggests the opposite—as the gods and the afterlife are unseen and miracles suspect. It does us no good to imagine that the meaning of life is to know, love, and serve the gods in this life, and to be with them forever in heaven, if there are no gods or heaven. Of course, we could imagine a world in which there was evidence for gods or an afterlife. If the sky normally talked to us, gods answered prayers, or dead persons regularly appeared and told us about post-mortem existence. But we live in no such world; the objective evidence seemingly contradicts all this. When people pray to the gods there is no effect in the world, the sky and the dead are silent. *Religious beliefs may just be wishful thinking.*

Still, any religious story or belief could be true. A god could have dictated the Koran to Mohammed or given commandments to Moses on a mountaintop. Persons long ago may have risen from the dead, walked on water, or ascended into heaven being pulled by winged horses and flown over Jerusalem accompanied by the angel Gabriel. An angel may have dictated sacred texts in an ancient language onto gold plates which were subsequently dug up in New York—and then translated by a man putting his face into a hat containing magic stones. Any of these stories could be true and their explanation of the meaning of life might then follow. But there seems a good chance that such stories are fictional.

We might make such stories more palatable to the intellect if we insist that they are to be understood, not literally, but allegorically or mythological. To interpret religious stories and beliefs in this fashion makes religion more defensible—since taking them literally often conflicts with what we know of science and history. For example, we might develop theologies consistent with modern science, such as Pierre Teilhard de Chardin's view of god-directed evolution as the meaning of life. Nevertheless, such attempts are still problematic, as they remain tethered to dubious philosophical claims about gods, souls, afterlives, and the like. Thus religious beliefs might solve the question of life's meaning if they are true, but if untrue they are seemingly of no help.

15. Should We Live As If Religious Claims Are True?

Some might reply that even if religious claims are false, we ought to live *as if* they are true. After all, what does it hurt to believe comforting stories that might be true? There may be something to this argument—life is hard so why not find comfort where you can as long as you do not force others to accept your beliefs. But there are many replies to this line of reasoning—that religious belief is basically a docile and good thing—that do not need to appeal to inquisitions, religious wars, human sacrifice, or other examples of religious cruelty over all of recorded history. Nor do they need to appeal to the anti-democratic, anti-progressive, misogynistic, authoritarian, medieval nature of many religious institutions, or to the personal guilt, shame, and fear that often result from those beliefs.

Religious belief may be just harmful in *general*. There is a strong correlation between religious belief and various measures of social dysfunction including homicides, the proportion of people incarcerated, infant mortality, sexually transmitted diseases, teenage births and abortions, corruption, income inequality, and more.[44] While no causal relationship has been established, the 2009 United Nations list of the twenty best countries to live in shows the least religious nations of the world generally at the top.[45] Only in the United States, which is ranked as the 13th best country to live in, would we say that religious belief is strong relative to other countries. Moreover, virtually all the countries with comparatively little religious belief ranked comparatively high on the list of best countries to live in, while the majority of countries with much religious belief ranked comparatively low on the list. In fact often the overlap is striking.[46] While correlation does not equal causation, such considerations should give pause to those who claim religious belief is beneficial. There is good reason to doubt that religious belief makes people's lives go better, and some powerful reasons to believe it makes their lives go worse.

Again none of the foregoing discussion shows that any particular religion is false. But at the very least it is debatable whether religious belief benefits humanity, or that we are better off living as if these stories are true. One could even maintain that religious beliefs are *the* most damaging kind of beliefs that humans can hold. Consider that Christianity rose in power as the Roman Empire declined in the 4th century, resulting in the marginalization of the Greek science the Romans had inherited. Had the scientific achievements of the Greeks been built upon throughout the Middle Ages, it is possible that we might live in an unimaginably better world today. Carl Sagan made this same point some thirty years ago:

> Something akin to laws of Nature was once glimpsed in a determinedly polytheistic society, in which some scholars toyed with a form of atheism. This approach of the pre-Socratics was, beginning in about the fourth century B.C., [quelled] by Plato, Aristotle, and the Christian theologians. If the skein of historical causality had been different—if the brilliant guesses of the atomists on the nature of matter, the

plurality of worlds, the vastness of space and time had been treasured and built upon, if the innovative technology of Archimedes had been taught and emulated, if the notion of invariable laws of Nature that humans must seek out and understand had been widely propagated—I wonder what kind of world we would live in now.[47]

It is conceivable then that had science continued to advance for those thousand years we would now live longer and better lives, or perhaps science might have conquered death altogether by now. It is conceivable we are not now immortal today because of the rise of religion. Granted such conjecture is speculative—our example may seem fantastic—but certainly the rise of religion was a major factor impeding scientific advance throughout the Middle Ages and its stifling effect on scientific advance may still be felt today.

The point is that religious belief is not innocuous. Religion may cause less harm today than it did in the medieval period, but this may be more a function of it having less power than it had previously. If that power were regained, we should not be surprised if the effect were again disastrous. (Anyone familiar with the Middle Ages does not long to go back.) We all may have paid, and could continue to pay, a heavy price for the consolation that religious beliefs provides to so many.

In sum, religious beliefs are problematic and living as if religion is true may be ill-advised. For these reasons it does not seem prudent to ground meaning in religious beliefs. Although any religious story, especially in their more sophisticated versions, could be true, *religious answers to the question of life's meaning are suspect because the truth of religion and its usefulness are suspect.* And if we are to ground meaning on a stable foundation, it is problematic to start with dubious claims.

16. What about Eastern Religions?

Our discussion so far has presupposed a typical Western theistic outlook, and our criticisms were directed primarily at classical western theism. But do our critiques apply to Eastern religions? While we do not have the time to investigate this question in detail, we can say that while some of our objections may not apply to Eastern religions many of them do.

For example consider that the meaning of life in Hinduism is connected with the ideas of karma, samsara, and moksha—all metaphysically dubious concepts. There may be no moral law of cause and effect, cycle of birth and rebirth, or liberation. In non-dualist Vedanta, the idea that atman is Brahman is crucial, but that too is metaphysically problematic. And some branches of Hinduism are openly monotheistic, opening themselves to the exact criticisms previously advanced. Jainism is also plagued by metaphysically doubtful ideas like reincarnation, souls and karma. It holds that the meaning of life is found by overcoming the desires of the physical body in order to achieve bliss and self-realization, but perhaps what a Jain will find after eliminating all desire is starvation and death instead of enlightenment. Again the connection between religious beliefs and practices and the meaning of life is uncertain.

Buddhism fares better since it is as much a philosophy of life as a religion, and hence it is less metaphysical than Hinduism or Jainism. To the extent it provides instructions for good living it is to be applauded, but Buddhism depends on the state of Nirvana and escaping the wheel of birth and rebirth for meaning—both controversial notions. It is also life-negating, with its goal of escaping the cycle of existence, and it requires that we be reborn numerous times. The Taoist idea that reality is one and the Confucian claim that meaning is found in ordinary experience are both problematic claims. So Eastern religions, like their Western counterparts employ dubious concepts to ground the meaning of life, and they are as problematic as Western religions in this regard.

17. Is Life Meaningful Even If Religion Is True?

However, there is another more basic argument that will be noted by a number of the authors we study which severs the connection between religious truth and the meaning of life. And that argument is *that the truth of religion is irrelevant to the question of life's meaning*. In other words, even if some religion is true, it does not matter for our concerns. We can see this if we try to state exactly how it is that religion gives life meaning, something surprisingly hard to formulate.

It does not take much thought to see the problem. For instance, if you are told that your meaning is to be part of a divine being's plan you might reasonably ask, how does being a part of someone else's plan give *my* life meaning? Being a part of your parent's or employer's or country's plan does not necessarily do so. And if you are told that the gods are such that they just emanate meaning, you might reasonably ask, how do they do that? If you cannot be the source of your own meaning, how can something else be? Or if you are told that the gods' love gives your life meaning, you might reasonably wonder why the love of people around you cannot do that. Or if you are told that life is meaningful because you will live forever, you might reasonably wonder how an infinite amount of time makes life meaningful. The point is not that it is impossible for the gods to give life meaning, but that it is not clear how they could do it. They may be irrelevant. If valid these objections completely undermine religious answers. Even if we became convinced there were gods we would still want to know if life had meaning.

In response one might claim that religious belief gives life meaning by positing a benevolent universe that is structured so as to provide meaning at its end or omega point. Perhaps it is eschatology—the branch of theology concerned with the end of the world or of humankind—more than anything else that most persons think of when they relate religion to meaning. So a believer might advance the following argument:

1. Life is fully meaningful if there is a heaven;
2. There is a heaven;
3. Thus life is fully meaningful.

The problem with this argument is that it is circular; it assumes what it is trying to demonstrate. The argument reduces to life is meaningful because it is meaningful. For the argument to work, we need an assurance that premise 2 is true. However we have no such assurance. Moreover, as we have already noted, it is not clear that premise 1 is true either. Alternatively we might try this argument:

1. Life cannot be fully meaningful without a (single?) god;
2. There is a god
3. Thus life is fully meaningful.

This is a valid deductive argument but again both premises are questionable. Moreover, the argument is blatantly question-begging, reducing roughly to the following: life cannot be fully meaningful unless something exists to make it fully meaningful. The upshot of both arguments and ones like them lands us back where we started in our discussion of religion. If religion is true, it *may not* provide meaning; if it is not true, it *cannot* ground meaning.

18. Why We Make No Religious Assumptions

For the foregoing reasons, we will conduct our search for meaning without appealing to invisible, hidden, supernatural entities. This is the natural starting point for those for whom religious answers are not available, but there are also reasons to adopt a neutral starting point even if one is a religious believer. That way if we do find evidence and reasons for life's meaningfulness, these reasons can appeal to believers and non-believers alike. Religious believers can always add gods to the equation if they think that makes life more meaningful; or they can invoke their gods to save meaning, if it appears life would otherwise be meaningless. The point is this. *By starting with a thin set of assumptions, rather than with more philosophically problematic ones that includes gods, souls, and afterlives, we will be more assured of our conclusions and they will have broader appeal.*

To better understand this, consider the parallels between our investigation of meaning in life without gods, and the search for a non-theistic, rational basis for morality. One might hold that morality, like meaning, is completely dependent on the gods' existence or commands. In that case there could be no such thing as morality without a supernatural basis. However, this view has been rejected by most philosophers and theologians, who maintain instead that right and wrong are in some sense independent of the gods. The gods cannot make the right wrong or the wrong right. The advantage of this approach—as in natural law theory for example—is that all rational beings have access to morality simply by virtue of being rational beings, i.e., everyone has access to understanding the basis of morality.

If it is true that morality has a non-theistic basis—say in reason, sympathy, evolution, or a social contract—then by analogy meaning might similarly have a non-theistic basis. In that case the existence of gods would not make any difference for meaning, since the gods could not make a meaningful situation meaningless or the reverse. Meaning would exist, or not exist, independent of whether gods exist or not, and all individuals could seek meaning by using their rational, emotional, or aesthetic faculties.

In the same way that all of us benefit when persons accept reasons to be moral that do not depend on problematic philosophical assumptions like the existence of gods, we would all benefit if persons believed that life was worth living without making extraordinary metaphysical claims. Of course the danger is that our investigation will reveal that there is no meaning, and this may have dire consequences for humanity.

But we can by no means be certain of this, especially when persons convinced that they know the meaning of life create all kinds of havoc in the world. For all we know the discovery of meaninglessness might propel human beings to create meaning, or it might not make any difference at all. People might just go along as they did before not being sure what life means. Since we cannot know what consequences will ensue from the conclusions we reach, I suggest we go forward seeking truth, making as few controversial philosophical assumptions as possible, and hoping that the truth will make us free.

CHAPTER 3 – AGNOSTICS: A MEANINGLESS OR UNANSWERABLE QUESTION

I am an agnostic; I do not pretend to know what many ignorant men are sure of.
~ Clarence Darrow

You see ... I can live with doubt and uncertainty and not knowing. I think it's much more interesting to live not knowing than to have answers which might be wrong. I have approximate answers and possible beliefs and different degrees of uncertainty about different things, but I am not absolutely sure of anything and there are many things I don't know anything about, such as whether it means anything to ask why we're here...I don't have to know an answer. I don't feel frightened not knowing things, by being lost in a mysterious universe without any purpose, which is the way it really is as far as I can tell. It doesn't frighten me.
~ Richard P. Feynman

Maybe philosophical problems are hard not because they are divine or irreducible or meaningless or workaday science, but because the mind of Homo sapiens lacks the cognitive equipment to solve them. We are organisms, not angels, and our minds are organs, not pipelines to the truth. Our minds evolved by natural selection to solve problems that were life-and-death matters to our ancestors, not to commune with correctness or to answer any question we are capable of asking.
~ Steven Pinker

Ubi dubium ibi libertas.
(Where there is doubt, there is freedom.)
~ Latin proverb

It you would be a real seeker after truth, it is necessary that at least once in your life, you doubt, as far as possible, all things.
~ Rene Descartes

Philosophy begins when one learns to doubt particularly to doubt one's cherished beliefs, one's dogmas and one's axioms.
~ Will Durant

Doubt is not a pleasant condition, but certainty is absurd.
~ Voltaire

Men become civilized, not in proportion to their willingness to believe, but in proportion to their readiness to doubt.
~ H. L. Mencken

We declare at the outset that we do not make any positive assertion that anything we shall say is wholly as we affirm it to be. We merely report accurately on each thing as our impressions of it are at the moment.
~ Sextus Empiricus

Trust a witness in all matters in which neither his self-interest, his passions, his prejudices, nor the love of the marvelous is strongly concerned. When they are involved, require corroborative evidence in exact proportion to the contravention of probability by the thing testified.
~ Thomas Henry Huxley

I would never die for my beliefs because I might be wrong.
~ Bertrand Russell

1. Agnosticism

Agnosticism is the idea that the truth or falsity of some claim is unknown or unknowable; it also denotes a basic skepticism toward answering certain questions. Typically agnosticism applies to religious belief, but in our case the idea applies to the meaning of life. The authors we call agnostic believe either that the question of the meaning of life is meaningless or that the answer, if one exists, is unknowable.

In our opening chapter, we refuted the claim that the word meaning properly applies only to words or signs, pointing out that it also applies to activities such as human lives. But there is a more substantive objection to the meaningfulness of our question—that our question is meaningless because it is not *possible* to answer it. Accordingly, a question for which there cannot possibly be an answer is said to be meaningless, at least by supporters of the validity of the objection. Note that this does *not* mean that there may be an answer which we don't know. Rather it means that the question asks for an answer which cannot be provided, thus rendering the question meaningless by definition. To understand this deeper objection we will consider three extraordinary twentieth-century philosophers who advocated this view: Paul Edwards, A.J. Ayer, and Kai Nielsen.

2. Paul Edwards: A Meaningless Question

Paul Edwards (1923 – 2004) was an Austrian American moral philosopher who was editor-in-chief of Macmillan's *Encyclopedia of Philosophy*, published in 1967. With eight volumes and nearly 1,500 entries by over 500 contributors it is one of the monumental works of twentieth century philosophy.

In his 1967 article entitled "Why," Edwards discusses whether or not the question of the meaning of life is itself meaningful.[1] He begins by pondering two issues regarding the use of the word why: 1) the contrast between how and why questions, and the prevalent view that science only deals with how questions; and 2) ultimate or cosmic why questions like "Why does anything at all exist?" or "Why is there something rather than nothing?"

Regarding the first issue, some thinkers insist on the contrast between how and why for religious or metaphysical reasons— maintaining that science answers how questions but only religion or metaphysics answers why questions. Other writers like Hume who are hostile to metaphysics, maintain that neither science, religion, nor metaphysics can answer why questions. Both groups agree that there are classes of meaningful why questions which cannot be answered by science; they disagree in that the former argue that religion or metaphysics can answer such questions, while the latter argue that they cannot be answered at all. In response Edwards makes a number of points. First, how and why questions are sometimes of the same type, as in cases where A causes B but we are ignorant of the mechanism by which it does this. In such cases it would be roughly equivalent to ask, why or how a particular drug works, or why or how some people who smoke get lung cancer but others do not. In these instances, science adequately deals with both why and how.

Still, there are cases when how and why ask different kinds of questions, as when we consider intentional human activity. How we robbed a bank is very different from why we robbed it, but it is false that empirical methods cannot answer both questions. In fact, the robbers probably know why they robbed the bank. True they might be lying or self-deceived about their aims, but still the answer is open to empirical methods. So we might ask the robbers friends about them or consult their psychoanalyst to find out why they did it.

For another case in which how and why questions differ, consider how we contrast questions about states or conditions as in "How cold is it?" or "How is his pain?" with questions about the causes of those conditions as in "Why is it cold?" or "Why is he in pain?" Clearly these are different types of questions. Edwards also notes that why questions are not always questions about the purposes of human or supernatural beings. To ask "Why are New York winters colder than Los Angeles winters?" is not necessarily to suppose that there is some conscious plan behind these phenomena. But it does appear we often answer both how and why questions without resorting to metaphysics.

To summarize Edwards thus far: how and why often are used to ask the same question; when dealing with human intentional actions they ask different questions—how asking about the means, why asking about the ends. Additionally, how questions often inquire about states or conditions, while why questions inquire as to the causes of those states or conditions. It does seem that we can in principle answer all these questions without resorting to religion or metaphysics.

Regarding our second issue, cosmic why questions, Edwards begins by considering what he calls "the theological why." The theological answer to the theological why posits that a god answers the question of meaning. Major difficulties here include how we could say anything intelligible about such disembodied minds, as well as all of the other difficulties involved with justifying such beliefs. Edwards focuses particularly on whether the theological answer really answers the question, mentioning a number of philosophers in this regard: "Schopenhauer referred to all such attempts to reach a final resting place in the series of causes as treating the causal principle like a 'hired cab' which one dismisses when one has reached one's destination. Bertrand Russell objects that such writers work with an obscure and objectionable notion of explanation: to explain something, we are not at all required to introduce a "self-sufficient" entity, whatever that may be...Nagel insists that it is perfectly legitimate to inquire into the reasons for the existence of the alleged absolute Being..."[2] Thus, the theological answer appears to be one of convenience that does not fully answer our query; rather, it stops the inquiry by asking no more why questions.

Edwards differentiates the theological why question—are there gods and do they provide the ultimate explanation?—from what he calls the "super-ultimate why." A person posing this latter question regards the theological answer as not going far enough because it does not answer questions such as "Why are there gods at all?" or "Why is there anything at all?" or "Why does everything that is, exist?" The theological answer simply puts an end to why questions arbitrarily; it stops short of pushing the question to its ultimate end. One might respond that it is obsessive to continually ask why questions, but most reflective persons do ask "Why does anything or everything exist?" suggesting that the question is basic to thoughtful persons. Of course it may be that we just don't know the answer to this ultimate mystery—all we can say is that the existence of anything is a mystery, its ultimate explanation remaining always beyond us.

According to Edwards, while some philosophers take the ultimate why question seriously many others argue that it is meaningless. The reason for this is that if a question cannot in principle be answered, as so many philosophers claim about this super ultimate why question, then that question is meaningless. Critics of this view agree that the question is radically different from all others but disagree that it is meaningless. They respond that ordinarily questions must in principle be capable of being answered to be meaningful, but not in the case of this ultimate question. Yet if a question really cannot be answered, and if all possible answers have been ruled out *a priori*, is that not the very definition of a meaningless question?

Another way of arriving at the conclusion that the question "why does everything exist?" is meaningless, is to consider how when we ordinarily ask "why x?" we assume the answer is something other than x. But in the case of "why anything at all?" it is not possible to find something outside of everything to explain everything. So meaningful why questions are those which are about anything in the set of all things, but if our why question is about something other than everything, then why has lost its meaning because it is logically impossible to have an answer.

Summary - How and why sometimes ask similar questions, sometimes they ask different questions. Theological whys ask meaningful questions, but this does not mean theological answers to such questions are true. Furthermore, theological answers do not answer the super-ultimate why question. The super-ultimate why question is meaningless since there cannot be something outside of everything that explains everything.

3. A.J. Ayer: A Meaningless Question and Subjective Values

A.J. Ayer (1910 – 1989) was the Grote Professor of the Philosophy of Mind and Logic at University College London from 1946 until 1959, when he became Wykeham Professor of Logic at the University of Oxford. He is one of the most important philosophers of the twentieth-century. Ayer is perhaps best known for advocating the verification principle, the idea that statements and questions are meaningful only if we can determine whether they are true by analytic or empirical methods.

In his 1947 article "The Claims of Philosophy," Ayer asks: does our existence have a purpose? According to Ayer to have a purpose means to intend, in some situation "to bring about some further situation which ... he [she] conceives desirable."[3] (For example, I have a purpose if I intend to go to law school because that leads to becoming a lawyer which is something I consider desirable.) Thus events have or lack meaning to the extent they bring about, or do not bring about, the end that is desired. But how does "life in general" have meaning or purpose? The above suggests that overall meaning would be found in the end to which all events are tending. Ayer objects that: 1) there is no reason to think that there is an end toward which all things are tending; and 2) even if there were such an end it would do us no good in our quest for meaning because the end would only explain existence (it is heading toward some end) not justify existence (it should move toward that end). Furthermore, the end would not have been one we had chosen; to us this end is arbitrary, that is, it is without reason or justification. So from our point of view, it does not matter whether we receive a mechanical explanation (the end is universal destruction) or a teleological explanation (the end is union with a god). Either way we merely explain *how* things are but we do not justify *why* things are—and that is what we want to know when we ask the meaning of life question. We want to know if there is an answer to this ultimate why question.

Now one might answer that the end toward which all is tending is the purpose of a superior being and that our purpose or meaning is to be a part of the superior being's purpose. Ayer objects that: 1) there is no reason to think that superior beings exist; and 2) even if there were superior beings it would do us no good in our quest for meaning because their purposes would not be *our* purposes. Moreover, even if superior beings had purposes for us, how could we know them? Some might claim this has been mysteriously revealed to them but how can they know this revelation is legitimate? Furthermore, allowing that superior beings have a plan for us and we can know it, this is still not enough. For either the plan is absolute—everything that happens is part of the plan—or it is not. If it is absolute then nothing we can do will change the outcome, and there is no point in deciding to be part of the plan because by necessity we will fulfill our role in bringing about the superior being's end. But if the plan is not absolute and the outcome may be changed by our choices, then we have to judge whether to be part of the plan. "But that means that the significance of our behavior depends finally upon our own judgments of value; and the concurrence of a deity then becomes superfluous."[4]

Thus invoking a deity does not explain the why of things; it merely pushes the why question to another level. In short even if there are deities and our purpose is to be found in the purposes they have for us, that still does not answer questions such as: why do they have these purposes for us? Why should we choose to act in accord with their plans? And regarding the answers to these questions we can simply ask why again. No matter what level of explanation we proceed to, we have merely explained how things are but not why they are. So the ultimate why question—why does anything at all exist—is unanswerable. "For to ask this is to assume that there can be a reason for our living as we do which is somehow more profound than any mere explanation of the facts..."[5] So it is not that life has no meaning. Rather it is the case that it is logically impossible to answer the question—since any answer to why always leads to another why. This leads Ayer to conclude that the question is not factually significant.

However, there is a sense in which life can have meaning; it can have the meaning or purpose we choose to give it by the ends which we choose to pursue. And since most persons pursue many different ends over the course of their lives there does not appear to be any one thing that is the meaning of life. Still, many search for the best end or purpose to pursue, hence the question of meaning is closely related to, or even collapses into, the question: how should we live? But that issue cannot be resolved objectively since questions of value are subjective. In the end each individual must choose for themselves what to value; they must choose what purposes or ends to serve; they must create meaning for themselves.

Summary - There is no reason to think there is a purpose or final end for all life and even if there were one, say it was to fulfill a god's purpose, that would be irrelevant since that purpose would not be ours. Regarding such a plan either we cannot help but be part of it—in which case it does not matter what we do—or we must choose whether to be part of it—which means meaning is found in our own choices and values. Moreover, all this leads us to ask what is the purpose or meaning of the gods' plans; but any answer to that question simply begets further why questions indefinitely. Thus it is logically impossible to answer the ultimate why question. In the end, the question of the meaning of life dissolves into or reduces to the question of how we should live.

4. Kai Nielsen: A Meaningless Question and Valuable Lives

Kai Nielsen (1926-) is professor emeritus of philosophy at the University of Calgary. Before moving to Canada, Nielsen taught for many years at New York University (NYU). He is a prolific writer, the author of more than 30 books and 400 articles.

In his 1964 article, "Linguistic Philosophy and The Meaning of Life" Nielsen begins by agreeing with Ayer that the purpose of life is the end at which all things aim. The trouble with this answer, as Ayer pointed, is that it only explains existence—but we want more. We want the end to be something we chose, not something dictated from the outside. In short when we ask what the meaning of life is we don't want an explanation of how things are; we want a justification of why things are. And no matter how completely we explain the facts about the world that does not tell us how we should live and die, it never tells us the meaning of it all.

Nielsen offers the example of discovering all sorts of facts about yourself. If after all this discovering you decide to continue to live as you had before, who can justifiably say that you are mistaken? No one is justified in saying that because all of these facts don't imply any values about how to live.

Now suppose we add a god. Even if we assume there are gods, that they have purposes for us, and that we know these purposes, this still does not provide meaning for our lives. Why? Because either we have to be part of that plan or we don't. If we have to be part of some god's plan then these purposes would be the god's purposes not ours, since the gods chose them and we did not. But if we do not have to be part of some god's purpose then we must judge if a god's plans are valuable, we must be the judge of whether to conform to the plan or not. So when we ask "what is the meaning of life?" we are not asking what our purpose is as a divine artifact. We don't want to know what we were made for, or that we were constructed for something which may or may not have value. We want to know if there is something within our lives that gives us purpose, we want to know why we should live one way instead of another. And whether there are gods with plans for us or whether there are some ends built into us by nature, these facts don't tell us how to live and die, they don't tell us the meaning of it all. Only we can decide this for ourselves.

So far Nielsen agrees with Ayer's analysis. But while Ayer concluded that we cannot reason about how to live, that value judgments are subjective, Nielsen argues that we can and do reason about morality—we do give reasons for saying one ought to do x or that x is good. But more importantly, Nielsen suggests that when we ask about meaning we really are asking for more than an answer to questions about what we ought to do or seek or value. Instead we are asking whether what we do matters at all. We are asking "Does anything matter?" But how do we answer such a question? If I say that love, conversation, and hiking are worthwhile to me, that they matter to me, I don't seem to really have answered the question. We want to know if these things are *really* worthwhile, that they ever really matter in some ultimate way.

But does it make sense to ask if anything is *really* worthwhile? For this question to be intelligible we need some standard of worthiness outside of our subjective preferences. Suppose for example that the standard for a worthwhile life is whether or not that life brings about the elimination of all human suffering. In that case one might legitimately say that life is worthless since nothing one does will likely achieve that goal. Such a criterion for worthiness is unrealistic. In contrast Nielsen argues that something is worthwhile not only if it ought to be achieved, but also that it *can* be achieved. If the goal cannot be achieved—eliminating all human suffering—one is bound to be frustrated, which means that one has set the bar too high. Instead we should set the bar more realistically by making our purpose, for example, to "help alleviate the sum total of human suffering."[6] This realistic goal is more conducive to our finding meaning. Often the frustration one feels from not being able to do more leads to questions about meaning. In this case we can probably not understand all suffering much less eliminate it, but we can find meaning by fighting against it. In short Nielsen counsels us to adopt the attitude that some things are valuable.

So what things are of value? Going to art museums or on fishing trips is valuable if you like art and fishing. And to say that such things are not eternal does not detract from their meaning. In fact it might add to it, since an eternity of doing these things would be boring. If we seek a more general answer to the question of why anything is worthwhile we might answer that people's preferences, desires, and interests are the *cause* of them finding certain things worthwhile. The *reason* certain things are worthwhile depends on the thing in question. So questions about the meaning of life do ultimately reduce to questions about ends that are worthwhile—we do find worthwhile what we desire, approve of, or admire. This may seem unsatisfactory, but all we can do is show that questions about what is meaningful or worthwhile are intelligible; they are amenable to general answers. If we value things, they are worthwhile to us.

But what if someone still wants an objective answer to the meaning of life question, an answer that is independent of a particular person's values? Nielsen argues that this question cannot be answered. There simply cannot logically be something that gives meaning to everything else but which is independent of human values. One way of understanding this point is to consider questions like "how hot is blue?" or "what holds the universe up?" These have the grammatical form of intelligible questions, but they are not intelligible. We can answer why certain things are valuable but the question of why things as a whole are valuable is non-sensible. Nielsen argues that if you continue to ask the meaning of life question after you have been told about subjective values, you will never be satisfied and something may be psychologically wrong with you. You may simply be expressing your own anxiety or insecurity.

Summary - We cannot know the answer to the question, why anything. As for the meaning of life, it is more than a question about what is valuable; it asks whether anything is valuable or anything matters. We might say that nothing matters since our efforts to effect change come to so little, but we should find meaning in the little we can do. Thus meaning reduces to subjective ends that we find worthwhile.

5. John Wisdom: A Meaningful but Mostly Unanswerable Question

Not all philosophers agree that the ultimate why question is meaningless. A notable exception was John Wisdom (1904–1993), who spent most of his career at Trinity College, Cambridge, and became Professor of Philosophy at Cambridge University.

In his article 1965 "The Meanings of the Questions of Life," Wisdom asks why some people think the question of the meaning of life is senseless. Because, he argues, answers to why questions appear to go on infinitely. (For example, if we ask what holds up the world and are told that it rests on a giant turtle, we may ask, what holds up the turtle? And if the answer we are given to that question is "super turtle," we can then ask, what holds that up? And if we are told the answer to that question is "super duper turtle," well, it is easy to see that we can just keep asking these questions forever and never resolve the issue.) Asking what supports everything is absurd and non-sensible; there cannot by definition be something outside of everything which supports everything. In short, there cannot be an answer to the ultimate why question.

Perhaps the meaning of life question cannot be answered because it asks for the why of everything rather than of just of a specific thing. Just because some particular thing supports some other particular thing does not mean that something supports everything. Similarly we can say that there is a meaning of something, but that does not mean there is a meaning for everything. Perhaps the meaning of life question is like this. If I tell you why I think something is meaningful, I always refer to something else and you can always ask: but why is that meaningful? So maybe the question of the meaning of life is like asking, what is the largest number? Or what supports everything? These all look for something outside everything but nothing is outside everything. Similarly, there cannot be a big meaning outside all the little inside meanings. (Essentially, this was the argument given by Edwards, Ayer, and Nielsen.)

So when we ask about the meaning of life we are asking about the meaning of the whole thing. And though there cannot be anything other than the whole thing, the question of what the whole thing means is *not* absurd. It's like coming in in the middle of a movie and not seeing the end. In that case, we want to know what went before and after to make sense of it. We want to go outside of our experienced meaning to see the whole. But we might have seen the whole movie and still not know the meaning. In that case we might ask, what did the whole thing mean? *And that is not an absurd question.* We might ask whether the play or movie is a tragedy, comedy, or farce. It is a tough question but it is not senseless. From an eternal perspective I could sensibly ask: what does it all mean?

Of course, we have only seen a small part of the movie or of life; we do not know much about what went before and what will come after. Nonetheless we want to know what the whole thing means; in Wisdom's words we are trying to find "the order in the drama of Time."[7] We don't know the answer but the question is sensible, and we may move toward an answer as we learn more. An answer, if there is one, lies not outside but within the complex whole that is life.

Summary - The question of the meaning of everything makes sense. There cannot by definition be anything outside of everything that gives it meaning, since there is nothing outside of everything, but we can still meaningfully ask: what does the whole thing mean? That question may be unanswerable, but if there is an answer it comes from within life.

6. R. W. Hepburn: An Unanswerable Question and Worthwhile Projects

R. W. Hepburn (1927-2008) grew up in Aberdeen Scotland and was Professor of Moral Philosophy at the University of Edinburgh. In his 1965 essay "Questions about the meaning of life," Hepburn claims that traditionally the question of the meaning of life tends to be conjoined with metaphysical, theological, and/or moral claims—that the gods have a plan; that the cosmos has a goal; that justice reigns, that death must be overcome, etc. What then is an analytic or naturalistic philosopher to do? Typically they argue either we: a) cannot talk intelligently about meaning of life; or b) must talk about meaning in a completely different way from the traditional way to make sense out of the question. Hepburn opts for the latter.

Hepburn asserts that meaningful lives are purposeful, or pursue valuable ends. This implies that meaning is not found but created—we must make value judgments—and this holds whether or not there are cosmic trends or a cosmic order. Moreover, the claim that there are gods is just a claim about the facts and nothing follows from that about what ought to be valued. So nothing about meaning follows from the truth or falsity of religion.

If we switch the question from what is the meaning of life to what is its purpose we encounter two problems. First the idea of the purpose of life presupposes a single purpose, whereas there are multiple purposes for a human life; and second the question suggests that we are a mere artifact, tool, or instrument. Second the issue is problematic because it is incompatible with moral autonomy, since on this account we simply are something to be used. Thus there are two reasons to disconnect questions about meaning from metaphysical and theological claims. First such claims are about facts only and not about values; and second if a life is given meaning by its role as divine artifact, this denies moral autonomy.

Additionally, two other thoughts lead to the separation of metaphysics from meaning. First, if we consider the familiar claim that life is meaningless if death is the end, then we see the irrelevance of metaphysics to our question. There is no obvious connection between finitude and disvalue or between infinity and value. Flowers that die have value while an eternity of meaninglessness is a plausible notion. Thus metaphysical concerns about death do not straightforwardly connect to meaning questions. And second the quest for meaning is often thought of as the possession of some esoteric metaphysical or theological knowledge. Tolstoy thought that peasants had such knowledge insofar as they were not generally as depressed as intellectuals. As a rejoinder Flew pointed out that this does not mean the simple-minded possess some knowledge that Tolstoy did not, but rather that they possess some peace of mind that Tolstoy lacked.[8] Hepburn agrees with this line of thinking which suggests that the answer to our query is not metaphysical but psychological or ethical. All these considerations weigh against the argument that meaning connects with metaphysical or theological claims.

Furthermore, if we consider Tolstoy's or John Stuart Mill's crisis of meaning we see that pursuing worthwhile projects is not enough for meaning either. We may think our projects valuable while still doubting they give our lives meaning. According to Hepburn finding meaning is not merely justifying our projects—we work to feed our children—but being energized and fulfilled by our projects. He contends that meaningful lives fuse these concerns; they pursue (morally) worthwhile projects that satisfy us. But it is not egoistic to want one's worthwhile projects to be compelling or interesting. In fact we often judge lives to be less meaningful because they fail to be morally worthwhile or personally compelling.

The foregoing considerations lead Hepburn to conclude: "The pursuit of meaning … is a sophisticated activity, involving a discipline of attention and imagination."[9] What then of Tolstoy's peasants? Hepburn argues that they possessed a *weak* sense of knowing how to live. They had not mastered techniques to deal with depression—they were not depressed—rather they were unaware of the kind of thoughts a Tolstoy or Mill might have. They knew *how* to live like babies know how to cry. But this weak sense of meaning is not enough if we see meaning as a *problem* that demands a reply. In that case we demand a *stronger* response to the question of how to live than the peasants gave; a response to the problematic context of life's difficulties and possible means of overcoming them.

All of this raises an interesting question: "Could a man's life have or fail to have meaning, without his knowing that it did or did not have meaning?"[10] On the one hand, Hepburn contends that lives could be meaningful without the people living those lives being aware of their meaning—for example if they did not realize the valuable contributions they made. On the other hand, it is odd to say that someone did not know the meaning of their life but that a biographer would discover it later. Regarding those who are "unreflectively happy or unhappy, it would be most natural to say that they have neither found nor failed to find the meaning of life."[11] Tolstoy's peasants are of the unreflective type, they have not found the meaning of life because they have never seen it as problematic; whereas if Tolstoy achieved their peace of mind he could be said to have found meaning, as he was aware of the problematic elements of life. Therefore those who have never been troubled by life's difficulties cannot be said to have solved a problem.

What is particularly difficult to reconcile with meaning is death. Some, like Tolstoy, believe that without immortality there is no meaning; others claim that death or immortality are irrelevant to meaning. Hepburn argues that though mortality and meaning may be compatible, one may still be troubled by the thought that death detracts from meaning. More generally we might be troubled that the effort we put forth in life is so great compared with the effect of our lives. (Yeats captured this thought: "When I think of all the books I have read, wise words heard, anxieties given to parents … my own life seems to me a preparation for something that never happens."[12])

Hepburn states that disappointment in life might take one of two forms. From an external standpoint an observer of your life would be disappointed that you did not fulfill your promise—in Hepburn's analogy they expected a symphony but only witnessed an overture—or from an internal perspective you might be disappointed in yourself, that you did not produce the music you wanted to. Philosophers sometimes argue that you should not be disappointed. Even if you are not immortal, even if you do not write a great symphony, a short piece of music has value nonetheless. Better not to worry about your shortcomings; better to enjoy a life and its small accomplishments. But what of endless suffering leading to death? Does this not make life futile and meaningless? Hepburn claims that some lives may afford the possibility of meaning, while others may not.

He also recognizes a fundamental difference between the naturalist and the theist. The naturalist will always find a tension between a subjective anthropocentric view in which a life can have meaning, and the objective *sub species aeternitatis* view from where it is hard to see meaning. For the theist there is a harmony between meaning in human life and eternal meaning. Without such harmony, the theist claims, there cannot be meaning in life.

Throughout his discussion Hepburn assumed that Christian theism provides a satisfactory answer to the meaning of life question. But now he notes two challenges to this view: 1) that no afterlife could compensate for the suffering in this world or, using the musical analogy, if the overture was bad enough no music that followed could compensate; and 2) that there it is morally objectionable that a god's plan give life meaning inasmuch as this conflicts with moral autonomy.

Hepburn regards this second objection as particularly strong. If the otherness and power of a god is stressed, then human moral judgment will be trivial compared to divine purpose. Nonetheless worshipping a god does not have to entail the abandonment of moral autonomy; it could be directed to the moral perfection and beauty of a god, and to actively internalizing that perfection as far as possible. So worshipping need not abrogate moral autonomy, and neither does acting in accord with what one believes is a god's will. All one needs are good reasons to believe that following a god's will is a better way to achieve some good than transgressing that will. Of course none of this shows that there are gods; that they have qualities one ought to worship; that these qualities are internally consistent or consistent with the world; that infinite gods have finite qualities; or that we could know their will. Thus the problem with the theistic conception of meaning is all of the difficulties with the plausibility of theism itself.

By contrast naturalistic philosophers seek a substitute for the immortality that gives the theist meaning. Rejecting religious metaphysics they try to find meaning only in beliefs they accept. This leaves naturalists open to the disturbing prospect that life may have no comprehensive, discoverable, or possible meaning. Hepburn concludes that we should consider the more limited notion of meaning—that there can be subjective purposes and better ways of living.

Summary - Hepburn maintains that theological and metaphysical realities are of little help in answering meaning questions. Instead we should focus on worthwhile projects that we find satisfying and interesting. We probably cannot answer the question of the meaning of life from a comprehensive, external point of view, but we can try to live as well as possible.

7. The Argument Thus Far

Edwards, Ayer, and Nielsen all argued that the *why anything* question cannot be answered. Edwards left it at that while Ayer and Nielsen were willing to take the argument a step further and ask how we should live. Ayer argued that this more practical question can only be answered subjectively, while Nielsen was more optimistic about our ability to reason objectively about moral matters. Wisdom claimed that the question is meaningful and intelligible, but probably unanswerable. Hepburn agrees that the question is meaningful and unanswerable, carefully explicating why religion and metaphysics cannot answer the question. Like these previous authors he also adds that meaning is best found in our subjective purposes.

8. Robert Nozick: How Can Anything *Glow* Meaning?

Robert Nozick (1938 – 2002) was an American political philosopher and professor at Harvard University. He is best known for his book *Anarchy, State, and Utopia* (1974), a libertarian answer to John Rawls's *A Theory of Justice* (1971). In chapter six of his 1981 book, Philosophical Explanations, Nozick addresses the question of the meaning of life.

"The question of what meaning our life has, or can have, is of utmost significance to us."[13] Yet we try to hide our concern about the question by making jokes about it. So what do we seek when asking this question? Basically we want to know how to live in order to achieve meaning. We may choose to continue our present life in the suburbs, change our lives completely by moving to a cave and meditating daily, or opt for a number of other possibilities. But how is one to know which life is really most meaningful from an infinite number of choices? "Could any formula answer the question satisfactorily?"[14]

A formula might be the meaning of life: seek union with a god, be productive, search for meaning, find love, etc. Nozick finds none of the proposed formulas satisfactory. Do we then seek some secret verbal formula or doctrine? Suppose there were a secret formula possessed by the sages. Would they give it to you? Would you be able to understand it? Maybe the sage will give you a ridiculous answer just to get you thinking. Perhaps it is not words at all but the physical presence of the sage that will convey the truth the questioner seeks. By being in their presence over time you may come to understand the meaning of life even if meaning transcends verbal formulas. Nozick doubts all of this.

Now what about the idea that the meaning of life is connected with a god's will, design or plan? In this case the meaning of life is to fulfill the role the gods have fashioned for us. If we were designed and created for a purpose connected to a plan then that is what we are for—our purpose would be to fulfill that plan. Different theological variants of your purpose might be to merge with the gods or enjoy eternal bliss in their presence.

Now let us suppose there are gods, that they have created us for a purpose, and that we can know that purpose. The question is, even knowing that all of the above is true, how does this provide meaning for our lives? Suppose for example that our role in the divine plan was trivial. Say it was to provide CO^2 for plants. Would that be enough? No, you probably think your role needs to be more important than that. Not just any role will do, especially not a trivial one.

Moreover, we want our role to "be positive, perhaps even exalted."[15] We don't want our role to be providing food for space aliens, however good we taste to them. Instead we want our role to focus on important aspects of ourselves like our intelligence or morality. But even supposing that we were to aid the space aliens by exercising our intelligence and morality that would not give us meaning if there was no point to us helping them. We want there to be a point to the whole thing.

Nozick argues that there are two ways we could be part of or fulfill a god's plan: 1) by acting in a certain way; or 2) by acting in any way whatsoever. Concerning the first we may wonder why we should fulfill the plan, and about both we may wonder how being a part of the plan gives our lives meaning. It may be good from the god's perspective that we carry out their plans, but how does that show it is good for *us*, since we might be sacrificed for some greater good? And even if it were good for us to fulfill their plan how does that provide *us* meaning? We might think it good to say help our neighbors and still doubt that life has meaning. So again how do the god's purposes give our lives meaning? Merely playing a role or fulfilling a purpose in someone else's plan does not give *your* life meaning. If that were the case your parent's plan for you would be enough to give your life meaning. So in addition to having a purpose, the purpose must be meaningful. And how do a god's purposes guarantee meaning? Nozick does not see how they could.

Accordingly you can: 1) accept meaninglessness, and either go on with your life or end it; 2) discover meaning; or 3) create meaning. Nozick claims 1 has limited appeal, 2 is impossible, so we are left with 3. You can create meaning by fitting into some larger purpose but, if you do not think there is any such purpose, you can seek meaning in some creative activity that you find intrinsically valuable. Engaged in such creative work, worries about meaninglessness might evaporate. But soon concerns about meaning return, when you wonder whether your creative activity has purpose. Might even the exercise of my powers be ultimately pointless? (This sends a chill through someone writing a book.)

Now suppose my creation, for example a book on the meaning of life, fits into my larger plan, to share my discoveries with others or leave something to my children. Does this give my creative activity meaning? Nozick doubts this solution will work since the argument is circular. That is, my creative activity is given meaning by my larger plan which in turn has meaning because of my creative activity. Moreover, what is the point of the larger plan? It was only chosen to give a meaning to life, but that does not show us what the plan is or what it should be.

This all brings Nozick back to the question of how our meaning connects to a god's purposes. If it is important that our lives have meaning, then maybe the god's lives are made meaningful by providing our lives with meaning, and our lives made meaningful by fitting into the god's plans. But if we and the gods can find meaning together, then why can't two people find it similarly? If they can then we do not need gods for meaning. Nor does it help to say that knowing the god's plan will give life meaning. First of all many religions say it impossible to know a god's plans, and even if we did know the plan this still does not show that the plan is meaningful. Just because a god created the world does not mean the purpose for creating it was meaningful, anymore than animals created by scientists in the future would necessarily have meaningful lives. It might be that directly experiencing a god would resolve all doubts about meaning. But still how can a god ground meaning? How can we encounter meaning? How can all questions about meaning end? "How, in the world (or out of it) can there be something whose nature contains meaning, something which just glows meaning?"[16]

Summary – A god's purposes do not guarantee meaning for you. Rather than accept meaninglessness or try to discover meaning, Nozick counsels us to create meaning. Still, this might not be enough to really give our lives meaning. In the end, does anything emanate meaning? Can anything glow meaning? Nozick is skeptical.

9. W.D. Joske: A Meaningful Question: A Meaningless Life

W.D. Joske (1928-) is professor emeritus at the University of Tasmania in Australia. In his 1974 article "Philosophy and the Meaning of Life," he notes that ordinary people often assume that philosophers think deeply about the meaning of life and related problems. Consequently they fear philosophy because they think it leads to the conclusion that life is meaningless. A typical response from professional philosophers is that this fear is unfounded since life "cannot be shown to be either significant or insignificant by philosophy."[17] But Joske argues that this view is mistaken and that one should indeed be afraid of philosophy. It may have something disconcerting to say about the meaning of life after all.

Joske claims that the question of the meaning of life is both vague (its meaning is unclear) and ambiguous (it has many meanings.) The questioner may be asking the meaning of: 1) all life; 2) human life; or 3) an individual life. Joske addresses this second issue only, not concerning himself with questions about the significance of history of Homo sapiens, but rather with the question of "whether or not the typical human life style can be given significance."[18] And what makes an activity significant or meaningful? Meaningful activities are ones with significance and that significance can be either intrinsic—from the activity itself—or derivative—from the end toward which that activity leads. Individuals want their activities to have both kinds of significance.[19]

Yet, Joske argues, even if there is an objective end for humans that end will have meaning for us only if we make it our own. It follows that the meaning of life is not to be discovered in an indifferent world, but must be provided or created by individuals. People who seek meaning in objective facts about the world are confused. The world is unsympathetic to us; it is neither meaningful nor meaningless—it just is. Yet Joske rejects this solution as facile and unsatisfying. The question of the meaning of life is a deep and real one which the simple injunction to create meaning does not adequately answer.

Joske proceeds to claim "that life may be meaningless for reasons other than that it does not contribute to a worthwhile goal, so that the failure to find meaning in life can be due to the nature of the world and not simply to failure of adequate commitment by an agent."[20] In other words, as opposed to the view of the optimists, the world may be intrinsically and deeply meaningless. Life may be like an activity but its significance can be challenged on many grounds. Joske labels four elements of meaninglessness: worthlessness, pointlessness, triviality, and futility. Activities can be: 1) worthless—lack intrinsic merit as in mere drudgery; 2) pointless—not directed toward any end; 3) trivial—have an insignificant end; or 4) futile—the end cannot be achieved. So activities lack meaning if they are worthless, pointless, trivial, or futile. At one extreme activities are fully meaningful if they lack none of these, that is, if they are intrinsically valuable, directed toward a non-trivial end, and not futile. At the other extreme, actions are fully valueless or meaningless if the lack all four element of meaning. In between are activities that are partially valuable. Joske says that most of us can never rid ourselves of the view that everything may be futile; and the few who do not think about this are lucky.

Joske now turns to showing how commonly held views lead to the conclusion that life is futile. To explain he clarifies what he means by "the typical human life style." While there is much diversity among human cultures and peoples, humans share certain traits such as being rationally reflective and having biological dispositions. So he wonders if we can assess the typical human lifestyle like we can assess activities. The main difference between them is that this core human nature is a given whereas we make choices about our activities. Notwithstanding this Joske thinks there are enough similarities so that we can assess the meaning of life by using the same criteria of judgment we use for activities. Judgments about pointlessness, futility, triviality, and worthiness are applicable to lives. Are there then any commonly held views about the world which would then lead us to view life as meaningless? Joske thinks there are.

CASE 1 – The Naked Ape – Many of our most supposedly noble endeavors are reducible to biology. Much of what we think we choose has been determined by our evolutionary history.

CASE 2 – Moral Subjectivism – Many of our moral choices are futile in the face of the world. With no objective moral reality much of what we do is futile.

CASE 3 – Ultimate Contingency– The reason for the laws of nature themselves is without reason, they are ultimately coincidences. There is no reason for what we call laws of nature; reality is not rational.

CASE 4 – Atheism– The gods have been thought to ground objective morality. Joske objects that gods and morality cannot be adequately connected, given Plato's famous question. (Is something right because the gods command it; or do the gods command it because it's right?)

Moreover, the purpose of the gods does not seem to give our lives meaning unless they become our own; and many find the idea that they can only find meaning in a god's plan degrading, as if man is an instrument for someone else's amusement. Nonetheless, many still feel that life without gods is meaningless. This is partly because people are indoctrinated to think this, yet Joske concedes that non-belief opens up another level of absurdity. While religious belief denies that life is futile, the non-believer has no such guarantee.

The point of all this is to show that philosophy is not neutral on the question of the meaning of life. It is also to show that there are analogies between futile activities—digging ditches and then filling them—and many things that people actually do as part of a human life. Examples of such futility include: Thinking our actions are noble when they are biologically motivated; dying for a cause which is ultimately unimportant; acting as if things are rational when in fact they are not; believing the gods give meaning when they do not do so or do not exist.

So what now? First Joske says that although we should not reject philosophical views that challenge our view of meaning, we may still question those views since the reasoning which led to them may have been unsound. Second "the futility of human life does not warrant too profound a pessimism. An activity may be valuable even though not fully meaningful…"[21] Although life may be futile—our ultimate ends cannot be achieved—we can still value them and give them our own meaning. However, this is not enough for Joske. If we cannot really be fulfilled, if our ultimate ends cannot really be achieved, life becomes grim. "A philosopher, even though he enjoys living, is entitled to feel some resentment towards a world in which the goals that he must seek are forever unattainable."[22]

Summary –The question of the meaning of life is both meaningful and dangerous. It is hard to rid ourselves of the view that life may be meaningless because of considerations related to biology, moral subjectivism, and a contingent, irrational and non-theistic metaphysics. We can try to value our lives, but we are justified in being dissatisfied with a life which might ultimately be futile and meaningless.

10. Oswald Hanfling: Harmless Self-Deception

Oswald Hanfling (1927-2005) was born in Berlin but when his parents had their business vandalized on Kristallnacht in 1938, he was sent to England to live with a foster family. He left school at the age of 14 and for the next 25 years worked as a businessman. Bored, he returned to school eventually earning a PhD in 1971. Hanfling was appointed as a lecturer at the Open University in 1970 and worked there until retiring as a professor in 1993.

Hanfling's book-length text, *The Quest for Meaning* (1987), begins by suggesting that our profound sounding question may admit of no answer. It is simply not clear what kind of answer we seek when we ask what the meaning of life or grass or an ocean is. A similar difficulty arises if we ask what *purpose* of life is.

Despite these worries Hanfling acknowledges that the notions of meaning and purpose regarding life arise in familiar ways. Depressed persons may say that their lives lack meaning, while others may say their lives are full of meaning. In either case we have a clear idea of what such persons mean. If someone says their life is meaningless they are telling us that something is wrong with it, that it is unsatisfactory, that it is somehow lacking. In addition people worry about the meaning of life as a whole too.

Hanfling devotes the first part of his book to aspects of life that may render it meaningless—general difficulties with the possibility of purpose, suffering, and death. He finds no conclusive argument that life is meaningless, but neither can he show that worries about meaninglessness are unfounded. The second part of the book considers the value of life and the possibility of finding meaning through self-realization. He is skeptical of the claim that life is valuable or that certain values are self-evident. Moreover, none of the arguments for self-realization are convincing, and no general prescription for the good life is available. The problem with trying to realize our nature is that we don't know what our nature is or even if one, as Sartre and other existentialists suggest.

One possible solution is to put all these questions out of our minds by devoting ourselves to our jobs, social roles, or other prescriptions of our traditions. However, radical questioning may return and destroy this stasis by undermining our uncritical acceptance of our traditions. In response we might hold on tighter to our traditions by keeping questions out of our minds. But is putting these questions out of our minds self-deception? When a waiter plays the role of a waiter is that self-deception? How about actors who lose themselves in their roles? Hanfling argues that we are better off if we play at being a waiter, actor, or philosophy professor. This may be self-deception, but it is of the benign kind.

These considerations lead Hanfling to consider that just as being rational, social, intellectual, aesthetic, or moral may lead to self-realization, so too may play. Hanfling has in mind an attitude opposed to seriousness, the free expression in an activity of what we are. (We will see this echoed later in the piece by Schlick.) We play by treating supposedly serious concerns with a playful outlook. All of this leads to Hanfling's conclusion:

The human propensity for playing, for finding meaning in play and for projecting the spirit of play into all kinds of activities, is a remedy for the existentialist's anguish, and for the lack of an ultimate purpose of life or prescription for living. If we can deduce such prescriptions neither from a natural nor from a supernatural source … we can still help ourselves through the spirit of play, finding fulfillment in the playing of a role or in regarding what we do as a kind of game. This is a kind of self-deception, but it is not irrational or morally wrong. We are, rather, taking advantage of certain properties of man, of *Homo ludens*, which make life more satisfying than it would otherwise be.[23]

Summary – While the question of the meaning of life may not make sense and there are no general answers, we will live better if we benignly deceive ourselves and play as if there is meaning to our lives.

11. Ludwig Wittgenstein: Meaningless Question or Ineffable Answer?

Ludwig Josef Johann Wittgenstein (1889 –1951) was an Austrian philosopher who held the professorship in philosophy at the University of Cambridge from 1939 until 1947. He first went to Cambridge in 1911 to study with Bertrand Russell who described him as: "the most perfect example I have known of genius as traditionally conceived, passionate, profound, intense, and dominating." Wittgenstein inspired two of the century's primary philosophical movements, logical positivism and ordinary language philosophy, and is generally regarded as one of most important philosophers of the twentieth century.

Given his stature as a 20th century giant of philosophy, we would be remiss if we did not mention Wittgenstein's doubt regarding the sensibility of our question, with the caveat that his positions are notoriously difficult to pin down and that we cannot, in this short space, due justice to the depth of his thought. To get the briefest handle on his thought on the question of the meaning of life, we will ruminate briefly upon the haunting lines that conclude his *Tractatus Logico-Philosophicus*:

> For an answer which cannot be expressed the question too cannot be expressed. *The riddle* does not exist. If a question can be put at all, then it *can* also be answered. Skepticism is *not* irrefutable, but palpably senseless, if it would doubt where a question cannot be asked. For doubt can only exist where there is a question; a question only where there is an answer, and this only where something *can be said*. We feel that even if *all possible* scientific questions be answered, the problems of life have still not been touched at all. Of course there is then no question left, and just this is the answer. The solution of the problem of life is seen in the vanishing of this problem. (Is not this the reason why men to whom after long doubting the sense of life became clear, could not then say wherein this sense consisted?) There is indeed the inexpressible. This *shows* itself; it is the mystical …Whereof one cannot speak, thereof one must be silent.[24]

One problem with these famous lines is that they are open to at least two different interpretations. On one interpretation the *question* of the meaning of life lacks meaning; hence there is no answer to a meaningless question. Worries about the question end when we forget it and start living, but this is not the same as learning an answer—there is no answer to a meaningless question. On the other interpretation there is an answer to the question but we cannot say what it is—the answer is ineffable. If we take the question in the first way, then we no longer have to worry about it since there is nothing to know. If we take the question the second way, then we are somewhat comforted by the existence of a truth which cannot be spoken.

The problem is that the two interpretations are in tension. How do we reconcile the claim that the question is meaningless with the claim that there is an ineffable answer? (One way to reconcile the two might be to say the inexpressible only reveals itself after the question has disappeared.) However we interpret Wittgenstein's enigmatic remarks, we can say this. If the question is senseless, then we waste our time trying to answer it. And if the answer is ineffable, then we waste our time trying to verbalize it. Either way there is nothing to say. Thus we probably ought to follow Wittgenstein's advice and simply "be silent." (As the following pages will attest, we will not follow this advice.)

12. Commentary on Agnosticism

Edwards, Ayer, and Nielsen all advance the most basic reason to be skeptical of an answer to the question of the meaning of life—there cannot logically be an answer to it, insofar as there cannot be anything outside of everything to give life meaning. In response we pose two questions: 1) should we be confident that the ultimate why question cannot be answered; and 2) should we be confident that we need to answer this question? I propose that the answer to both is no.

Regarding the first question, the first reason to reject these authors' conclusion is that we simply do not know whether the question is meaningless or meaningful, answerable or unanswerable. I am skeptical of the capacity of our minds to wrap themselves around this ultimate question, as our minds did not evolve to answer it. These authors may well be correct that if it *were* impossible to answer a question that question would be meaningless. But how can we know that it is impossible to answer the question? We cannot rule out all possible answers beforehand; we cannot even know all the possible answers. Thus we should draw no conclusions whatsoever about answers to the ultimate why question; in other words, we should be skeptical of skepticism.

A second reason to reject the view that the question is meaningless is found in the essay by Wisdom. His argument that the question is meaningful as well as possibly answerable is a strong one. I think he is correct; the question is meaningful. It is a relatively straightforward question even if we cannot answer it. There is nothing outrageous about asking what the whole thing means, with the caveat that that answer cannot come from outside of everything but must come from within everything.

A third reason to reject the claim that the question is meaningless has to do with our intuition. It is philosophically problematic to appeal in this way, but there would be something very strange and irrational about the world if such a universal question turned out to be baseless. Of course the nihilists will draw this exact conclusion but the counter-intuitive nature of the claim that the question is meaningless counts slightly against the claim. Putting all these reasons together, we have not been given sufficient rationale for concluding that our question is meaningless.

Turning to our second question—do we need to answer the question—Ayer's claim that we can reduce our big question to littler ones is instructive. Perhaps we don't need to answer the super ultimate why question; perhaps we need mostly concern ourselves with how we should live. After all we can know *something* about how to live without knowing everything about the universe. We may not know why there is something rather than nothing, but we know many things—what makes us happy or what we find worthwhile. In short this second question is more manageable. So we can say something about the meaning of life— how we should live given what we know about ourselves and the world—without having to say everything about the meaning of life.

Nielsen agrees that we cannot answer the ultimate why question and he also agrees with Ayer that the meaning question reduces to the question of what we find valuable. But he goes a bit further than Ayer's appeal to subjective values, claiming that we can at least give reasons why we value one thing or another. Nevertheless, we cannot answer the question: what gives value to all things that is independent of human choices and attitudes? Thus we cannot ultimately ground value objectively outside of ourselves. Furthermore, if our values ultimately come from us asking for objective value or meaning invites despair and reveals our insecurity. We should be content with finding reasons for doing one thing rather than another, even if such a distinction is not based on objective values.

Given the above considerations it is not surprising that so many of our thinkers will turn to subjective value. For example Hepburn argues that the question is likely to be both meaningless and unanswerable objectively, forcing him to turn to subjective values as the only source of meaning. Like many of the thinkers we have examined, he sheds serious doubt that meaning can be grounded on some metaphysical or theological concerns. Thus Hepburn must reduce the abstract question of universal meaning to more concrete issues concerning subjective values. Nozick also rejects external meaning from the gods, leaving meaning to be found in subjective values. But Nozick goes further than Hepburn or Nielsen by considering that creating meaning may not really be enough. He asks: How can meaning exist at all, in any form? How can meaning, by itself, just shine? He hints that the answer to both questions is—it cannot. If he is correct we are left forlorn.

The pessimism hinted at by Nozick is picked up by Joske. While he agrees with Wisdom that the question is meaningful, there are multiple reasons why life is probably meaningless. What a depressing thought. No wonder that Joske thinks that philosophy is dangerous; it effectively removes all our moorings. If we combine Nozick's concern that subjective values are not enough to satisfy our thirst for meaning with Joske's radical skepticism about meaning in life, we are left with a skeptical cynicism regarding the very possibility of living a meaningful life. Hanfling suggests putting these questions out of our minds and just pretending or playing at life. But could we really sustain such an outlook? Would not existential concerns intrude in our merriment? Perhaps such questions motivate Wittgenstein to conclude that we might as well remain silent; remain skeptics; remain agnostics.

Since we cannot say that our question is definitely meaningless or unanswerable, we ought to be skeptical of those conclusions. Yet even if there cannot be an answer or we cannot know an answer to our big question, we can meaningful ask and propose answers to the queries: How should we live? And, what should we value? These questions are not overwhelming or unsolvable. Still, we remain deeply disturbed by Nozick's insinuation that answers to these questions may not be enough, and by Joske's implication that all may be for naught. And nothing Hanfling or Wittgenstein says comforts either. We don't want to deceive ourselves and we don't want to remain silent. In the end then it is not agnosticism that disturbs us, but the indication that it hints at something worse—at nihilism. What terrifies us is not that there is no answer or that we don't know it. What terrifies is that there is an answer and that answer is that life is meaningless. It is to nihilism that we now turn.

CHAPTER 4 – NIHILISTS: LIFE IS MEANINGLESSNESS

Tomorrow, and tomorrow, and tomorrow,
Creeps in this petty pace from day to day
To the last syllable of recorded time;
And all our yesterdays have lighted fools
The way to dusty death. Out, out brief candle!
Life's but a walking shadow, a poor player
That struts and frets his hour upon the stage
And then is heard no more. It is a tale
Told by an idiot, full of sound and fury,
Signifying nothing.
~ William Shakespeare

Life is warfare and a stranger's sojourn.
And after fame is oblivion.
~ Marcus Aerulius

'God', 'immortality of the soul', 'redemption', 'beyond'.
Without exception, concepts to which I have never devoted any
attention, or time; not even as a child. Perhaps I have never been
childlike enough for them? I do not by any means know atheism
as a result; even less as an event: It is a matter of course with
me, from instinct. I am too inquisitive, too questionable, too
exuberant to stand for any gross answer. God is a gross answer,
an indelicacy against us thinkers—at bottom merely a gross
prohibition for us: you shall not think!
~ Friedrich Nietzsche

There is something which, for lack of a better name, we will
call the tragic sense of life, which carries with it a whole
conception of life itself and of the universe, a whole philosophy
more or less formulated, more or less conscious.
~ Miguel De Unamuno

1. Nihilism

Nihilism is the philosophical doctrine which denies the existence of one or more of those things thought to make life good such as knowledge, values, or meaning. A true nihilist does not believe that knowledge is possible, that anything is valuable, or that life has meaning. Nihilism also denotes a general mood of extreme despair or pessimism toward life in general.

The historical roots of contemporary nihilism are found in the ancient Greek thinkers such as Demosthenes, whose extreme skepticism concerning knowledge is connected with epistemological nihilism. But as historians of philosophy point out, many others including Ockham, Descartes, Fichte, and the German Romanticists contributed to the development of nihilism.[1] The philosophy of Frederick Nietzsche is most often and most closely associated with nihilism, but it is not clear that Nietzsche was a nihilist. So we will begin our study of nihilism with the philosopher who had the most influence upon Nietzsche, and who was definitely a nihilist, Arthur Schopenhauer.

2. Arthur Schopenhauer: "On the Sufferings of the World"

Arthur Schopenhauer (1788 – 1860) was a German philosopher known for his atheism and pessimism—in fact he is the most prominent pessimist in the entire western philosophical tradition. Schopenhauer's most influential work, The World as Will and Representation, emphasized the role of humanity's basic motivation, which Schopenhauer called will. His analysis led him to the conclusion that emotional, physical, and sexual desires cause suffering and can never be fulfilled; consequently he favored a lifestyle of negating desires, similar to the teachings of Buddhism and Vedanta. Schopenhauer influenced many thinkers including Nietzsche, Wittgenstein, Einstein, and Freud.

In "On the Sufferings of the World" (1851), Schopenhauer boldly claims: "Unless suffering is the direct and immediate object of life, our existence must entirely fail of its aim."[2] In other words suffering and misfortune are the general rule in life, not the exception. Contradicting what many philosophers had stated previously, Schopenhauer argued that evil is a real thing, with goodness being the lack of evil. We can see this by considering that happiness or satisfaction always imply some state of pain or unhappiness being brought to an end; and by the fact that pleasure is not generally as pleasant as we expect, while pain much worse than imagined. To those who claim that pleasure outweighs pain or that the two balance out, he asks us "to compare the respective feelings of two animals, one of which is engaged in eating the other."[3] And he quickly follows with another powerful image: "We are like lambs in the field, disporting themselves under the eye of the butcher, who choose out first one and then another for his prey. So it is that in our good days we are all unconscious of the evil Fate may have in store for us—sickness, poverty, mutilation, loss of sight or reason."[4]

Schopenhauer continues by offering multiple ideas and images meant to bring the reality of human suffering to the fore: a) that time marches on and we cannot stop it—it stops only when we are bored; b) that we spend most of life working, worrying, suffering, and yet even if all our wishes were fulfilled, we would then either be bored or desire suicide; c) in youth we have high hopes but that is because we do not consider what is really in store for us—life, aging, and death. Of our old age Schopenhauer says: "It is bad today, and it will be worse tomorrow; and so on till the worst of all."[5] d) it would be much better if the earth were lifeless like the moon; life interrupts the "blessed calm" of non-existence; f) if two persons who were friends in youth met in old age, they would feel disappointed in life merely by the sight of each other; they will remember when life promised so much, in youth, and yet delivered so little; g) "If children were brought into the world by an act of pure reason alone, would the human race continue to exist?"[6] Schopenhauer argues that we should not impose the burden of existence on children. He describes his pessimism thus:

> I shall be told ... that my philosophy is comfortless—because I speak the truth; and people preferred to be assured that everything the Lord has made is good. Go to the priests, then, and leave the philosophers in peace ... do not ask us to accommodate our doctrines to the lessons you have been taught. That is what those rascals of sham philosophers will do for you. Ask them for any doctrine you please, and you will get it.[7]

Schopenhauer also argues that non-human animals are happier than human beings, since happiness is basically freedom from pain. The essence of this argument is that the bottom line for both human and non-human animals is pleasure and pain which has as it basis the desire for food, shelter, sex, and the like. Humans are more sensitive to both pleasure and pain, but have much greater passion and emotion regarding their desires. This passion results from human beings ability to reflect upon the past and future, leaving them susceptible to both ecstasy and despair. Humans try to increase their happiness with various forms of luxury as well as desiring honor, other persons praise, and intellectual pleasures. But all of these pleasures are accompanied by the constant increased desire and the threat of boredom, a pain unknown to the brutes. Thought in particular creates a vast amount of passion, but in the end all of the struggling is for the same things that non-human animals attain—pleasure and pain. But humans, unlike the animals, are haunted by the constant specter of death, a realization which ultimately tips the scale in favor of being a brute. Furthermore, non-human animals are more content with mere existence, with the present moment, than are humans who constantly anticipate future joys and sorrows.

And yet animals suffer. What is the point of all their suffering? You cannot claim that it builds their souls or results from their free will. The only conclusion we should come to is "that the will to live, which underlies the whole world of phenomena, must, in their case satisfy its cravings by feeding upon itself."[8] Schopenhauer argues that this state of affairs—pointless evil—is consistent with the Hindu notion that Brahma created the world by a mistake, or with the Buddhist idea that the world resulted from a disturbance of the calm of nirvana, or even with the Greek notion of the world and gods resulting from fate. But the Christian idea that a god was happy with the creation of all this misery is unacceptable. Two things make it impossible for any rational person to believe the world was created by an omniscient, omnipotent, and omnibenevolent being: 1) the pervasiveness of evil; and 2) imperfection of human beings. Evil is an indictment of such a creator but since there is no such creator it is ultimately an indictment of reality and of ourselves.

Schopenhauer continues: "If you want a safe compass to guide you through life, and to banish all doubt as to the right way of looking at it, you cannot do better than accustom yourself to regard this world as a penitentiary, a sort of penal colony."[9] He claims this is the view of Origen, Empedocles, Pythagoras, Cicero, as well as Brahmanism and Buddhism. Human life is so full of misery that if there are invisible spirits they must have become human to atone for their crimes.

> If you accustom yourself to this view of life you will regulate your expectations accordingly, and cease to look upon all its disagreeable incidents … as anything unusual or irregular; nay, you will find everything is as it should be, in a world where each of us pays the penalty of existence in [their] own particular way.[10]

Ironically there is a benefit to this view of life; we no longer need look upon the foibles of our fellow men with surprise or indignation. Instead we ought to realize that these are our faults too, the faults of all humanity and reality. This should lead to pity for our fellow sufferers in life. Thinking of the world as a place of suffering where we all suffer together reminds us of "the tolerance, patience, regard, and love of neighbor, of which everyone stands in need, and which, therefore, every [person] owes to [their] fellows."[11]

Summary - Schopenhauer thinks life, both individually and as a whole, is meaningless, primarily because of the fact of suffering. It would be better if there was nothing. Confronted with this situation, the best we can do is to extend mercy to our fellow sufferers.

3. Commentary: "On the Sufferings of the World"

I think Schopenhauer's philosophical insights are generally underrated by philosophers, which is in large part due to their supposed pessimism. They should be considered as a clarion call to look at life more realistically and improve it. Seen thus, his philosophy is not so pessimistic after all.

Schopenhauer is correct that suffering is real; philosophers who think it merely a privation of good are deceiving themselves. If we bring pain or evil to an end we experience happiness—surely this suggests that suffering is real. There is also something intuitive about the idea that the pleasure we look forward to often disappoints, whereas pain is often unendurable. How often have you looked forward to something whose reality disappointed? In Schopenhauer's graphic image the pleasure of eating does not compare with the horror of being eaten. However, this comparison is unfair, since we eat many times and can only be eaten once— naturally eating a single time cannot compare in pleasure to the terror of being eaten. A better comparison would be a lifetime of eating versus one moment of being eaten. We can certainly imagine that one would opt for multiple culinary pleasures in exchange for being quickly eaten at some later time

Schopenhauer's idea that we are like lambs waiting to be slaughtered is an even more powerful image. We are sympathetic to the lambs, cows, and pigs as they await their fates, but ours is not much different. We typically wait longer for our death, and the field in which we are fenced may be larger and more interesting, but our end will be similar, even worse if we linger and suffer at the end of life. Just like the animals awaiting slaughter we too cannot escape. Surely there is some sense in which our impending death steals from the joy of life. We are all terminal, all in differing stages of the disease of aging which afflicts us. And this it seems is what holds together his many images and ideas. We cannot stop time; we worry; we slowly realize many of our dreams will never be realized; and we recognize that each day we will grow older and more feeble, leading to an inevitable outcome. It may have been better if we had never existed at all.

It is this consciousness of suffering and death which makes human life worse than animal life, according to Schopenhauer. Yet this argument is not quite convincing, inasmuch as that same consciousness provides benefits for us as opposed to non-human animals. So Schopenhauer's argument is not completely convincing. Still, although he has not established that the life of the brute is better than that of the human, he has shown something quite powerful—*it is not obvious that human animal life is better than non-human animal life*. This is no small achievement and ought to be taken seriously. If this argument is correct then humans should change their own nature from an animal one if possible—by using their emerging technologies.

Schopenhauer is also correct that non-human animal suffering is hard to reconcile with Christian theism, as generations of Christian apologists have discovered. Moreover, his Stoic response to the evils of the world is commendable, as is his call for tolerance for the foibles of our fellow travelers. In the end Schopenhauer is correct in his essential message: *the sufferings of the world count strongly against its meaningfulness, even if not definitively so.*

4. Arthur Schopenhauer: "On the Vanity of Existence"

In "On the Vanity of Existence," Schopenhauer argues that life's futility:

> is revealed in the whole form existence assumes: in the infiniteness of time and space contrasted with the finiteness of the individual in both; in the fleeting present as the sole form in which actuality exists; in the contingency and relativity of all things; in continual becoming without being; in continual desire without satisfaction; in the continual frustration of striving of which life consists. *Time* and that *perishability* of all things existing in time that time itself brings about is simply the form under which the will to live, which as thing in itself is imperishable, reveals to itself the vanity of its striving. Time is that by virtue of which everything becomes nothingness in our hands and loses all real value.[12]

The past is no longer real and thus "it exists as little as does that which has never been."[13] The present compares to the past as something does to nothing. We came from nothing after eons of time and will shortly return to nothing. Each moment of life is transitory and fleeting and quickly becomes the past—in other words, vanish into nothing. The hourglass of our lives is slowly emptying. In response one might simply try to enjoy the present, but since the present so quickly becomes the past it "cannot be worth any serious effort."[14]

Existence rests in the fleeting present; it is thus always in motion, resembling "a man running down a mountain who would fall over if he tried to stop and can stay on his feet only by running on... Thus existence is typified by unrest."[15] Such a life is one of striving continually for what can seldom be attained or what, when attained, quickly disappoints. We live life hurrying toward the future but also regretting what is past—while the present we regard as merely the way to the future. When looking back on our lives we find that they were not really enjoyed, but instead experienced as merely the way to the future. Our lives were all those present moments that seemed so impossible to enjoy.

What is life then? It is a task where we strive to sustain our lives and avoid boredom says Schopenhauer. Such a life is a mistake:

> Man is a compound of needs which are hard to satisfy; that their satisfaction achieves nothing but a painless condition in which he is only given over to boredom; and that boredom is a direct proof that existence is in itself valueless, for boredom is nothing other than the sensation of the emptiness of existence. For if life, in the desire for which our essence and existence consists, possessed in itself a positive value and real content, then there would be no such thing as boredom: mere existence would fulfill and satisfy us. As things are, we take no pleasure in existence except when we are striving after something—in which case distance and difficulties make our goal look as if it would satisfy us (an illusion which fades when we reach it)—or when engaged in purely intellectual activity, in which case we are really stepping out of life so as to regard it from outside, like spectators at a play. Even sensual pleasure itself consists in a continual striving and ceases as soon as its goal is reached. Whenever we are not involved in one or other of these things but directed back to existence itself we are overtaken by its worthlessness and vanity and this is the sensation called boredom.[16]

That our will to live will eventually be extinguished is "nature's unambiguous declaration that all the striving of this will is essentially vain. If it were something possessing value in itself, something which ought unconditionally to exist, it would not have non-being as its goal."[17] We begin our lives in the bodily desires of other persons and end as corpses.

> And the road from the one to the other too goes, in regard to our well-being and enjoyment of life, steadily downhill: happily dreaming childhood, exultant youth, toil-filled years of manhood, infirm and often wretched old age, the torment of

the last illness and finally the throes of death—does it not look as if existence were an error the consequences of which gradually grow more and more manifest?[18]

Summary - The finitude of existence, the ephemeral nature of the present, the contingency of life, the non-existence of the past, the constancy of need, the experience of boredom, and, most importantly the inevitability of death, all lead to the conclusion that life is pointless.

5. Commentary: "On the Vanity of Existence"

In focusing upon the movement of time Schopenhauer has zeroed in on a fundamental fact of life which may render it meaningless—the sense in which we can never be in the present and savor it, as life is always slipping through our grasp. I do not think he is correct when he says that the past is no longer real—the present is partly the result of what happened in the past; the past is partly instantiated in the present. But he is correct that the present is ephemeral, disappears quickly, and much of it seems to vanish into nothingness. Enjoying the present is difficult for these very reasons. Life does hurry us along, and we are incapable of stopping its relentless march. Life is fleeting.

Schopenhauer is also correct that we do strive for successes to avoid boredom, but I think this says more about us than it does about life—life may not be boring, we may be! Those with rich and passionate inner lives find many things interesting. The fact that our striving can be so compelling to us suggests that life does not have to be boring; we may choose to make our lives interesting.

But Schopenhauer has a response to all this. All our striving is in vain because of death; the goal of our being is non-being. He may be mistaken that death implies that our lives have *no* value, but certainly they have *less* value because of death. If you honestly consider the trajectory of our lives from birth to infirmity and death—there is a vanity to life. In the end Schopenhauer's analysis is fundamentally right: *suffering, the transience of the present, the awareness of death, and fact of death, all detract from the possibility of a meaningful life*. His case against meaningfulness is strong indeed.

6. Albert Camus: Revolting Against Nihilism

Albert Camus (1913 – 1960) was a French author, philosopher, and journalist who was awarded the Nobel Prize for Literature in 1957. He was a major philosopher of the 20th-century, with his most famous work being the novel L'Étranger (The Stranger). He is often cited along with Jean Paul Sartre as an existentialist, although Camus rejected the label. He died in a car accident in France.

In *"The Myth of Sisyphus"* (1955) Camus claims that the only important philosophical question is suicide—should we continue to live or not? That all the rest is secondary is obvious, says Camus, because no one dies for scientific or philosophical arguments; they usually abandon them when their life is at risk. Yet people do die because either they judge their lives meaningless or for reasons that give their lives meaning. This suggests that questions of meaning supersede all other scientific or philosophical questions. "I therefore conclude that the meaning of life is the most urgent of questions."[19]

What interests Camus is what leads to suicide. He argues that "beginning to think is beginning to be undermined … the worm is in man's heart."[20] The rejection of life emanates from deep within, and this is where its source must be sought. For Camus killing yourself is admitting that all of the habits and effort needed for living are not worth the trouble. As long as we accept reasons for life's meaning we continue, but as soon as we reject these reasons we become alienated—we become strangers from the world. This feeling of separation from the world Camus terms absurdity, and it is this feeling that leads to the contemplation of suicide. Still, most of us go on because we are attached to the world; we live out of habit.

But is suicide a solution to the absurdity of life? For those who come to believe in life's absurdity it is the only honest answer; one's conduct must follow from one's beliefs. Of course conduct does not always follow from belief. Individuals argue for suicide but continue to live; others profess that there is a meaning to life and choose suicide. Yet most persons are attached to this world by instinct, by a will to live that precedes philosophical reflection. Thus they elude questions of suicide and meaning by combining instinct with the hope that something gives life meaning. Yet the repetitiveness of life brings absurdity back to consciousness. In

Camus' words: "Rising, streetcar, four hours in the office or factory, meal, four hours of work, meal, sleep, and Monday, Tuesday, Wednesday, Thursday, Friday, and Saturday..."[21] So the question of suicide returns, forcing a person to confront and answer this essential question.

And what of the death to which suicide leads? Of death we know nothing. "This heart within me I can feel, and I judge that it exists. This world I can touch, and I likewise judge that it exists. There ends all my knowledge, and the rest is construction."[22] Furthermore, I cannot know myself intimately anymore than I can know death. "This very heart which is mine will forever remain indefinable to me. Between the certainty I have of my existence and the content I try to give to that assurance, the gap will never be filled. Forever I shall be a stranger to myself ..."[23] We know that we feel but our knowledge of ourselves ends there.

What makes life absurd then is our inability to have knowledge of ourselves and the world's meaning even though we desire such knowledge. "...what is absurd is the confrontation of this irrational and the wild longing for clarity whose call echoes in the human heart."[24] The world could have meaning: "But I know that I do not know that meaning and that it is impossible for me just now to know it."[25] This tension between our desire to know meaning and the impossibility of knowing it is the only important truth we can utter. Humans are tempted to leap into faith, but the honest ones will answer that they do not understand; they will learn "to live without appeal..."[26] In large part this means recognizing that one does not have to live up to any higher purposes. In this sense we are free—living without appeal, living the best we can in the face of the absurd. Aware of our condition we exercise our freedom and revolt against the absurd—this is the best we can do.

Nowhere is the essence of the human condition made clearer than in the Myth of Sisyphus. Condemned by the gods to roll a rock to the top of a mountain whereupon its own weight would make it fall back down again, Sisyphus was condemned to this perpetually futile labor. His crimes had seemed slight, yet his preference for the natural world as compared to the darkness of the underworld was enough to incur the wrath of the gods: "His scorn of the gods, his hatred of death, and his passion for life won him that unspeakable penalty in which the whole being is exerted toward accomplishing nothing."[27] For this he was condemned to everlasting torment. Camus describes the toil of Sisyphus and the accompanying despair he must have felt knowing his labor was futile.

Yet Camus sees something else in Sisyphus at that moment when he goes back down the mountain. Consciousness of his fate is the tragedy; yet consciousness also allows Sisyphus to scorn the gods which provides a small measure of satisfaction. Tragedy and happiness go together; this is the state of the world that we must accept. Fate decries that there is no purpose for our lives, but one can be the master of their response—that nothing can take away: "This universe henceforth without a master seems to him neither sterile nor futile. Each atom of that stone, each mineral of that night-filled mountain, in itself forms a world. The struggle itself toward the heights is enough to fill a man's heart. One must imagine Sisyphus happy."[28]

Summary – Life is essentially meaningless and absurd yet we can revolt against it and find some happiness for ourselves. Essentially Camus asks if there is a third alternative between acceptance of life's absurdity or its denial by accepting hopeful metaphysical propositions. Can we live without the hope that life is meaningful but without the despair that leads to suicide? If the contrast is posed this starkly it seems an alternative appears—we can proceed defiantly forward. We can live without faith, without hope, and without appeal. And we can be happy.

7. Thomas Nagel: Irony as a Response to Nihilism

Thomas Nagel (1937-) is a prominent American philosopher, author of numerous articles and books, and currently University Professor of Philosophy and Law at New York University where he has taught since 1980.

In "The Absurd," (1971) Nagel asks why people sometimes feel that life is absurd. For example people sometimes say that life is absurd because nothing we do now will matter in the distant future. But Nagel points out that the corollary of this is that nothing in the distant future matters now: "In particular, it does not matter now that in a million years nothing we do now will matter."[29] Furthermore, even if what we do now *does* matter in a distant future, how does that prevent our present actions from being absurd? In other words, if our present actions are absurd then their mattering in the distant future can hardly give them meaning. For the mattering in the distant future to be important things must matter now. And if I claim definitely that what I do now will *not* matter in a million years then either: a) I claim to know something about the future that I do not know; or b) have simply assumed what I'm trying to prove—that what I do will not matter in the future. Thus the real question is whether things matter now—since no appeals to the distant future seem to help us answer that question.

Consider next the argument that our lives are absurd because we live in a tiny speck of a vast cosmos or in a tiny sliver of time. Nagel argues that neither of these concerns makes life absurd. This is evident because even if we were immortal or large enough to fill the universe, this would not change the fact that our lives are absurd, if they are absurd. Another argument appeals to death, to the fact that everything ends, and reasons to the conclusion that there is no final purpose for our actions. Nagel replies that many of the things we do in life do not need any further justification than their justification at the moment—when I am hungry I eat! Moreover, if the chain of justification must always lead to another justification, we would be caught in an infinite regress. In short since justification must end somewhere if it is to be justification at all, it might as well end in life. Nagel concludes that the arguments just outlined fail but adds: "Yet I believe they attempt to express something that is difficult to state but fundamentally correct."[30]

For Nagel the discrepancy between the importance we place on our lives from a subjective point of view and how gratuitous they appear objectively is the essence of the absurdity of our lives. "… the collision between the seriousness with which we take our lives and the perpetual possibility of regarding everything about which we are serious as arbitrary, or open to doubt."[31] And, short of escaping life altogether, there is no way to reconcile the absurdity resulting from our pretensions and the nature of reality. This analysis rests on two points: 1) the extent to which we must take our lives seriously; and 2) the extent to which, from a certain point of view, our lives appear insignificant. The first point rests on the evidence of the planning, calculation, and concerns with which we invest in our lives.

> Think of how an ordinary individual sweats over his
> appearance, his health, his sex life, his emotional honesty, his
> social utility, his self-knowledge, the quality of his ties with
> family, colleagues, and friends, how well he does his job,
> whether he understands the world and what is going on in it.
> Leading a human life is full-time occupation to which
> everyone devotes decades of intense concern.[32]

The second point rests on the reflections we all have about whether life is worth it. Usually after a period of reflection, we just stop thinking about it and proceed with our lives.

To avoid this absurdity we try to supply meaning to our lives through our role "in something larger than ourselves... in service to society, the state, the revolution, the progress of history, the advance of science, or religion and the glory of God."[33] But this larger thing must itself be significant if our lives are to have meaning by participating in it; in other words, we can ask the same question about meaning of this larger purpose as we can of our lives—what do they mean? So when does this quest for justification end? According to Nagel it ends when we want it to. We can end the search in the experiences of our lives or in being part of a divine plan. But wherever we end the search, we end it arbitrarily. Once we have begun to wonder what the point of it all is; we can always ask of any proposed answer—and what is the point of that? "Once the fundamental doubt has begun, it cannot be laid to rest."[34] In fact there is no imaginable world that could settle our doubts about its meaning.

Nagel further argues that reflection about our lives does not reveal that they are insignificant compared to what is really important, but that our lives are only significant by reference to themselves. So when we step back and reflect on our lives, we contrast the pretensions we have about the meaning of them with the larger perspective in which no standards of meaning can be discovered.

Nagel contrasts his position on the absurd with epistemological skepticism. Skepticism transcends the limitations of thoughts by recognizing the limitations of thought. But after we have stepped back from our beliefs and their supposed justifications we do not then contrast the way reality appears with an alternative reality. Skepticism implies that we do not know what reality is. Similarly when we step back from life we do not find what is really significant. We just continue to live taking life for granted in the same way we take appearances for granted. But something has changed. Although in the one case we continue to believe the external world exists and in the other case we continue to pursue our lives with seriousness, we are now filled with irony and resignation. "Unable to abandon the natural responses on which they depend, we take them back, like a spouse who has run off with someone else and then decided to return; but we regard them differently..."[35] Still, we continue to put effort into our lives no matter what reason has to say about the irony of our seriousness.

Our ability to step back from our lives and view them from a cosmic perspective makes them seem all the more absurd. So what then are our options? 1) We could refuse to take this transcendental step back but that would be to acknowledge that there was such a perspective, the vision of which would always be with us. So we cannot do this consciously. 2) We could abandon the subjective viewpoint (our earthly lives) and identify with the objective viewpoint entirely, but this requires taking oneself so seriously as an individual that we may undermine the attempt to avoid the subjective. 3) We could also respond to our animalistic natures only and achieve a life that would not be meaningful, but at least less absurd than the lives of those who were conscious of the transcendental stance. But surely this approach would have psychological costs. "And that is the main condition of absurdity—the dragooning of an unconvinced transcendent consciousness into the service of an imminent, limited enterprise like a human life."[36]

But we need not feel that the absurdity of our lives presents us with a problem to be solved, or that we ought to respond with Camus' defiance. Instead Nagel regards our recognition of absurdity as "a manifestation of our most advanced and interesting characteristics."[37] It is possible only because thought transcends itself. And by recognizing our true situation we no longer have reason to resent or escape our fate. He thus counsels that we regard our lives as ironic. It is simply ironic that we take our lives so seriously when nothing is serious at all; this is the incongruity between what we expect and reality. Still, in the end, it does not matter that nothing matters from the objective view, so we should simply chuckle at the absurdity of our lives.

Summary – Life has no objective meaning and there is no reason to think we can give it any meaning at all. Still, we continue to live and should respond, not with defiance or despair, but with an ironic smile. Life is not as important and meaningful as we may have once suspected, but this is not a cause for sadness.

8. Westphal & Cherry: Critique of Nagel

Jonathan Westphal, adjunct professor of philosophy, received his B.A. from Harvard College, M.A. from the University of Sussex, and PhD from the University of London. Christopher Cherry is Honorary Senior Research Fellow at the University of Kent in Canterbury England. Their 1990 article "Is Life Absurd" offers a critique of Nagel's influential work, particularly his claim that life is absurd.[38]

The authors claim first that Nagel offers no reason why we should take the external perspective from which the value of every human concern is cast into doubt. More importantly some values are immune to Nagel's critique. Westphal and Cherry give the example of someone absorbed in music. Such an individual cannot entertain the idea that music is worthless and their attention to music destroys the external point of view. If you are moved by Bach you cannot at the same time claim the music is pointless. In fact the only way to truly describe this musical experience is by its subjective emotional value. If we describe Bach's Brandenburg concertos as soothing or harmonious, these are evaluations from the internal perspective which cannot be captured or negated by the external perspective.

However, this analysis does not apply only to music. If we consider lives lived with humanity and integrity, what is there about the external perspective that damages them or renders them meaningless? After all, many lives are lived without pretension and without any claim that music or art or literature is objectively valuable. Thus the external perspective has nothing ostentatious or pretentious to negate. Think of the passionate butterfly collector collecting butterflies or the patient astronomer chronically stars. In neither of these cases is there a hint of pretension nor of the eternal perspective. Such persons are just emotionally engaged.

Nagel's solution to all this is irony, which the authors suggest may appeal to a New York intellectual but not too many others. Why not rather simply ignore the eternal perspective, or dine, have fun, and play backgammon as Hume claimed was the cure for too much metaphysics? Or just engage in interesting play or work. Life does not call for a grand response such as defiance or scorn or irony. Instead why not just be absorbed subjectively in music or tennis? Such absorption is far away from the eternal perspective.

Summary – There is no incongruity between our aspirations and pretensions, and reality from the eternal perspective. If we engage ourselves in things in front of us we find that the eternal perspective does not concern us and we can ignore it.

9. Walter Stace: Responding to Nihilism with Contentment

Walter Terence Stace (1886 - 1967) was a British civil servant, educator and philosopher who wrote on Hegel and Mysticism. In "Man Against Darkness" (1948), Stace claims that the loss of faith in god and religion is responsible for the bewildering state of the world today. This loss of religious faith is depressing, since it leaves us without a scaffold upon which to build ethics. But he also agrees with Sartre and Russell—there are no gods, there is no source for morality, and we live in a universe that is purposeless and indifferent to our values. Thus the only possible values for human beings are those they create.

The cause of the decline of the influence of religion is modern science, but not a particular discovery of science. Rather it is the spirit and assumptions of science that have undermined religious belief. The world view of science propagated by Galileo and Newton prefigured 18th century skepticism by removing the idea of final causes and purposes from the heavens. In essence western civilization was turning its back on the notion of a cosmic order, plan, and purpose. Henceforth astronomy would be understood in terms of the kind of causes that allow us to predict and control, and "the concept of purpose in the world was ignored and frowned upon."[39] In this context Stace quotes Whitehead claim that nature is "merely the hurrying of material, endlessly, meaninglessly."[40]

This highlights the fundamental division in Western thought: those before Galileo thought the world had a purpose; many after him did not. This destruction of purpose in the universe is the key event that signaled the end of religion's preeminence in culture, inasmuch as religion cannot survive in a world where everything is thought futile. Science has left us with no reason for things to be as they are: "Belief in the ultimate irrationality of everything is the quintessence of what is called the modern mind."[41] Another consequence of the decline of the religious view was the ruin of morality, for if morality could not be anchored beyond humankind then it must be our own invention. But as humans differ in their desires and preferences, inevitably morality would be seen as relative. It was in Hobbes that this moral philosophy first flowered and, despite the attempts of Kant and others, the objective basis for morality has been lost. In short moral relativism follows from the world view first illuminated by Galileo—a cosmos devoid of final causes and thus meaningless.

Another consequence of the scientific world view is the loss of belief in free will. Once the idea of a chain of causation is understood it is but a short leap to seeing human action as predictable as a lunar eclipse, to a fatalistic account of human action. And though the subtle arguments of the philosopher may be able to undermine the determinist's case, the belief in various sorts of determinism—the belief that human beings are puppets in a vast cosmic drama—has penetrated the modern mind.

In response to the present condition philosophers have advanced subtle arguments that are not understood by laypersons; religious leaders have sought to revive religion but their pleas do not move modern people, accustomed as they are to a vast, uncaring universe. A religious revival calling for a return to a pre-scientific religion will ultimately fall on deaf ears; the world has grown up too much for that. And science will not save us either: "though it [science] can teach us the best means for achieving our ends, it can never tell us what ends to pursue."[42] The masses must "face the truth that there is, in the universe outside of man, no spirituality, no regard for values, no friend in the sky, no help or comfort for man of any sort."[43]

While we may have justifiably suppressed this truth before it was known, it is now too late. So we must learn to live without the illusion that the universe is good, moral, and follows a plan. We need to learn to live good and decent moral lives without the illusion of religion and a purposeful universe. "To be genuinely civilized means to be able to walk straightly and to live honorably without the props and crutches of one or another of the childish dreams which have so far supported men."[44] Such a life will not be completely happy but "it can be lived in quiet content, accepting resignedly what cannot be helped, not expecting the impossible, and being thankful for small mercies,"[45] Humankind must grow up, put away its childish fantasies, and strive "for great ends and noble achievements."[46]

Summary – There is no objective meaning, but we can be content and noble.

10. Joel Feinberg: Almost Embracing Nihilism

Joel Feinberg (1926 -2004) was an American political and social philosopher. He is known for his work in the fields of individual rights and the authority of the state, thereby helping to shape the American legal landscape. He taught at Brown, Princeton, UCLA, Rockefeller University, and at the University of Arizona, where he retired in 1994.

In "Absurd Self-Fulfillment" (1992) Feinberg begins by considering Richard Taylor's suggestion that Sisyphus could be compelled or addicted to pushing stones. (We will discuss Taylor in the next chapter.) Let us suppose the gods make this part of his nature like walking or speaking; suppose further that Sisyphus gets self-fulfillment from rock pushing as it expresses something basic to his genetic nature. Now Sisyphus' work is typically thought absurd because it is pointless labor that comes to nothing. Philosophers have had differing responses to these issues. Pessimists regard all lives as absurd and respond with scorn, despair, cynicism, etc. Optimists think lives can be partly or wholly fulfilled and therefore good; they respond with hope, satisfaction, positive acceptance, etc. While absurdity and self-fulfillment are different,. Taylor suggests that lives can be both absurd and self-fulfilling, like Sisyphus' rock pushing. So Feinberg asks: what is the relationship between absurdity and self-fulfillment? Can they go together?

Absurdity in individual lives for Feinberg is characterized by: 1) extreme irrationality, as in obviously false beliefs; or the disharmony or incongruity between two things such as means and ends, premises and conclusions, or pretentions and reality; 2) Nagel's account, the clash between the subjective and objective view of our lives. Nagel's absurdity is not relevant to Sisyphus, but if added to the story it would add to the absurdity of his situation; 3) pointlessness—activities with no point or meaning; 4) futility—activities with a point but incapable of achieving their goal; and 5) triviality—activities that produce some trivial advantage but are not worth the cost of their labor. So the absurd elements in life fall into one of five categories: 1) pointless, 2) trivial, 3) futile, 4) Nagel's absurdity, and 5) incongruous or irrational. As for the alleged absurdity of human life in general, Feinberg considers the sense of the absurd in Taylor, Camus, and Nagel.

For *Taylor* life is absurd (pointless, meaningless) because our repetitive activity ultimately comes to nothing. And even if we do achieve something, say build a cathedral, this does not cancel out the absurdity since in the end they all come to nothing; all our achievements ultimately vanish. But what would a non-absurd existence be like? This is important because unless we know what non-absurdity is like, we have nothing to contrast an absurd situation with. Initially Taylor suggests this would entail Sisyphus building an enduring and beautiful temple. But from a distance of a million years all lives seem pointless and all achievements are temporary—they do not overcome meaninglessness. So the building of the temple does not seem to remove absurdity. Suppose then, Taylor argues, that the gods allow Sisyphus to finish his temple and admire it? Taylor argues that then Sisyphus would be eternally bored, so again this would be absurd. Feinberg suggests that Sisyphus could enjoy his achievement and then die, thus not having to endure the boredom; or even better the gods could preserve him and his temple forever. But then Taylor could respond that Sisyphus would still be bored since he would have nothing left to do. Either nothing we do lasts or, if it does, we are bored when we have finished. In the end any conceivable life would be absurd for Taylor.

For *Camus* humans want a cosmic order, significance for their labor, and an intelligible life. But life has no order, destroys our work, and is alien to us. In short the things we want—a caring universe with which one is connected and in which we are immortal—are precisely the things we cannot have. What we get is death. This confrontation between the things one needs—most notably immortality—and the thing one gets—death—is the birthplace of the absurd. There is also the absurdity of the cycle of working for money to buy food so that one can work for money and round and round. You could say that these activities are intrinsically valuable, but Camus argues that we are simply driven to do all these things. And then there is the absurdity of so much animal life—they reproduce and then die. Their lives seem to have no other reason than to perpetuate their species. Are not human lives similar? What these examples show is that "life is pointless because justification for any of its parts or phases is indefinitely postponed..." [47] We do A for the sake of B, and B for the sake of C, etc. Camus's response to absurdity is to rebel, revolt, and live the best one can, since there will always be a divide between what our nature wants—intelligibility and immortality—and the little we can get. For Camus, self-fulfillment may be construed as being "intensely and continuously conscious of my absurdity..." [48] We fulfill ourselves by recognizing the absurdity of our situation.

For *Nagel* the absurd derives from the incongruity between our serious view of ourselves and our apparent triviality from the universal perspective. As Feinberg points out, following Nagel, the life of a mouse might not seem absurd to the mouse but it is absurd from our point of view. According to Nagel our lives are like that too, seeming to matter from the inside but absurd from the outside. Feinberg captures this idea with a distinction between absurd persons—who have a flawed assessment of their importance—and absurd situations—which are a property of one's situation. However, whatever the difference in the details between the three authors for all of them life is absurd: for Taylor because achievements do not last and effort and outcome are in tension; for Camus because the universe is indifferent to our needs; and for Nagel because of the clash between our pretensions and reality.

Feinberg now introduces a new kind of absurdity—when the situation one is in differs from the situation one thinks they are in. For example, if Sisyphus thought his rock pushing was important he would be woefully mistaken about the true nature of his predicament. We are all in the situation of being much less important than we think we are. Thus we should not take ourselves too seriously. Still, Feinberg concludes that while some elements of life are absurd, the arguments that all life is absurd are not convincing. Within life some things seem absurd and some things do not.

Turning to *self-fulfillment*, there are at least four models of self-fulfillment in the ordinary sense: 1) satisfying one's hopes or desires; 2) achieving one's goals; 3) bringing closure to things; and 4) doing the natural or realizing potential. It is this last conception that philosophers have focused upon primarily—so much so that to not fulfill one's nature indicates a wasted life whereas a fulfilling life is often defined as using one's natural talents. Feinberg now explores how Sisyphus might be wired to fulfill his nature by rock pushing. He might have: 1) an appetite for it; 2) a peculiar talent for it; 3) an instinct for it; 4) a general drive to do it; or 5) a compulsive impulse to do it as Taylor suggests. Feinberg argues that no matter how the gods wired Sisyphus his life does not seem capable of being fulfilled, precisely because the gods fixed his life, not allowing him discretion in living his life. As Feinberg says, "If he can fulfill his nature without these discretionary activities, then he has really assumed the nature of a different species."[49] However, if the gods told him to do it in his own way, to exercise discretion in how to push his rocks, then he could be fulfilled, although his life would still be pointless. Thus life can be absurd and fulfilling at the same time.

Feinberg now asks whether it would matter if one found fulfillment in something that from the outside appeared trivial. Suppose one enjoys playing ping-pong and socializing with others who like to play. If that tendency follows from one's nature, then one will probably be fulfilled by playing. Now suppose that someone does not succeed in finding playing partners or others interested in ping-pong and instead goes to philosophy discussion groups weekly, something one finds boring. Now their lives seem unfulfilled. While this may not be bad from an objective point of view—philosophy may be more important than ping-pong—for them it is really bad; they do not like philosophy, they like ping pong! Even if it is objectively absurd to like to hit ping pong balls all day, they naturally enjoy doing it; it is good for them to fulfill their nature in this way precisely because the desire is natural to them. Moreover, self-fulfillment necessitates that we have self-love. "And the truest expression of self-love is devotion toward one's own good, which is the fulfillment of one's' own (who else's) nature—absurd as that may be."[50] Thus, self-fulfillment matters because without it we cannot have self-love as well as the reverse.

We see then that our lives are *not* absurd from the inside—we have goals and purposes—but may be so from the outside. What attitude should we take toward a fulfilling life that we decide is absurd from the outside, that will come to nothing in the end? These attitudes Feinberg calls "cosmic attitudes," ones we have toward the entire universe. Feinberg agrees with Nagel that irony is the appropriate attitude; it is "an attitude of detached awareness of incongruity...a state of mind halfway between seriousness and playfulness."[51] Feinberg argues that one can appreciate this incongruity, like one appreciates humor, and there is a kind of bittersweet pleasure in it. Feinberg says we ought to respond not with tears, anger, or amusement, but with a "tired smile." Thus neither pessimism—the view that all lives are worthless—nor optimism—the view that all lives are worthwhile—is warranted. After having a good life and then considering Camus, Taylor, and Nagel, Feinberg sees the cosmic joke and is tickled. "Now he can die not with a whine or a snarl, but with an ironic smile."[52]

Summary – There is no objective meaning. We can find some subjective meaning by acting in accord with our nature; our lives can be both fulfilling and absurd. All we can do is passively accept this nihilistic state of affairs with an ironic smile. Feinberg goes a bit further than Nagel, nearly embracing nihilism.

11. Simon Critchley: Affirming Nihilism

Simon Critchley (1960 -) was born in England and received his PhD from the University of Essex in 1988. He is series moderator and contributor to "The Stone," a philosophy column in The New York Times. He is also currently chair and professor of philosophy at The New School for Social Research in New York City.

In his recent book, *Very Little Almost Nothing*, Critchley discusses various responses to nihilism. Those responses include those who: a) *refuse* to see the problem, like the religious fundamentalist who doesn't understand modernity; b) are *indifferent* to the problem, which they see as the concern of bourgeoisie intellectuals; c) *passively accept* nihilism, knowing that nothing they do matters; d) *actively revolt* against nihilism in the hope that they might mitigate the condition.[53] He rejects all views that try to overcome nihilism—enterprises that find redemption in philosophy, religion, politics or art—in favor of a response that embraces or affirms nihilism. For Critchley the question of meaning is one of finding meaning in human finitude, since all answers to the contrary are empty. This leads him to the surprising idea that "the ultimate meaning of human finitude is that we cannot find meaningful fulfillment for the finite."[54] But if one cannot find meaning in finitude, why not just passively accept nihilism?

Critchley replies that we should do more than merely accept nihilism; we must *affirm* "meaninglessness as an achievement, as a task or quest … as the achievement of the ordinary or everyday without the rose-tinted spectacles of any narrative of redemption."[55] In this way we don't evade the problem of nihilism but truly confront it. As Critchley puts it:

> The world is all too easily stuffed with meaning and we risk suffocating under the combined weight of competing narratives of redemption—whether religious, socio-economic, scientific, technological, political, aesthetic or philosophical—and hence miss the problem of nihilism in our manic desire to overcome it.[56]

For models of what he means Critchley turns to playwright Samuel Beckett whose work gives us "a radical de-creation of these salvific narratives, an approach to meaninglessness as the achievement of the ordinary, *a redemption from redemption.*"[57] Salvation narratives are empty talk which cause trouble; better to be silent as Pascal suggested: "All man's miseries derive from not being able to sit quietly in a room alone." What then is left after we are saved from the fables of salvation? As his title suggests; very little … almost nothing. But all is not lost; we can know the happiness derived from ordinary things.

Critchley finds a similar insight in what the poet Wallace Stevens called "the plain sense of things."[58] In Stevens' famous poem, "The Emperor of Ice Cream," the setting is a funeral service. In one room we find merriment and ice cream, in another a corpse.

The ice cream represents the appetites, the powerful desire for physical things; the corpse represents death. The former is better than the latter, and that this is all we can say about life and death. The animal life is the best there is and better than death—the ordinary is the most extraordinary.

For another example Critchley considers Thornton Wilder's famous play "Our Town" which exalts the living and dying of ordinary people, as well as the wonder of ordinary things. In the play young Emily Gibbs has died in childbirth and is in an afterlife, where she is granted her wish to go back to the world for a day. But when she goes back she cannot stand it; people on earth live unconscious of the beauty which surrounds them. As she leaves she says goodbye to all the ordinary things of the world: "to clocks ticking, to food and coffee, new ironed dresses and hot baths, and to sleeping and waking up."[59] It is tragic that while living we miss the beauty of ordinary things. Emily is dismayed but we are enlightened—we ought to appreciate and affirm the extraordinary ordinary. Perhaps that is the best response to nihilism—to be edified by it, to find meaning in meaninglessness, to realize we can find happiness in spite of nihilism.

Summary – We should reject philosophies of meaning and affirm nihilism, enjoying nonetheless the pleasures that life offers.

12. Milan Kundera: Nihilism as Unbearable

Critchley advocates a kind of *lightness* about life. Perhaps we should not take life too seriously, enjoy the sensual or other pleasures it affords, and reject all *heavier* philosophies of meaning. But is this solution satisfactory? This is the fundamental question posed Milan Kundera in his novel *The Unbearable Lightness of Being*. Kundera (1929 -) is a writer of Czech origin who has lived in exile in France since 1975, where he became a naturalized citizen. His books were banned by the Communist regimes of Czechoslovakia until the downfall of the regime in the Velvet Revolution in 1989.

Kundera begins his novel by asking the meaning of Nietzsche's idea of eternal recurrence—the notion that everything that has already happened will recur ad infinitum. Although it is hardly Nietzsche's interpretation, Kundera remarks: "Putting it negatively, the myth of eternal return states that a life which disappears once and for all, which does not return, is like a shadow, without weight, dead in advance, and whether it was horrible, beautiful, or sublime, its horror, sublimity, and beauty mean nothing."[60]

For Kundera a life lived only once has a kind of lightness, triviality or unimportance about it; by contrast, if all recurred infinitely, a tremendous weight or heaviness would be imposed on our lives and choices. He contrasts the heaviness and lightness of life as follows: "If the eternal return is the heaviest of burdens, then our lives can stand out against it in all their splendid lightness. But is heaviness truly deplorable and lightness splendid?"[61] Kundera answers:

> the heaviest of burdens crushes us, we sink beneath it, it pins us to the ground. But ... the heavier the burden, the closer our lives come to the earth, the more real and truthful they become. Conversely, the absolute absence of a burden causes a man to be lighter than air, to soar into the heights, take leave of the earth and his earthly being, and become only half real, his movements as free as they are insignificant.[62]

The problem with the light life is that it is insignificant. If everything happens only once it might as well not have happened at all. (This is eerily reminiscent of Schopenhauer's remarks about how the fleetingness of life undermines its significance.) The problem is that we find the insignificance of our lives and decisions unbearable; it is the unbearable lightness of being. In a world that lacks objective meaning, we must accept nihilism, unless we can act as if our actions eternally recur, but then the heaviness of our actions and choices crushes us under their weight. Moreover, there is nothing heavy or eternal about life.

Despite these conundrums the main characters in his novel that pursue the weightiness of love end up happy, whereas those that do not suffer the unbearable lightness of being. This suggests that heaviness may be better after all, but there is no return and there is nothing eternal for Kundera, and even if there were this would make our lives and choices too burdensome. Perhaps the fact that some of his characters find love is enough; but it is hard to see how even that ultimately mattered, since nothing matters ultimately. In the end nihilism is, for conscious beings, both true and unbearable.

Summary – A life lived heavily is disingenuous and crushes us; a life lived lightly is unbearable.

13. Commentary on the Varieties of Nihilism

Suffering and death count strongly against meaning; the challenge of nihilism may be *the* challenge for contemporary individuals and culture. We have argued that rejecting or denying nihilism, by accepting a religious metaphysics for example, is philosophically problematic, inasmuch as there are good reasons to doubt the truth of these systems. Accepting nihilism is either self-defeating, useless, or both. Finding meaning by affirming nihilism is a brave response but it is not all that different than accepting nihilism in the end. So questions remain. Why give up so easily? What do we gain by embracing nihilism?

Camus' Sisyphus supposedly found happiness in his revolt, but one has to wonder whether that suggestion is mere romanticism. And neither Nagel's nor Feinberg's irony provides solace; they merely counsel passive acceptance. Maybe we should simply reject meaning and all salvific narratives, reveling in the pleasures and joys of this world, the extraordinary ordinary. But can we really do it? In *Our Town* Wilder suggests we cannot, it is too hard to appreciate life while you live it. When responding to Emily's query as to whether human beings can appreciate life every minute while they live it, the narrator tells her: "No—saints and poets maybe—they do some."[80] But even if we could affirm nihilism would this be satisfactory? If we think of Critchley as advocating living lightly, Kundera responds that such a life is unbearable; perhaps even more so than living heavily.

We thus find ourselves at an impasse. Nihilism looms large and none of our responses are completely viable. Rejecting nihilism seems intellectually dishonest, passively accepting it appears fatalistic, actively rejecting it with Camus is futile, embracing it looks pointless, and realizing it is unbearable. The only way forward—if we do not want to accept the verdict of nihilism—is to consider other responses. It is to these responses that we now turn.

CHAPTER 5 – NATURALISTS: SUBJECTIVE MEANING

The living thing is not the clay molded by the potter, nor the harp played upon by the musician. It is the clay modeling itself.
~ Edward Stuart Russell

You ask me what satisfaction I get out of life, and why I go on working. I go on working for the same reason that a hen goes on laying eggs. There is in every creature an obscure but powerful impulse to active functioning. Life demands to be lived. Inaction, save as a measure of recuperation between bursts of activity, is painful and dangerous to the healthy organism—in fact, it is almost impossible. Only the dying can be really idle.
~ H. L. Mencken

Have you been able to think out and manage your own life? Our great and glorious masterpiece is to live appropriately.
~ Michel de Montaigne

I do not know to what great end Destiny leads us, nor do I care very much. Long before that end, I shall have played my part, spoken my lines, and passed on. How I play that part is all that concerns me. In the knowledge that I am an inalienable part of this great, wonderful, upward movement called life, and that nothing, neither pestilence, nor physical affliction, nor depression, nor prison, can take away from me my part, lies my consolation, my inspiration, and my treasure.
~ Owen C. Middleton (after being sentenced to life imprisonment in 1932.)

There is no golden rule which applies to everyone: every man must find out for himself in what particular fashion he can be saved.
~ Sigmund Freud

1. Naturalism and Subjective Meaning

Assuming that none of our previous answers completely satisfies, we now consider the idea that meaning is not something you stumble upon, receive, or discover, but something you fashion, invent or create. This is probably the most prevalent view among contemporary philosophers. On this account life can still be meaningful even though there is no supernatural reality—but only if individuals *give* meaning to their lives in the natural world in which they live. Therefore subjectivists believe that meaning is relative to their desires, attitudes, interests, wants, preferences, etc., and there are no invariant standards of meaning. Something is meaningful to individuals to the extent that they find that thing meaningful, in other words, meaning is constituted by human minds and varies between persons.

2. Jean Paul Sartre: The Classic Statement of Subjective Meaning

Jean-Paul Sartre (1905-1980) was a French existentialist philosopher, playwright, novelist, screenwriter, political activist, biographer, and literary critic. He was one of the leading figures in 20th century French philosophy, particularly Marxism, and was one of the key figures in literary and philosophical existentialism. Sartre was also noted for his long personal relationship with the feminist author and social theorist Simone de Beauvoir. He was awarded the 1964 Nobel Prize in Literature which he refused.

In his famous public lecture "Existentialism Is a Humanism" (1946) Sartre set out the basic points of his existential philosophy and its relationship to the question of the meaning of life. He begins by noting that the communists have criticized his philosophy as bourgeois; others have described it as sordid, unappreciative of beauty, and subjective; and Christians have rejected it as morally relative. In response Sartre explains that existentialism is based upon the doctrine that *existence precedes essence*; that our concrete subjective existence comes before whatever essence we develop.

To more fully elucidate this idea Sartre asks us to consider an artifact such as a paper-knife (letter opener). In this case its essence—to open letters—precedes its existence. The artisan had this essence in mind before it existed. When we think of God as creator of human beings we are reasoning similarly. God had our nature or essence in mind first, and then creates us in accord with that human nature. Sartre's atheistic existentialism implies the reverse. For human beings our existence precedes our essence since there is no God to give us an essence, and we freely choose what we will become. Unlike chairs and tables we have to make ourselves, and in so doing we alone are responsible for the essence we create.

Along with this responsibility comes the anguish that accompanies our decisions. We never know which action we should perform but perform them we must. Furthermore, as there are no gods or objective moral guidelines, we alone must choose, be responsible for our choices, and accept the accompanying anguish that choice brings. Thus we cannot escape our freedom; we have no excuses. When deciding between staying with our mother or going off and fighting the Nazis, in Sartre's example, no theory of human nature or objective moral values help. We must simply exercise our freedom, choose, and accept the responsibility and anguish that follows.

The benefits of an existential view are first, that it begins with individual consciousness, the only certain beginning for any philosophy; and second, it is compatible with human dignity, as it respects humans as subjects rather than making them objects. Individuals are artists or moral agents who have no a priori rules to guide them in creating art or living moral lives. And we should not judge others for the choices they make, unless they hide behind doctrine and dogma which is to deny one's freedom.

In the end to be human means precisely to recognize oneself as sole legislator of values and meaning, which for Sartre is the logical conclusion of his atheistic position. But even if there were gods it would make no difference, human beings would still have to create their own values and meanings for their lives to be valuable and meaningful.

Summary – Human beings are not artifacts with a pre-existing essence; they are subjects who must freely choose to create their own meaning.

3. Kurt Baier: Subjective Meaning Without Gods

Kurt Baier (1917 – 2010) was an Austrian moral philosopher who received his DPhil at Oxford in 1952. He spent most of his career at the University of Pittsburgh, authored the influential, *The Moral Point of View*, and was one of the most important moral philosophers of the second half of the twentieth century.

In his 1957 lecture, "The Meaning of Life," Baier claims that Tolstoy's crisis of meaning would have been incomprehensible to medieval Christians who thought themselves the center of the cosmic drama, and for whom the meaning of life was to gain eternal bliss. However, the modern scientific worldview conflicts with this medieval view. The earth and humans are not at the center of the solar system and the cosmos is billions of years old, not a mere six thousand. But the conflict runs much deeper. In the Christian view god is "a kind of superman… [who] acts as a sort of playwright-cum-legislator-cum-judge-cum-executioner."[1] This god writes the play, makes the rules, and punishes misbehavers. According to this view all is for the best even if it appears otherwise, and humans ought to worship, venerate, praise, and obey the creator. But with the rise of science the universe is explained better and more reliably without gods, leading many educated persons to reject the Christian view and conclude that individuals and the universe are without meaning.

Explaining the Universe - In response to this apparent conflict between science and religion one might argue that the two are in fact complimentary. Science, it might be said, gives precise explanations of small parts of the universe; religion gives vague explanations for the whole universe. The devoid-of-meaning conclusion comes about only because one is confusing the two explanations. Scientific explanations tell us *how* things are but not *why* they are. The ultimate explanation is that which explains the purpose or the why of something. While both types of explanations are needed and work well in their own domain, if we are looking for answers to the ultimate why questions we need religious answers.

Baier argues instead that both scientific and religious explanations involve an infinite regress—they are both equally incomplete. Saying that gods caused the universe merely raises the question of what caused the gods; saying the gods are the reason there is something rather than nothing just raises the question of why the gods exist. Thus scientific explanations lack nothing that religious explanations possess; neither type of explanation explains completely. Scientific explanations differ from religious ones by being precise, capable of falsification, and amenable to slow improvement. These considerations lead Baier to the main conclusion of the first section:"that scientific explanations render their explicanda as intelligible as pre-scientific explanations; they differ from the latter only in that, having testable implications and being more precisely formulated, their truth or falsity can be determined with a high degree of probability."[2]

The Purpose of Existence - Despite the conclusion reached above—that scientific explanations are better than religious ones—it might still be argued that scientific explanations lead to the conclusion that life is meaningless. After all humans and their planet are not at the center of creation, the universe appears doomed, humans were not specially created, and the entire universe is a hostile place. In such conditions humans try to seize a few moments of joy until their lives end in death. Science explains such a world but what meaning does it find in it? Whereas the medieval worldview provided purpose, the scientific worldview does not. Or so it seems.

Baier responds by distinguishing between two different senses of purposes. 1) Purposes that persons and their behavior have (to build factories to make cars) and 2) purposes that things have (the purpose of a car is to provide transportation.) People do many things without purpose or meaning, pointless labor for example, but the scientific worldview does not force us to regard our lives in this way. Instead it provides better ways of achieving our purposes. As for the other kind of purpose—the purpose of things—to be used this way is degrading and implied by the Christian worldview, viewing a human as a divine artifact here to serve the purpose of its maker. Moreover, those who reject the scientific worldview because they think it renders life pointless from the outside, forget that life can still be meaningful from the inside. They "mistakenly conclude that there can be no purpose *in* life because there is no purpose *of* life."[3]

Baier notes that many long for the medieval worldview where a gentle father watches over and cares for them, but he stresses that rejecting this view does not render life meaningless. Rather one can find meaning for oneself; one can become an adult and stand on their own feet. The Christian replies that being part of a god's plan assures that life is meaningful, that life is moving toward an end that transcends the individual. What then is this noble plan or end for which the gods have created the world? Two problems immediately confront us: 1) how can the purpose be grand enough to justify all the suffering in the world? And 2) the story of how the plan is brought to fruition involves morally objectionable concepts. The whole story of a taboo on the fruit of a tree, punishment given for violating said taboo, blood sacrifice, sacraments and priests to administer them, judgment day, and eternal hellfire are all grossly objectionable. Baier concludes "that god's purpose cannot meaningfully be stated."[4] And even if they could be stated coherently they require humans to be totally dependent on the gods, which Baier finds inconsistent with humans as independent, free, and responsible individuals.

The Meaning of Life - But how can life have meaning if all ends in death, if there is no paradise? In the Christian worldview life has meaning because, though it is filled with the suffering that follows from the curse the gods sent after the fall, it is followed by a paradise after we die. However, if we accept that life is filled with suffering but deny the afterlife, then life appears meaningless. Why endure it all if there is no heaven? According to Baier if we reject the afterlife, then the only way to find meaning is in this life.

Of course we do not normally think life is worthless, a thing to be endured so as to get to heaven. If we did we would kill our friends and ourselves quickly in order to get to heaven, but the gods forbid such acts so we must accept the pain and suffering that accompany our lives. As for murder, most of us think that it does deprive persons of something valuable, their lives. And how do we decide if our lives are valuable? Most of us regard our lives as worth living if they are better than the average life, or closer to the best possible life than the worst possible life. By contrast the Christian view compares life to some perfect paradise, promises believers that they can enjoy this paradise, and denigrates the pleasures of this life as vile and sinful. Baier elaborates on the point:

> It is now quite clear that death is simply irrelevant. If life can be worthwhile at all, then it can be so even though it be short. And if it is not worthwhile at all, then an eternity of it is simply a nightmare. It may be sad that we have to leave this beautiful world, but it is so only if and because it is beautiful. And it is no less beautiful for coming to an end. I rather suspect that an eternity of it might make us less appreciative, and in the end it would be tedious.[5]

The upshot of all this is that the scientific worldview helps us see meaning in this life, since the worth of this life need no longer be maligned in comparison with a perfect idealized afterlife.

Conclusion - Baier states that persons who reject a traditional religious view often assume that life is meaningless because they think there are three conditions of meaning that *cannot* be met given the scientific worldview. Those conditions are: 1) the universe must be intelligible; 2) life must have a purpose; and 3) human hopes must be satisfied. For Christians these conditions can be met, thus one must either adopt a worldview incompatible with modern science, the Christian view, or accept that life is meaningless. But Baier argues that a meaningful life can be lived even without these three conditions being met. Life does have meaning on the scientific worldview—the meaning we give it—and besides there are multiple reasons for rejecting the Christian worldview.

Summary – Science explains existence better than religion. Religion gives purpose to existence but does so in morally objectionable ways. Although there is no objective meaning to life, we can give subjective meaning to it. A religious worldview hinders our doing this by its emphasis on an idealized afterlife, thereby belittling the beauty and meaning of this life.

4. Paul Edwards: Terrestrial Meaning is Enough

In "The Meaning and Value of Life" (1967) Paul Edwards, to whom we have already been introduced, notes that many religious thinkers argue that life cannot have meaning unless our lives are part of a divine plan and at least some humans achieve eternal bliss.

Non-believers are divided, some maintaining that life can have meaning without these religious provisos and others that it cannot. Edwards refers to these latter individuals as pessimists but wonders "whether pessimistic conclusions are justified if belief in God and immortality are rejected."[6]

Schopenhauer's Arguments - Edwards begins by examining Schopenhauer's claims that life is a mistake, that non-existence is preferable to existence, that happiness is fleeting and unobtainable, and that death is a final destruction: "nothing at all is worth our striving, our efforts, and struggles…All good things are vanity, the world in all its ends bankrupt, and life a business which does not cover its expenses."[7] Schopenhauer reinforces these conclusions by emphasizing the ephemeral and fleeting nature of pleasures and joys: "which disappear in our hands, and we afterwards ask astonished where they have gone … that which in the next moment exists no more, and vanishes utterly, like a dream, can never be worth a serious effort."[8] Edwards thinks that this pessimism mostly reflects that Schopenhauer was a lonely, bitter, and miserable man. Still, persons of more cheerful dispositions have reached similar conclusions so we should not dismiss Schopenhauer's too quickly.

The Pointlessness of It All - Next Edwards briefly considers the famous trial attorney Clarence Darrow's pessimism:

> This weary old world goes on, begetting, with birth and with living and with death … and all of it is blind from the beginning to the end … Life is like a ship on the sea, tossed by every wave and every wind; a ship headed for no port and no harbor, with no rudder, no compass, no pilot; simply floating for a time, then lost in the waves…[9]

Not only is life purposeless but there is death: "I love my friends … but they all must come to a tragic end."[10] For Darrow attachment to life makes death all the more tragic.

Next he considers the case of Tolstoy. Perhaps no one wrote so movingly of the overwhelming fact of death and its victory over us all as Tolstoy. "Today or tomorrow … sickness and death will come to those I love or to me; nothing will remain but stench and worms. Sooner or later my affairs, whatever they may be, will be forgotten, and I shall not exist. Then why go on making any effort?"[11] Tolstoy if you remember compared our situation to that of a man hanging on the side of a well holding on to a twig. A dragon waits below, a beast above, and mice are eating the stem of the twig. Would a small bit of honey on the twig really provide comfort? Tolstoy thinks not. Refusing to be comforted by life's little pleasures as long as there were no answers to life's ultimate questions, he saw but four possible answers to his condition: 1) remain ignorant; 2) admit life's hopelessness but partake of its pleasures; 3) commit suicide; or 4) weakness, seeing the truth but clinging to life anyway. Tolstoy argues that the first solution is not available to the conscious person; the second he rejects because there is so little pleasures and to enjoy pleasures while others lack them would require "moral dullness;" he admires the third solution which is chosen by strong persons when they recognize life is no longer worth living; and the fourth solution is for those who lack the strength and rationality to end their lives. Tolstoy thought himself such a person.

Edwards wonders if those who share the pessimists' rejection of religion might nonetheless avoid their depressing conclusions. He admits that there is much truth to the claims of the pessimists—that happiness is difficult to achieve and fleeting, that life is capricious, that death ruins our plans, that all these things cast a shadow over our lives—and we should consider these arguments well-founded. But does meaninglessness follow as Darrow and Tolstoy suggested?

Comparative Value Judgments About Life and Death - Edwards begins to answer by pointing to inconsistencies in the pessimist's arguments. For instance pessimists often argue that death is bad because it puts an end to life, but this amounts to saying that life does have value or else its termination would not be bad. In other words if life had no value—say one was in state of persistent, unending pain—then death would be good. One might say that life has value until the realization of death becomes clear, but this argument too is flawed—such a fixation on death is obsessive. Furthermore, claims that death is better than life or that it would have been better had we not been born appear incongruous. One can make comparisons between known things—that A is a better scientist or pianist than B—but if there is no afterlife as the pessimists contend, then death cannot be experienced and comparisons with life are meaningless.

The Irrelevance of the Distant Future - Edwards also attacks the claims of those who appeal to a "distant future" in which to find life's meaning. He does not find it obvious that eternally long lives would be more meaningful than finite ones, for what is the meaning of everlasting bliss? And if future bliss needs no justification then why should bliss in this life need any?

The issue of the distant future also comes up regarding value judgments. Edwards argues that it makes sense to ask if something is valuable if we do not regard it as intrinsically valuable, or it is being compared to some other good. But it does not make sense to ask this of something that we do consider intrinsically valuable and which is not in conflict with attaining some other good. We may meaningfully ask if the pain we experienced at the dentist is worthwhile, since that is not the kind of thing we ordinarily do for fun, but we should not ask such questions about being happy or in love because we think such experiences intrinsically valuable. In addition Edwards finds concerns about the distant future irrelevant to most human concerns—we are typically concerned with the present or near future. Even if you and the dentist are both dead in a hundred years that does not mean that your efforts now are worthless.

The Vanished Past - Some claim that life's worthlessness derives from the fact that the past is gone forever, which implies that the past is as if it had never been. Others claim that the present's trivialities are more important than the past's most important events. To the first claim Edwards replies that if only the present matters then past sorrows, as well as past pleasures, do not matter. To the second claim he points out that this is simply a value judgment about which he and others differ. While the pessimist might lament the passing years and the non-existence of the past, the optimist may take pride in realities actualized as opposed to potentialities unfulfilled. Still, Edwards admits that there is a sense in which the past does seem less valuable than the present, as evidenced by how little consolation to the sick or aged would be the fact that they used to be healthy. Thus the issue of the relative value of past and present is debatable.

To recap Edwards' main points: 1) comparative judgments about life versus death are unintelligible; 2) the experience of a distant future will not necessarily make life worthwhile; 3) it makes no sense to ask if intrinsically valuable things are really valuable; and 4) the vanished past does not say much about life's meaning. In sum, the pessimists have not established their arguments convincingly.

The Meanings of the "Meaning of Life" - If the pessimistic conclusions do not necessarily follow from the rejection of gods and immortality is there reason for optimism? Can there be meaning without gods or immortality? To answer these questions Edwards appeals to Baier's distinction between: 1) whether we have a role in a great drama or whether there is objective meaning to the whole thing—what Edwards calls meaning in the *cosmic* sense; and 2) whether or not our lives have meaning from within or subjectively—what Edwards calls the *terrestrial* sense. It is easy to claim that someone's life has meaning *for them*, but harder to defend the claim that life has meaning in the cosmic sense. It is important to note that to say one's life has meaning in the terrestrial sense does not imply that such a life was good. A person might achieve the goals of their life, to be a good murderer, but it is easy to see that such a life is not good.

While it is easy enough to reject cosmic meaning—the pessimists view—it does not follow that rejection of cosmic meaning eliminates terrestrial meaning. It is perfectly coherent to proclaim that there is no cosmic plan but that one nevertheless finds their terrestrial life meaningful. Many individuals have achieved such meaning without supernatural beliefs. Moreover, the existence of cosmic meaning hardly guarantees meaning in the terrestrial sense. Even if there is an ultimate plan for my life I would need to know it, believe in it, and work toward its realization.

Is Human Life Ever Worthwhile? - Turning to the question of whether life is ever worthwhile, Edwards wonders what makes individuals ask this question and why they might answer it negatively. To say that life is worthwhile for a person implies that they have some goals and the possibility of attaining them. While this account is similar to the notion of meaning in the terrestrial sense, it differs because worthiness implies value whereas terrestrial meaning does not. In other words terrestrial meaning implies only subjective value, whereas the notion of a worthwhile life implies the existence of objective values. In the latter case we have goals, the possibility of their attainment, *and* the notion that those goals are really valuable. But Edwards claims that he doesn't need objective values to determine the worthiness of a life, inasmuch as even the subjectivist will allow some distinction between good and bad conduct. He bases his argument on the agreement of "rational and sympathetic human beings."

Still, the pessimists are dissatisfied. They grant that person's lives may have meaning in the subjective sense but claim this is not enough "because our lives are not followed by eternal bliss."[12] Edwards counters that pessimists have unrealistic standards of meaning that go beyond those of ordinary persons—who are content with subjective meaning. According to the standards of pessimists life is not worthwhile because it is not followed by eternal bliss, but this does not imply that it is not worthwhile by other less demanding standards. And why should we accept the special standards of the pessimist? In fact Edwards notes that ordinary standards of living such as achieving our goals do something that the pessimists' standards do not—they guide our lives.

Moreover, there are a number of questions we might ask the pessimist. Why does eternal bliss bestow meaning on life, while bliss in this life does not? Why should we abandon our ordinary standards of meaning for the special standards of the pessimists? This latter question is particularly difficult for the pessimist to answer—after all nothing is of value to the pessimist. Still, pessimists usually do not commit suicide, suggesting that they believe there is some reason for living. And they often have principles and make value judgments as if something *does* matter. Thus there is something disingenuous about their position.

Is the Universe Better with Human Life Than Without It? - All of this leads to the ultimate question: is the universe better with or without human life in it? Edwards thinks that without an affirmative response to this question, no affirmative response can be given to the meaning of life question. He quotes the German phenomenologist, Hans Reiner, in this regard: "Our search for the meaning of our lives ... is identical with the search for a logically compelling reason why it is better for us to exist than not to exist. ... whether it is better that mankind should exist than that there should be a world without any human life."[13] A possible answer to this question appeals to the intrinsic meaning of the morally good a pre-condition of which demands the existence of moral agents and a universe. In that case it is better that the universe and humans exist so that moral good can exist. Of course this claim is open to the objection that a universe and moral agents introduce physical and moral evil which counterbalances the good. In that case whether it is better that the universe exists or not would depend on whether more good than evil exists.

Why the Pessimist Cannot be Answered – The upshot of all this is that one cannot satisfactorily answer the pessimist. Why? Because questions such as whether life is better than death or whether the universe would be better if it had not existed have no clear meaning. Is it better for humans and the universe to exist than not to? Philosophers have answered the question variously: Schopenhauer answered in the negative, Spinoza in the positive. But Edwards concludes that there are no knock-down arguments either way. It is simply impossible to prove that "coffee with cream is better than black coffee," or "that love is better than hate."[14]

Summary – Human life can have subjective, terrestrial meaning and some lives are worthwhile as long as standards of meaning are not set too high. But pessimists ultimately cannot be answered if we need to show them that human existence is better than non-existence. We cannot know if, all things considered, it is better if there is life than not.

5. Kai Nielsen: Meaning in the Face of Death

Kai Nielsen (1926 -) is professor emeritus of philosophy at the University of Calgary. Before moving to Canada, Nielsen taught for many years at New York University. He is a prolific author and a well-known contemporary philosopher.

In a 1978 essay, "Death and the Meaning of Life," Nielsen argues that for intellectuals in the modern world belief in an afterlife is virtually impossible to hold. Nonetheless he wants to resist the common view that death renders our lives meaningless. He claims to feel no terror or dread when contemplating death, despite the fact that he is convinced it means his utter annihilation. He admits to enjoying life and not wanting to die but, powerless to prevent the inevitable, he "takes rational precautions against premature death and faces the rest stoically ... Death should only be dreadful if one's life has been a waste."[15] He also wonders why must we "suffer angst, engage in theatrics and create myths for ourselves. Why not simply face it and get on with the living of our lives?"[16]

Of course critics claim that life is meaningless without an afterlife, gods and morality. Concerning morality Nielsen argues that things are right and wrong independent of gods. To support this claim he summons Plato's famous argument against equating the god's power with what is right. The key is that naked power does not imply goodness—we do not want to reduce morality to power worship. "The crucial thing to see is that there are things which we can recognize on reflection to be wrong, God or no God, and that we can be far more confident that we are right in claiming that they are wrong, than we can be in claiming any knowledge of God's or God's order."[17]

Furthermore, the absence of a god and an afterlife does not mean that life is pointless. True there may be no meanings *of* life, but that does not mean there are no purposes *in* life. It may be that the cosmos does not grant the former but that hardly denies us the latter. And the goals and ends that we seek in this life are sufficient "to make life meaningful in the sense that there are in our lives and our environment things worthwhile doing, having or experiencing, things that bring joy, understanding, exhilaration or contentment to ourselves or to others."[18] That such things are not eternal does not make them meaningless.

He admits that critics will argue that something is missing in this account—namely an objective meaning independent of the success of our subjective projects. This had led some to postulate hope in an afterlife that fulfills their aspirations, and has led others to abandon hope altogether. Nielsen advocates a different position. Why not hope that through our strivings we can make this world a better place: "a truly human society without exploitation and degradation in which all human beings will flourish?"[19] Such hope is consistent with both secular and religious ideals, and is far more intellectually respectable than positing other worlds to give life meaning.

Summary – We can have subjective meaning primarily found by creating a better world, even if there is no objective meaning.

6. Hazel Barnes: We Must Create Meaning

Hazel Barnes (1915-2008) was a longtime professor of philosophy at the University of Colorado at Boulder. She played a major role in introducing French existentialism to the English-speaking world through her translations and scholarship.

In her 1967 essay, "The Far Side of Despair," Barnes asks why people assume that a lack of meaning or a grand purpose for the universe is bad. She argues that individuals project meaning onto a meaningless universe because of a desire for immortality, a desire to share in the eternal goodness of the gods and their reality. The positive side to these beliefs is that it follows from them that what we do really matters, and a heaven awaits those who act correctly. The negative side is that there is a hell which corresponds to this promise of heaven. Of course not all views of higher meaning depend on the idea of personal immortality—Aristotelianism and Hebraism do not—but they still suggest there is some proper place for humankind in the world.

Existentialism rejects all pronouncements of meaning. "Humanistic existentialism finds no divine presence, no ingrained higher meaning, no reassuring absolute."[20] Still, it is a fallacy to draw the inference that my life is not worth living from the fact that the universe has no meaning. Our lives may have intrinsic value both to ourselves and to others, although the universe does not care about us. In this context Barnes quotes Merleau-Ponty: "Life makes no sense, but it is ours to make sense of."[21] And Sartre argues: "To say that we invent values means nothing except this: life has no meaning a priori. Before you live it, life is nothing, but it is for you to give it a meaning. Value is nothing other than this meaning which you choose."[22]

To contrast traditional views of meaning with existentialist ones, Barnes compares life to a blank game board with pieces but no instructions. Theological, rational, and nihilistic views all suggest that unless we can discover the correct pattern of the board and the correct instructions or rules, there is no reason to play the game. In contrast the existentialists maintain that though there is no pre-existing pattern imprinted on the board and no set of rules provided, we are left free to create our own game with its own patterns and rules. There is no objective truth about how to construct the game or live a life, but if the individual who constructs a life finds value in the creating, making, and living of a life then it has been worthwhile. Creating our own lives and values gives us satisfaction, elicits the approval of others, and may make it easier for others to live satisfying lives.

Still, for many this is not enough, they want some eternal, archetypical measurement for their lives. Barnes acknowledges that life is harder without belief in such things, but wonders if the price we would pay for this ultimate authority is too high. Given such an authority, humans would be measured and confined by non-human standards. We would be like slaves or children with our futures, not open to our choices, but prescribed for them. Humans "in the theological framework of the medieval man-centered universe has only the dignity of the child, who must regulate his life by the rules laid down by adults. The human adventure becomes a conducted tour … The time has come for man to leave his parents and to live in his own right by his own judgments."[23]

Another problem for many with creating your own meaning is the implied subjectivity of value. How do we understand that what some people find meaningful others think deplorable? Barnes responds that she welcomes the fact that we possess the freedom to create our own values and live uniquely, it is part of the growing up process.

A final difficulty manifests itself when we contemplate the future. What difference will it make in the end whether I live one kind of life rather than another? What is the point of it all if there is no destination, no teleology? Barnes counters: "If there is an absolute negative quality in the absence of what will not be, then there is a corresponding positive value in what will have been."[24] In other words if nothingness is bad, it is so only because some existing things were good. Moreover, "The addition of positive moments does not add up to zero even if the time arrives when nothing more is added to the series."[25]

Barnes rejects the view that human life is worthless and meaningless just because it is not connected to a non-human transcendent authority. We are right to rebel against the fact that our lives must end, but still we do continue to exist in a sense because

> We live in a human world where multitudes of other consciousnesses are ceaselessly imposing their meaning upon

[the external world]…and confronting the projects which I have introduced. It is in the future of these intermeshed human activities that I most fully transcend myself. In so far as "I" have carved out my being in this human world, "I" go on existing in its future.[26]

Summary – We must grow up and create meaning for ourselves, rather than imagining some outside agency can do this. And through our projects we have a limited immortality.

7. Raymond Martin: A Fast Car and a Good Woman

Raymond Martin is Crichton Professor of Philosophy at Union College. He spent most of his career at the University of Maryland. In his 1989 piece, "The Meaning of Life" Martin notes that problems come with life—poverty, sickness, suffering, pain, etc—that challenge the meaning of our lives. If we can avoid these problems, we should; if we cannot avoid them, we must accept them. Learning the difference between the two is part of the problem of life. Death is a special problem that challenges meaning in life, but Martin is unsure it is related to the question of whether our lives are worth living.

For Martin, the problem of the meaning of life is in determining how our lives can be worth living. This question is related to speculative questions about whether there is objective meaning in reality, but more importantly the question is a practical one—how to live our lives so that they are as worthwhile as possible. However, for some people the problem of how to live well includes demanding an answer to the speculative meaning of life question. Tolstoy is the classic example of a man whose existential angst leaps from his pages, causing us to wonder—what is it all for?

While many things challenge our belief in life's meaning—bad times, death, having our beliefs disputed—Martin wonders if philosophical questions are typically a source of psychological despair when things are going well. He cites Nagel as a philosopher who thinks that questions about the meaning of life can lead to deep psychological distress, if we consider for example how insignificant our lives appear from an objective perspective. In fact Nagel argues that questions about the meaning of life will often result in psychological crisis, and Tolstoy thought such questions could destroy you if you did not have faith.

But Martin thinks the foregoing analysis suspect, asking us to consider "a time when your life was at its subjective best ... Whatever your peak experience, were you worried then about the meaning of life?" [27] He thinks answer is no. At such moments we had solved the problem of life and questions of meaning did not arise. This indicates that happiness is the crucial issue, primarily because happy people do not turn questions into problems. If there is a problem of life then it is how to be happy.

Martin now turns to Taylor's view that meaning and values derive from actions in which we are truly engaged. But Martin finds Taylor's optimism too easy, just as he had found Nagel's pessimism too hard. As a middle way he argues that meaning is neither inevitable nor impossible but meaningful "largely to the degree that you are doing what you love to do."[28] Or, to go even further, life is meaningful when you get all the things that you want. So if we reflect on a time when we were really satisfied, we realize that then the meaning of life question did not arise. But still such satisfaction does not last. And that is because even when you get what you want, you always want more or you want something different or you want what you have in a different way. In short we are not easily satisfied. And that was largely Tolstoy's problem. He had everything but even when he got it he found that it did not last, that it was not completely satisfying.

Since getting what you want will satisfy you, we are led to Buddha's answer—do not want anything. Martin claims that while this may have worked for Buddha, it does not work for most of us. Moreover, not wanting just adds another thing to our list of wants; we want to not want! So we may have to accept that life offers only fleeting satisfactions and that doing what we love is the best we can do. Of course this does not solve the basic problem that satisfaction does not last—we are often dissatisfied with our lives even when they are going well. In that case the best we can do is whatever satisfies us: "a fast car and a good woman, or whatever you think will do it for you."[29] In the end it is disappointing to realize that we will never get the deep and lasting satisfaction we crave.

Finally, Martin believes his analysis illuminates the relationship between death and meaning. Why do we think that death threatens meaning? Because death puts an end to our search for satisfaction;

and the nearness of death shows us that we will never be fully satisfied. Death symbolizes defeat in our struggle for serenity. But in moments of complete satisfaction, in the ecstasy of love for example, death seems not to matter and we temporarily defeat death. But soon our desires return, our struggle to be satisfied continues: "Until death ends the struggle—perhaps forever."[30]

Summary – The only meaning life has comes from doing what you love. But in the end we cannot attain complete satisfaction.

8. John Kekes: Immoral Lives Can Be Meaningful

John Kekes is Professor Emeritus at SUNY-Albany. He begins his essay "The Meaning of Life" as follows: "Most of our lives are spent in routine activities ... It is natural to ask then why we should continue on this treadmill."[31] One answer is that nature, instinct, and training impel us to struggle. To seek more is to "misuse the respite we occasionally enjoy from the difficult business of living."[32] Many throughout the world struggle for the basics of life, without much time to worry about the meaning of life. Those in first world countries struggle instead for wealth, honor, and prestige, but when there is time left over for reflection they often wonder whether such things really do matter; they wonder about the meaning of it all.

What Gives Life Meaning? - Maybe life has no meaning. We may have evolved to ask questions, and have the time to ask them, but this doesn't mean we can answer them. Life may just be a brute fact, to be explained only by laws of nature. There may be no other meaning. We could respond to all this with cynicism or despair, but these poison the enjoyment of life. "Despair and cynicism cleave us into a natural self and a preying, harping, jeering, or self-pitying self. We are thus turned us against ourselves. Reflection sabotages our own projects."[33] This is why so many avoid deep questions and go on living as best they can. However, such avoidance is possible only if we are doing well. For as soon as the young look forward, the old look backward, or the sick look at their present state, the question of meaning will arise. But even if we are doing well, shouldn't we ask about meaning? Would it not be foolish to engage in projects which may not be valuable? In short, no matter what our situation, we are brought back to the question of the meaning of life.

Kekes now turns to the famous crisis of meaning experienced by John Stuart Mill's. Mill had meaning in his life— he wanted to improve the world—and then lost it as he recounts in his autobiography. He thought that even if all his desires for a better world were satisfied he would still not be happy because, of any proposed meaning, one can always ask: "and why does that have meaning?"[34] What happened was that Mill became disengaged from his projects, he became disillusioned. It was not that his life was worthless, pointless, destructive, trivial or futile—from an objective point of view his life was meaningful. What happened was that he no longer cared about or identified with his projects. Kekes responds that even if Mill's life was intrinsically meaningful and subjectively engaging, that would still not be sufficient for meaning because one can always conclude that all projects are ultimately absurd.

A similar notion is captured by Nagel's sense of the absurd—the pretension with which we take ourselves internally versus the apparent external insignificance of our lives. Still, many have taken the eternal perspective and remained concerned about human welfare; thus merely taking that perspective does not necessarily lead to the conclusion that life is meaningless. For Mill the issue was not that his life appeared absurd from a universal perspective but rather that he stopped caring about it, and he became desultory precisely because he stopped caring. Thus sometimes we lose commitment to our projects, not because they lack something, but because our will and emotions are not engaged in them. This leads Kekes to ask: "what is it that engages our will and emotions, and gives meaning to our lives, given that our projects are not defective and we do not suffer from a sense of absurdity?"[35] Typically we respond to this question with religious and moral answers.

The Religious Answer - The religious approach says value must come from the outside in terms of a cosmic order. Specific religions are interpretations of the cosmic order through revelation, scripture, miracles, church authority, religious experience, etc. While science tells us something of this order, it does not tell us everything. But we want to know everything about the cosmic order gives meaning to our lives. Furthermore, the better we know the order, the better our lives will go. If we are like dogs tied to carts drawn by horses, if that is the cosmic order, then the best we can do is to go along with the order and not oppose it. The Stoics thought we must conform to the order, while religious thinkers generally believe that the order is good. The key to meaning then is to find this order and live in harmony with it.

But there are problems with religious answers. First of all we have no direct access to the cosmic order since all evidence comes from the natural world. Thus we cannot know if there is cosmic order or, if there is, what form it takes. Moreover, even if the natural world did point to a cosmic order, this would not be enough to give us meaning, since we still would not know anything about the nature of that cosmic order. Furthermore, even if we could infer something of the cosmic order from the natural world that still would not be enough. Think again of Sisyphus. He knows his fate but temple building was not his purpose, it was the gods. He was enslaved by them. How then can their purposes give his life meaning? Sisyphus, pyramid builders, and dogs tied to carts—none of their lives have meaning.

So not only must there be a cosmic order but that order must be both necessary and good. Do we have any reason to believe this? Kekes thinks not. Can we derive inferences about the cosmic order from the natural world? No. If we are hones we must accept that the cosmic order, if it really is reflected by the natural world, is good, bad, and indifferent. So if the cosmic order must be good for our lives to have meaning, then they do not have meaning, since the cosmic order is at most partly good. In sum, the religious answer fails because 1) we have no reason to believe there is a cosmic order; 2) if there is one we know nothing about it; and 3) if we did infer something about the cosmic order from the natural world, reasonable persons would conclude it was not exclusively good.

The Moral Answer - The moral approach concerns the good independent of the gods, even if a god's will might reflect that good. We need to know what is good if we are to know how pursuing it gives meaning to life, and ethics looks for this in the natural world. Here we are concerned not with ethics in the narrow sense of what is right, but in the wide sense of what is good. To better understand this let us go back to Taylor. He thought meaning for Sisyphus could be subjective if he wanted to push rocks; that would make his life meaningful independent of the fact that the project seemed meaningless from an objective point of view. So it is wanting to do our projects that makes them meaningful, meaning comes from us. In other words meaning is subjective; it does not come from the projects themselves. Therefore the *subjective* view of meaning is that "a life has meaning if the agent sincerely thinks so, and it lacks meaning if the agent sincerely denies it."[35] By contrast the *objective* view states that "lives may lack meaning even if their agents think otherwise, for they may be mistaken."[36]

There are three reasons to reject the subjective view and accept the objective. *First*, if meaning is subjective, then there is no difference whether we want to pursue a project because we are being indoctrinated or manipulated, or because we truly think it meaningful after reflection. On this view discovering that we were simply wired to want something, say to push boulders up hills forever, would not change our minds about an activity's meaningfulness. But this seems wrong; discovering any of this should change our minds about meaning! Subjective desire or active engagement may be part of the meaning of life, but it does not seem to be all of it.

Second, even if we truly want to roll rocks, and have not been manipulated into wanting this, such a desire alone does not make the act meaningful unless it *matters* to us that rocks are rolled. We could still ask of this non-manipulated desire, why do it? So even if we are not manipulated, and want to do something that matters to us, we still do not have enough for meaning because questions about the value of our desires remain. Are we being manipulated by gods, media, or indoctrination? Do things matter to us because of upbringing, education, or society? We simply cannot answer questions like these without considering how reality is independent of us. This leads us back to the objective view.

Third, we pursue projects because we think they would make our lives better but they may not do so. We may change our minds about a project when it does not make our lives better, concluding that the project was not meaningful after all. But if believing a project meaningful were sufficient to making it meaningful, the subjective view of meaning, then we would not change our minds like this. All of this counts against the subjective view of meaning.

Now it might be said in defense of the subjective view that these three objections show that the truth of our beliefs does not affect whether our lives are meaningful. This is partly right and partly wrong. It is true we may find our projects meaningful even if we are manipulated or our projects are not good, but it is false that meaning is subjective. Objective considerations about wants being manipulated and beliefs being false still matter, since knowledge of these may destroy our belief in meaning. Thus in addition to subjective considerations, objective ones matter as well, for example that we have non-manipulated desires and true beliefs. Subjective willing, whether of a god or human, is not enough for meaning; for a meaningful life we must subjectively want some objective things that really make our lives better. However, none of this presupposes a cosmic order; there can be things that are really good without positing a cosmic order. In summary the moral approach says that our lives are meaningful if: 1) they are not worthless pointless, futile, etc; 2) we reject the view that all projects are absurd; 3) there are projects we want to pursue; 4) our desired projects will actually make our lives go better.

Conclusion - But when we ask about making our lives go better, do we have in mind morally or non-morally better? We could follow Socrates and say the morally good life is both the satisfying and the meaningful life, but this will not do and the moral answer fails. Why? First, morally good projects may not be satisfying; and second, even if morally good projects are satisfying it does not follow that *only* morally good lives are satisfying. It could be that either immoral or non-moral projects give meaning. That people can get meaning from immoral projects shows that the moral answer is mistaken.

Both moral and religious answers fail because they seek a general answer to the question, thereby failing to sufficiently emphasize individual differences. This seems to lead us back to the subjective view but, as we saw earlier, we had multiple reasons for rejecting that view. Since neither the subjective nor objective approach works we might be led to again consider the religious or moral approaches but, as we saw previously, they both failed. The former because there is no reason to think there is a cosmic order that confers meaning, and the latter because immoral lives can be meaningful.

This all leads Kekes to advancing a pluralistic approach to meaning in life—meaningful lives take a plurality of forms. A central claim of the pluralistic approach is that all approaches giving general answers are mistaken. The other basic claim is that morally bad lives may be meaningful and morally good lives may not be. Thus contrary the orthodox view, what makes a life meaningful and what makes it good are distinct.

Summary – Meaningful lives are not pointless, futile, trivial, or absurd and involve pursuing activities agents find engaging and life-bettering. These activities are found in the natural world, thus excluding a religious answer; and these activities may be immoral, thus excluding the moral answer. There are no general answers as to what activities or projects a subject will find rewarding and engaging.

9. David Schmidt: Engagement in Little Things

David Schmidt (1955-) is Kendrick Professor of Philosophy and joint Professor of Economics at the University of Arizona. In "The Meanings of Life" (2002) he admits that philosophy may not be able to deal with the question of the meaning of life, but he'll try to understand "life's meaning by reflecting on what it has been like to live one."[37] Schmidt begins by contrasting the existential attitude—that life's meaning is of extreme importance and that we must give meaning to our lives—with the Zen attitude—that meaning is not something to worry about and that meaning is found simply by being mindful in the present. Schmidt doesn't take sides on this matter, admitting that he is no sage and that it is hard to talk profoundly about such matters.

He next notes that while some lives mean more than others, meaning has *limits*. Why? Because: 1) meaning in life does not last; 2) meaning changes; 3) meaning may not be deep enough to fulfill our longings; 4) life may be the kind of thing that cannot have deep meaning; and 5) life is short. Ultimately our most lasting achievements are ephemeral. Although there are limits to meaning, that does not mean life is meaningless. Schmidt agrees with Taylor that being fully engaged in our lives, however trivial they might seem from a universal perspective, is what gives them limited meaning. Still, sadness accompanies knowing that the meaning of our lives is limited.

Schmidt now lists some of the components of meaningful lives, although he admits there are many ways to live them. First they have impact, maybe not on the cosmos, but on something important to you like your family. So you should not look for an impact where you don't have any, but where you do. Schmidt wonders about Nozick's claim that you need to leave permanent traces in the world—a higher standard for meaning—but suggests that we should probably be content with less. Features of meaningful lives are:

1) Meanings are symbolic – For example, we can give meaning to simple worms if we want. Meanings need not be intrinsic, only meaningful to us. Of course two persons could have the same experience with one finding it meaningful, the other finding it meaningless.

2) Meanings are choices – We choose whether our lives have sufficient meaning for us. If we choose to view them as meaningless, then we should not worry about it since that is meaningless too. And if we can't enjoy meaninglessness, then we should choose to treat life as meaningful.

3) Meanings track relationships – Our lives derive meaning when they mean something to the people around us. Our lives communicate things to others—that they are important or we care about them—and maybe their meaning is in what they communicate.

4) Meanings track activity – Most of us don't want to plug into "the matrix-like happiness machine" which suggests we want more than experiences; we want the meaning that comes from activities. This raises questions as to whether you would think life in the machine was objectively or only subjectively meaningful. Meaning also seems related to the activity of making contact with external reality, something we cannot do in the machine.

In order to experience deep meaning, we need to bring a personal touch to life or decorate our house in Schmidt's metaphor. Life is the picture we put on the bare walls. As we age we may lament the path we chose, or regret that we could only choose one path. Maybe meaning is being attentive to the path we chose and, though we cannot state what the meaning of life is, we can still enjoy the process. Just engaging in certain activities—coaching little league football in his example—is sometimes sufficient.

Schmidt wrote a postscript to his original article after he was diagnosed with a brain tumor. In it he claimed that the encounter with death had not changed his view of the meaning of life. You cannot live each day as if it is your last and it is hard to make permanent traces in the world. Some say that life is meaningful if we finish painting one big picture which has an impact; others maintain that meaning comes from painting many smaller pictures, which has the advantage of something being done if the brush is taken away unexpectedly. Schmidtz says that our lives can be meaningful because of the little pieces of our lives that slowly add up, even if they never produce a completed work of art.

Summary – Being engaged in our lives is what gives them meaning. There are a few things we can say about life's meaning, but we can never state its meaning with clarity. The best we can do is find meaning in what we are engaged in.

10. Robert Solomon: Live According to Your Vision

Robert C. Solomon (1942 – 2007) received his PhD from the University of Michigan and was Quincy Lee Centennial Professor of Philosophy and Business at the University of Texas at Austin for many years until his death. In a chapter of his book, *The Big Questions,* Solomon asks: "What is the meaning of life? This is *the* big question—the hardest to answer, the most urgent and at the same time the most obscure."[38] The question usually arises when we something has gone wrong in our lives, whereas if our everyday lives are filled with activity we seldom think about the question.

Solomon first considers the meaning of the word meaning in the question. Often the meaning of something is what it refers to—like a word or a sign—but what do our lives refer to? We might say they refer to other people or the universe or a god, but this does not seem to be the same kind of reference. Nonetheless, many people do think of their lives as having meaning by reference to something outside themselves like their children, or gods, or an afterlife.

Regarding children, Solomon argues that if the meaning of someone's life is their children we can immediately ask, what is the meaning of your children's lives and their children, ad infinitum? It is hard to see how this all makes your own life meaningful. Regarding gods, it is again hard to see how this answers the question. For now we must ask: why did gods create us? If for some purpose, what was it? Why do gods need worlds anyway, what is the meaning of the world? It is not clear how gods would solve the problem. Regarding the afterlife, similar questions emerge. Is this life so insignificant that only reference to another one could make it significant? Why does the fact that the next life lasts longer make it more meaningful? What should we do in this life to be rewarded in the next? So the questions re-emerge: what should we do, what is important, how should we live? So while it is true that people dedicate their lives to their children or their gods or a possible afterlife, none of these answers really answer the question—they just raise more questions like: What is the meaning of our children's lives? How do I live to serve a god? What is the purpose of an afterlife?

Perhaps then life is meaningless, since nothing external can give it meaning. Solomon replies that the fact that there is no external meaning outside of life does not imply that there is no meaning in life. In the same way that words have meaning in context, our lives may have meaning in context. If we truly devote them to our children or our gods, we can give our lives meaning.

Solomon further argues that the question of meaning in life does not require a specific answer so much as a vision of life in which you have a role. This vision is important since it colors the way you see the world. For example if you think life is a business contract you will probably see it differently than someone who sees it as a gift from the gods. Some of these grand images of life which can give it meaning include life as: a game, tragedy, mission, story, art, adventure, disease, desire, nirvana, altruism, honor, learning, frustration, relationships, or an investment.

If live is a *game,* you might not take it too seriously but still want to win or be a good sport. If life is a *story*, you might see yourself as the hero of an unfolding narrative to be judge by the quality of the role you played. If life is a *tragedy,* living one's life bravely in the face of our inevitable death may be the best we can do. If life is a *joke*, we could see our lives less seriously and laugh at them. If life is a *mission,* you might convert others, bring about revolution, raise children, advance science or promote morality. If life is an *art,* we may want to create our lives as ones with beauty, style or class. If life is an *adventure,* we would live life to the fullest, taking risks and enjoying challenges. If life is a *disease,* then all ends in death. If life is *desire,* the satisfaction of desire brings meaning; if life is *nirvana,* then the goal is to eliminate desire and achieve tranquility. If life is *altruism,* we live for others even if they do not reciprocate. If life is *honor,* then we must fulfill expectations and do our duty. If life is *learning,* we derive satisfaction from learning, from growing and developing our potential. If life is *suffering*, perhaps the best we can do is detach ourselves through contemplation or self-denial. If life is an *investment,* we think of the time of our lives as capital invested to gain a reward—say money or fame. And if life is *relationships,* then love and friendship are most important.

Solomon does not prescribe any one of these over another; instead he presents them as various images or visions which can give meaning to human life. Thus meaning is something we create, by choosing to live in accord with a vision of life of our own choosing.

Summary – We create meaning by living in accord with our vision of life.

11. David Lund: Our Search for Meaning is Meaningful

David Lund is Professor Emeritus of Philosophy at Bemidji State University in Bemidji, Minnesota where he taught for many years. His 1999 textbook, *Making Sense Of It All: An Introduction to Philosophical Inquiry*, concludes with a chapter devoted to the meaning of life. He asks: What is the point of it all? Is this point found in our daily lives, or is there a higher purpose to our lives? How can anything matter if all ends in death? The basic problem with answering such questions is that they depend upon our answers to other philosophical questions such as: Is there objective truth? Are we free? Is there personal identity over time? Does a non-natural realm exist? Do we survive death?

It is tempting to think of the meaning of life as something beyond life, and we do say meaning *of* life instead of meaning *in* life. Yet, from the cosmic standpoint, it does not seem to matter much whether we lived or not, as all ends in universal death. Of course our day to day lives seem significant, as we concern ourselves with happiness, self-actualization, love or other aspects of our lives. But the universe does not care about our interests: "It is indifferent to our ideals, our achievements, our values, our very existence. It is a vast spiritual emptiness. There is no cosmic plan in which our lives have a permanent value."[39]

In response we might look to the gods' purposes, but this merely pushes the question back. How does fulfilling the god's purposes make our lives meaningful? For this answer to terminate our search for meaning, we must embrace the god's purposes, they must become our own. So meaning comes largely from within us. The same with an afterlife, either it is intrinsically meaningful or not. If it is not meaningful, then we would have to look to some other world for its meaning; if it is meaningful, then this life could be too. This suggests that the meaning of life must be found within us, in this life. In fact most of us do think our lives are intrinsically valuable and most of us try to live well no matter what. Questions about the meaning of life then are about whether our lives are valuable beyond their intrinsic value.

Lund proceeds by distinguishing activities that have intrinsic value for people but which are not goal oriented, with activities that are not intrinsically valuable but which have derivative value because they are goal directed. Lund concludes that for an activity to be meaningful:

> It must have enough intrinsic value to be worthwhile in itself; it must also have derivative value in virtue of being directed toward a goal; and this goal must be important and achievable. An activity would be meaningless if it lacked all of these features. And though it may still have meaning, it would be meaning-deficient to some degree if it lacked at least one of them.[40]

Unfortunately our lives may be futile because of the nature of the world itself. If we cannot achieve our goals, the goals that if achieved would prevent life from being meaningless, then we can say that life is futile. We may think that our lives have value beyond their intrinsic value, but if they do not then our lives are futile whether we know it or not. Perhaps it is only our illusions that prevent us from seeing them this way. We might assume that there is objective truth and pursue it, but if we found there was no such truth our pursuit of it would be futile. Or it might be that moral values are subjective. If we had lived as if values were objective, then we gave our lives for things which were ultimately insignificant. Of course we could simply accept that moral subjectivism holds and find meaning in our subjective values.

The loss of theism makes the meaning problem worse for many people since the truth of theism solves the problem of the indifferent universe, and the futility that accompanies it. This is why atheism is so devastating for meaning and why it is so difficult to accept. In response, Lund suggests we face our probable fate with honor.

> It is unbecoming of us, indeed unworthy of us, to be unwilling or unable to face the truth, whatever that should turn out to be. If a more uplifting view of the world—one more in accord with our hopes—can be sustained only with a faith that has no concern for the truth, then it is not worth having; and we should have the intellectual courage to reject it.[41]

The quest for meaning is a quest for understanding and truth—a truth we must find for ourselves.

> … there are churches and other institutions or organizations that would have us passively accept, without critical reflection, the dogmas they foist upon us. But we must not succumb to this, even if what we hear from these sources is what we would very much like to believe. We must insist on thinking things out for ourselves and on having our beliefs reflect our understanding of truth, rather than our desires or the opinions of some self-proclaimed authority.[42]

To live this way is courageous and wise; it is to reject the dogma imposed by authority. It also evokes compassion at the real suffering and lack of meaning that we all endure. "Such compassion, especially in conjunction with courage and wisdom, will help us to live so as to leave a good legacy, and to see that one's legacy is of great importance, despite the likelihood that it be short-lived."[43] The search for truth and meaning may never succeed, but the search itself is all the meaning that there probably is, and is as close to the meaning of life as we will probably come.

Summary – Our lives may well be futile, but we can find some small meaning by searching for truth, accepting whatever it is that we find.

12. Julian Baggini: We Give Life Meaning By Loving

Julian Baggini (1968 -) is a British philosopher, author of several books about philosophy written for a general audience, and co-founder and editor-in-chief of The Philosophers' Magazine. He was awarded his PhD in 1996 from University College London. His 2004 book, *What's It All About: Philosophy & The Meaning of Life,* conducts a secular and non-hubristic inquiry into the question of the meaning of life. Secular because we cannot know if religion is true, and not hubristic since it does not claim there is some secret answer to the question. Were there such an answer we would probably have discovered it by now. Baggini begins by looking at some of the proposed answers.

Can living life *forward* give life meaning? Instead of looking into the past why not look to some future goal, like avenging your brother's death? The problem with this answer is that we can always ask of this future, or any future, why bring it about? And that question leads to the quest for some final end. In short any why/because series can be extended infinitely into either the past or future and never definitively and finally puts an end to our questions. Other problems with looking to the future include: 1) we might die before we reach our goal; 2) even if we are immortal this does not solve our problem since meaning would always be in our future; and 3) if we do reach our goal, then what?

The main problem with a future-oriented life is that it locates meaning in a specific moment in time. This raises an obvious question: shouldn't we expect some meaning from the present too? It seems then that meaning involves something enduring, something about which no further why questions need be asked, and this something must in some sense exist now. In other words the key to meaning must be found in something that is an end in itself.

Baggini now turns to the notion that gods or an afterlife give life meaning. While believing in a god is no answer to the question of the meaning of life, we could stop worrying and accept that the gods provide meaning. However, this is to give up the search. In this case you don't know the meaning of life, you just stop asking the question. As for an afterlife, is there such a thing? The evidence suggests there is no afterlife and even if there were what would be the meaning of it? The more important question is whether life can be meaningful without this assumption.

To fully answer our question we need to find a way that life can be meaningful that is not derived from the gods, or the past or the future, but from within. Baggini proceeds to investigate six ways (helping others, serving humanity, being happy, becoming successful, enjoying each day, and freeing your mind) that might provide life with meaning. His concludes that all of them may be part of a good or meaningful life, but they are not all of it. They do not guarantee that our lives are meaningful because, of any of them, we can still ask: is such a life meaningful?

What all this means is that we are threatened with meaninglessness. According to Baggini our choices are to accept that: 1) life is meaningless; 2) the question is meaningless; or 3) meaning is impossible to discover. Regarding 1—while life is not meaningful in an objective sense, it can still be subjectively meaningful. Regarding 2—while life is not the kind of thing that can bear meaning, it cannot bear meaning anymore than sound can bear color, it can have meaning for the person living it. Regarding 3—although we cannot know the meaning of life with certainty, we can still find our lives meaningful by living them. One might say that such a life is not sufficiently examined and thus not worth living, but that is mere intellectual snobbery. Unexamined lives can be worth living if the people living them find them worthwhile. So a life can be subjectively meaningful despite the lack of any objective meaning.

Baggini's admits "This kind of rationalistic-humanistic approach leaves many unsatisfied."[44] A fundamental objection to such an approach is that it separates morality from meaning. Can human values really be enough to ground value? In response Baggini says: 1) we might say that certain people have meaningful but immoral lives; or 2) we could say that subjective meaning is a necessary but not sufficient condition for meaningful life—the life must also be moral. As to the charge that this second response is ad hoc, Baggini reminds the reader that life is meaningful only if it is worth living. And this is to recognize that all humans have an equal claim to a good life and to make someone's life go worse is a moral wrong. Baggini also reminds readers that simply because life has to have value in itself and for the person living it "does not … mean that the only person able to judge the value is the person living the life…"[45] Individuals may be mistaken about the value of their lives; just because they think they have meaningful lives does not make them so.

Another objection to a humanistic account of meaning says that we should accept and be attuned to the mystery in life and that the rationalistic humanistic account does not do this. Baggini responds that this is merely a plea from those who like mystery. He has not said that there are no gods or that people cannot get meaning from them; he just does not think there are good reasons to believe in the transcendent and he finds his meaning elsewhere. Furthermore, there is plenty of mystery about how to actually have meaningful lives; discovering what is meaningful to us is quite mysterious. Baggini thinks that attunement to the mystery that we are alive at all is a reason to be thankful. In fact this is a more noble kind of mystery than believing in the mystery of a god or afterlife, which Baggini thinks are motivated by fear that without gods we would have to take responsibility for our lives.

The tragedy and fragility of life suggests that love, a topic on which philosophers are notoriously silent, is the answer to the problem of human existence. The desire to do good things is motivated not by reason but by love. What then of love and happiness? They are connected, Baggini asserts, but love is not the same as happiness. Love persists thru unhappiness and its object is the beloved. Love shows the value we place in authenticity since we want to be loved for who we are. Love provides insight into true success, the kind that makes life meaningful. Love requires us to seize the day; otherwise we might let it pass us by. Love shows that we can have meaningful lives without philosophy, without a careful examination of our lives.

Philosophy is not good at examining love or the non-rational components of human life which reveals the limits of philosophical insight. In the end love is not motivated by reason. The rational-humanistic approach is not misguided however; rather, it shows the limits of our ability to understand life. And it also shows loves' limits, mortality and fragility. "Sadly, it is not true that all you need is love. Love, like life, is valuable, but fragile and subject to no guarantees. It is fraught with risk and disappointment, as well as being the source of great elation and joy."[46] In the end the humanist accepts that morality, mystery, meaning, and love exist without transcendental support."The transcendentalist's desire for something more is understandable, but the humanist's refusal to succumb is, I believe, a sign of her ability to confront and accept the limits of human understanding and, ultimately, human existence."[47]

Baggini concludes his deflationary account of meaning by saying that the meaning of life is available to all, not only to the guardians who claim a monopoly on it. His view thus challenges the power of those who would control us, and gives us the responsibility of determining meaning for ourselves. But knowing about the meaning of life does not provide a recipe for living it. It is hard to live meaningfully, it is an ongoing project, and one is never finished with the task. Baggini concedes that his is not the last word on the subject, that we need more than philosophers to work our problem out, and that no book is ever the final word on the subject. Also people are different so we cannot offer an instruction manual for all—only suggest a framework within which persons might live meaningfully.

In the end the meaning of life is not that mysterious, it is something within our grasp, and we can live meaningfully. Hope rather than despair is called for, since there are many ways to live meaningful lives. We can recognize all the good and bad things in life and still see that there are lots of ways to live meaningful lives.

> We can see the value of happiness ... We can learn to appreciate the pleasures of life ... We can see the value of success ... We can see the value of seizing the day ... We can appreciate the value in helping others lead meaningful lives ... And finally, we can recognize the value of love, as perhaps the most powerful motivator to do anything at all.[48]

Summary – We can give our lives meaning by doing meaningful things and recognizing the value of love.

13. Bertrand Russell: Worshipping as a Free Man

Bertrand Arthur William Russell, 3rd Earl Russell, (1872 – 1970) was a British philosopher, logician, mathematician, historian, atheist, and social critic. He is considered, along with his protégé Ludwig Wittgenstein, one of the founders of analytic philosophy and is widely held to be one of the 20th century's most important logicians. He co-authored, with A. N. Whitehead, *Principia Mathematica*, an attempt to ground mathematics in logic. His writings were voluminous and covered a vast range of topics including politics, ethics, and religion. Russell was awarded the Nobel Prize in Literature in 1950 "in recognition of his varied and significant writings in which he champions humanitarian ideals and freedom of thought." Russell is thought by many to be the greatest philosopher of the 20th century.

Russell's view of the meaning of life is set forth most clearly in his 1903 essay: "A Free Man's Worship." It begins with an imaginary conversation about the history of creation between Mephistopheles, the devil, and Dr. Faustus, a man who sells his soul to the devil in return for power and wealth. In this account god had grown weary of the praise of the angels, and thought it might be more amusing to gain the praise of beings that suffered. Hence god created the world.

Russell describes the epic cosmic drama and how after eons of time the earth and human beings came to be. Humans, seeing how fleeting and painful life is before their inevitable death, vowed that there must be purpose outside of this world. And though following their instincts led to sin and the need for god's forgiveness, humans believed that god had a good plan leading to a harmonious ending for humankind. God, convinced of human gratitude for the suffering he had caused, destroyed man and all creation.

Russell argues that this not so uplifting story is consistent with the world-view of modern science. To elaborate he penned some of the most pessimistic and often quoted lines in the history of twentieth-century philosophy:

> That man is the product of causes which had no prevision of
> the end they were achieving; that his origin, his growth, his
> hopes and fears, his loves and his beliefs, are but the outcome
> of accidental collocations of atoms; that no fire, no heroism, no

intensity of thought and feeling, can preserve an individual life beyond the grave; that all the labors of the ages, all the devotion, all the inspiration, all the noonday brightness of human genius, are destined to extinction in the vast death of the solar system, and that the whole temple of Man's achievement must inevitably be buried beneath the debris of a universe in ruins--all these things, if not quite beyond dispute, are yet so nearly certain, that no philosophy which rejects them can hope to stand. Only within the scaffolding of these truths, only on the firm foundation of unyielding despair, can the soul's habitation henceforth be safely built.[49]

Still, despite the ultimate triumph of vast universal forces, humans are superior to this unconscious power in important ways—they are free and self-aware. This is the source of their value. But most humans do not recognize this, instead choosing to placate and appease the gods in hope of reprieve from everlasting torment. They refuse to believe that their gods do not deserve praise, worshiping them despite the pain the gods inflict. Ultimately they fear the *power* of the gods, but the god's power is not a reason for respect and worship. For respect to be justified, creation must really be good. But the reality of the world belies this claim; the world is not good and submitting to its blind power enslaves and ultimately kills us.

Instead let us courageously admit that the world is bad, but nevertheless love truth, goodness, beauty, and perfection, despite the fact that the universe will destroy such things. By rejecting this universal power and the death it brings, we find our true freedom. While our lives will be taken from us by the universe, our thoughts can be free in the face of this power. In this way we maintain our dignity.

However, we should not respond to the disparity between the facts of the world and its ideal form with indignation, for this binds our thoughts to the evil of the universe. Rather we ought to follow the Stoics, resigned to the fact that life does not give us all we want. By renouncing desires we achieve resignation, while the freedom of our thoughts can still create art, philosophy and beauty. But even these goods ought not to be desired too ardently or we will remain indignant; rather we must be resigned to accept that our free thoughts are all that life affords in a hostile universe. We must be resigned to the existence of evil, to the fact that death, pain, and suffering will take everything from us. The courageous bear their suffering nobly and without regret; their submission to power an expression of their wisdom.

Still, we need not be entirely passive in our renunciation either. We can actively create music, art, poetry and philosophy, thereby incorporating the ephemeral beauty of this world into our hearts, achieving the most that humans can achieve. Yet such achievements are difficult, for we must first encounter despair and dashed hopes so that we may be somewhat freed from the Fate that will engulf us all—freed by the wisdom, insight, joy, and tenderness that our encounter with darkness brings. As Russell puts it:

> When, without the bitterness of impotent rebellion, we have learnt both to resign ourselves to the outward rule of Fate and to recognize that the non-human world is unworthy of our worship, it becomes possible at last so to transform and refashion the unconscious universe, so to transmute it in the crucible of imagination, that a new image of shining gold replaces the old idol of clay.[50]

In our minds we find the beauty that we create in the face of Fate and tragedy, and in this way we master the power of nature. Life is tragedy, but we need not give in; instead we can find the "beauty of tragedy" and embrace it. In death and pain there is sanctity, awe, and a feeling of the sublime. In the experience of such feelings we forget petty and trivial desires and, at least temporarily, transcend the loneliness and futility of being a human confronted with vast forces over which one has no control, and which do not care for us. To take the tragedy of life into one's heart, to feel it, but to respond with renunciation, wisdom, and charity, is the ultimate victory for man: "To abandon the struggle for private happiness, to expel all eagerness of temporary desire, to burn with passion for eternal things—this is emancipation, and this is the free man's worship."[51] For Russell the contemplation of Fate and tragedy are the way we subdue them.

As for our fellow companions, all we can do is to ease their sorrow and sufferings and not add to the misery that Fate and death will bring. We can take pride that we did not add to their pain. Nonetheless the universe continues its inevitable march to universal death and humans are condemned to lose everything. All we can do is to cherish those brief moments when thought and love ennoble us, and reject the cowardly terror of less virtuous persons who worship Fate. We must ignore the tyranny of reality that continually undermines all of our hopes and dreams and aspirations. As Russell so eloquently puts it:

> Brief and powerless in man's life; on him and all his race the slow, sure doom falls pitiless and dark. Blind to good and evil, reckless of destruction, omnipotent matter rolls on its relentless way; for man, condemned today to lose his dearest, tomorrow himself to pass through the gate of darkness, it remains only to cherish … the lofty thoughts that ennoble his little day; disdaining the coward terrors of the slave of Fate, to worship at the shrine that his own hands have built; undismayed by the empire of chance, to preserve a mind free from the wanton tyranny that rules his outward life; proudly defiant of the irresistible forces that tolerate, for a moment, his knowledge and condemnation, to sustain alone, a weary but unyielding Atlas, the world that his own ideals have fashioned despite the trampling march of unconscious power.[52]

Summary – There is no objective meaning in life. We should be resigned to this, not believing otherwise just because it is comforting, but strive nonetheless to actively create beauty, truth, and perfection. In this way we achieve some freedom from the eternal forces that will destroy us.

14. Richard Taylor: Engaging Our Wills

Richard Taylor (1919 – 2003) was an American philosopher renowned for his controversial positions and contributions to metaphysics. He advocated views as various as free love and fatalism, and was also an internationally-known beekeeper. He taught at Brown, Columbia and the University of Rochester, and had visiting appointments at about a dozen other institutions. His best known book was *Metaphysics* (1963).

In the concluding chapter of his 1967 book, *Good and Evil: A New Direction*, Taylor suggests that we examine the notion of a meaningless existence so that we can contrast it with a meaningful one. He takes Camus' image of Sisyphus as archetypical of meaninglessness—pointless and eternal toil. Taylor notes that it is not the weight of the rock or the repetitiveness of the work that makes Sisyphus' task unbearable, it is rather its pointlessness. The same pointlessness may be captured by other stories—say by digging and then filling in a ditch forever. Crucial to all these stories is that nothing ever comes of such labor.

But now suppose that Sisyphus' work slowly built a great temple on his mountaintop: "then the aspect of meaninglessness would disappear."[53] In this case his labors have a point, they have meaning. Taylor further argues that the subjective meaninglessness of Sisyphus' activity would be eliminated were the Gods to have placed within him "a compulsive impulse to roll stones."[54] Implanted with such desires, the gods provide him the arena in which to fulfill them. While we may still view Sisyphus' toil meaningless from the outside, for externally the situation has not changed, we can now see that fulfilling this impulse would be satisfying to Sisyphus from the inside. For now he is doing exactly what he wants to do—forever.

Taylor now asks: is life endlessly pointless or not? To answer this question he considers the existence of non-human animals—endless cycle of eating and being eaten, fish swimming upstream only to die and have offspring repeat the process, birds flying halfway around the globe only to return and have others do likewise. He concludes that these lives are paradigms of meaninglessness. That humans are part of this vast machine is equally obvious. As opposed to non-human animals we may choose our goals, achieve them, and take pride in that achievement. But even if we achieve our goals, they are transitory and soon replaced by others. If we disengage ourselves from the prejudice we have toward our individuals concerns, we will see our lives to be like Sisyphus'. If we consider the toil of our lives we will find that we work to survive, and in turn pass this burden on to our children. The only difference between us and Sisyphus is that we leave it to our children to push the stone back up the hill.

And even were we to erect monuments to our activities, they too would turn slowly turn to dust. That is why, coming upon a decaying home, we are filled with melancholy:

> There was the hearth, where a family once talked, sang, and made plans; there were the rooms, here people loved, and babes were born to a rejoicing mother; there are the musty remains of a sofa, infested with bugs, once bought at a dear price to enhance an ever-growing comfort, beauty, and warmth. Every small piece of junk fills the mind with what once, not long ago, was utterly real, with children's voices, plans made, and enterprises embarked upon.[55]

When we ask what it all was for, the only answer is that others will share the same fate, it will all be endlessly repeated. The myth of Sisyphus' then exemplifies our fate, and this recognition inclines humans to deny their fate—to invent religions and philosophies designed to provide comfort in the face of this onslaught.

But might human life still have meaning despite its apparent pointlessness? Consider again how Sisyphus' life might have meaning; again if he were to erect a temple through his labors. Notice not only that the temple would eventually turn to dust, but that upon completion of his project he would be faced with boredom. Whereas before his toil had been his curse, now its absence would be just as hellish. Sisyphus would now be "contemplating what he has already wrought and can no longer add anything to, and contemplating it for an eternity!"[56] Given this conclusion, that even erecting a temple would not give Sisyphus meaning, Taylor returns to his previous thought—suppose that Sisyphus was imbued with a desire to labor in precisely this way? In that case his life would have meaning because of his deep and abiding interest in what he was doing. Similarly, since we have such desires within us, we should not be bored with our lives if we are doing precisely what we have an inner compulsion to do: "This is the nearest we may hope to get to heaven…"[57]

To support the idea that meaning is found in this engagement of our will in what we are doing, Taylor claims that if those from past civilizations or the past inhabitants of the home he previously described were to come back and see that what was once so important to them had turned to ruin, they would not be dismayed.

Instead they would remember that their hearts were involved in those labors when they were engaged in them. "There is no more need of them [questions about life's meaning] now—the day was sufficient to itself, and so was the life."[58] We must look at all life like this, its justification and meaning come from persons doing what "it is their will to pursue."[59] This can be seen in a human from the moment of birth, in its will to live. For humans "the point of [their] living, is simply to be living..."[60] Surely the castles that humans build will decay, but it would not be heavenly to escape from all this, that would be boredom: "What counts is that one should be able to begin a new task, a new castle, a new bubble. It counts only because it is there to be done and [one] has the will to do it."[61]

Philosophers who look at the repetitiveness of our lives and fall into despair fail to realize that we may be endowed, from the inside, with the desire to do our work. Thus: "The meaning of life is from within us, it is not bestowed from without, and it far exceeds in both beauty and permanence any heaven of which men have ever dreamed or yearned for."[62]

Summary – We give meaning to our lives by the active engagement our wills have in our projects.

15. R. M. Hare: Nothing Matters?

R.M. Hare (1919 – 2002) was an English moral philosopher who held the post of White's Professor of Moral Philosophy at the University of Oxford from 1966 until 1983 and then taught for a number of years at the University of Florida. He was one of the most important ethicists of the second half of the twentieth century.

Hare begins by telling the story of a happy 18 year old Swiss boy who stayed with Hare in his house at Oxford. After reading Camus' *The Stranger* the boy's personality changed, becoming withdrawn, sullen, and depressed. (*The Stranger* explores existential themes like death and meaning; its title character Meursault is emotionally alienated, detached, and innately passive.) The boy told Hare that after reading Camus he had become convinced that *nothing matters*. Hare found it extraordinary that the boy was so affected.

As a philosopher concerned with the meaning of terms, Hare asked the young boy what "matters" means, what does it mean to be matter or be important? The boy said that to say something matters "is to express concern about that something."[63] But Hare wondered whose concern is important here? When we say the something matters, the question arises, "matters to whom?" Usually it's the speakers concern that is expressed, but it could be someone else's concern. We often say things like "it matters to you" or "it doesn't matter to him." In these cases we refer not to our own concern, but to someone else's.

In Camus' novel the phrase "nothing matters" could express the view of the author, the main character, or the reader (the young boy.) It's not Camus' unconcern that is being expressed, since he was concerned enough to write the novel—writing the novel obviously mattered to Camus. It is clear in the novel that the main character does think that nothing matters—he doesn't care about hardly anything. Still, Hare thinks that even Meursault is concerned about some things.

Hare doesn't think it possible to be concerned about nothing at all, since we always choose to do one thing rather than another thereby revealing, however slightly, what matters to us. At the end of Camus' novel Meursault is so upset by the priest's offer of religion that he attacks him in a rage. This display of passion shows that something did matter to Meursault, otherwise he would have done nothing. Yet even supposing that nothing does matter to a fictional character: why should that matter to the Swiss boy? In fact the boy admitted that he cares about many things, which is to say that things do matter to him. Hare thinks the boy's problem was not to find things that matter, but to prioritize them. He needed to find out what he valued.

Hare claims that our values come from our own wants and the imitation of others. Maturing in large part is bringing these two desires together—the desire to have our own values and to be like others with the former taking priority. "In the end...to say that something matters for us, we must ourselves be concerned about it; other people's concern is not enough, however much in general we may want to be like them."[64] Nonetheless we often develop our own values by imitating others. For instance we may pretend to like philosophy because we think our philosophy professor is cool, and then gradually we develop a taste for it. This process often works in the reverse; my parents want me to do x, so I do y. Eventually, through this process of conforming and non-conforming, we slowly develop our own values.

Hare concludes that things did matter to the young boy and he was just imitating Meursault by saying that nothing matters, just as he was imitating him by smoking. What the boy did not understand was that matter is a word that expresses concern; it is not an activity. Mattering is *not* something things do, like chattering. So the phrase "my wife chatters," is not like the phrase "my wife matters." The former refers to an activity; the latter expresses my concern for her. The problem comes when we confuse our concern with an activity. Then we start to look in the world for mattering and when we do not find things actively doing this mattering, we get depressed. We do not observe things mattering, things matter to us if we care about them. Mattering doesn't describe something things do, but something that happens to us when we care about things. To say nothing mattes is hypocritical; we all care about something. (Even if what we care about is that nothings seems to matter.)

As for his Swiss friend, Hare says he was no hypocrite; he was just confused about what the word matter meant. Hare also suggests that we are the kinds of beings who generally care about things, and those who sincerely care about almost nothing are just unusual. In the end we cannot get rid of values—we are creatures that value things. Of course when confronted with various values, so many different things about which to be concerned, it is easy to through up our hands and say that nothing matters. When confronted with this perplexity about what to be concerned about, about what to value, Hare says we might react in one of two ways. First, we might reevaluate our values and concerns to see if they are really ours; or second, we might stop thinking about what is truly of concern altogether. Hare counsels that we follow the former course, as the latter alternative leads to stagnation: "We content ourselves with the appreciation of those things, like eating, which most people can appreciate without effort, and never learn to prize those things whose true value is apparent only to those who have fought hard to achieve it..."[65]

Summary – We all generally care about some things, some things do matter to us. We don't find this mattering in the world; it is something we bestow upon things and persons. Hare suggests we find value (or meaning) in things which are really worthwhile.

16. Irving Singer: Creating Value

Irving Singer is Professor of Philosophy at MIT where he has taught since 1958. He is a voluminous writer and the author of *Meaning in Life* in three volumes, as well as the three volume trilogy, *The Nature of Love.*

Singer says there are basically three positions regarding the meaning of life: a) traditional religious answers; b) nihilistic answers; and c) create our own meaning answers. Singer grants that religious answers provide many persons with meaning but he rejects them:

> this pattern of belief is based on non-verifiable assumptions that exceed the limits of natural events and ordinary experience. Take away the transcendental props, which nowadays have become wobbly after centuries of criticism, and the grand edifice cannot stand. The challenge in our age is to understand how meaning can be acquired without dubious fantasying beyond the limits of our knowledge.[66]

Singer also rejects nihilism, especially the idea that the universe is indifferent to whatever we value. Singer counters that what we want is valuable to us whether or not the universe cares. Our values originate in our human condition; they spring from, but do not contradict, a world that we should not expect to care about us anymore than we expect this of other inanimate things. One can consistently hold that they both act with purpose and that the universe is purposeless. Our values do not exist from the eternal perspective, but they are not arbitrary, irrational, or absurd; our values emanate from our evolved nature.

While Singer's thoughts on the topic are vast and complex, the secret to understanding it is found in the title of his first major book on the subject, *Meaning in Life: The Creation of Value.* Meaning is something we *create.* Yet he is sensitive to the rejoinder that regardless of what matters to us subjectively, nothing matters objectively. Here he notes two responses: 1) if something matters to an individual then it matters, period; and 2) if nothing matters then it doesn't matter that nothing matters. However, neither response reassures. That things matter only to us is not enough, and that things do not matter at all provides no comfort.

In response to this conundrum we might welcome the notion that nothing matters. If we embrace this thought we may no longer be tormented by a social faux pas or even by the fact that all our efforts will finally come to nothing. We may no longer need to contrast the meager with the important; we could leave self-righteousness behind, accepting ourselves and others. But what then should we do, what then should we value? The idea that nothing matters is ultimately unhelpful.

Instead Singer argues that accepting that nothing matters is to lose touch with one's instincts, as we naturally find things matter to us. By simply being alive we reveal that things do matter to us; in large part being alive is about choosing what does and does not matter to us. That something matters is a prerequisite for life, and specifically what matters is what brings happiness and meaning to individuals.

Yet none of this means there is a reality behind the appearances that gives meaning to life as the optimists claim. "Our mere existence in time, as creatures whose immersion in past and future prevents us from adequately realizing the present, convinces me that the optimists are deluding themselves."[67] Like Emily Gibbs in Wilder's *Our Town,* we seem incapable of realizing life while we life it. And while some like Plato and Whitehead have posited eternal objects as a solution to the passage of time, Singer rejects these as mere abstractions and static—unlike life.

All of this leads Singer back to the question: Is life worth living? He answers that we must participate in significant creative acts to make our lives meaningful. To clarify what he means Singer quotes George Bernard Shaw:

> This is the true joy in life, the being used for a purpose recognized by yourself as a mighty one; the being thoroughly worn out before you are thrown on the scrap heap; the being a force of Nature instead of a feverish selfish little clod of ailments and grievances complaining that the world will not devote itself to making you happy. And also the only real tragedy in life is the being used by personally minded men for

purposes which you recognize to be base. All the rest is at worst mere misfortune or mortality: this alone is misery, slavery, hell on earth; and the revolt against it is the only force that offers a man's work to the poor artist, whom our personally minded rich people would so willingly employ as pander, buffoon, beauty monger, sentimentalizer and the like.[68]

Singer grants that Shaw does not tell us how to be forces of nature or what it means to be true to our nature. But for Singer this includes at a minimum an acceptance of our nature and self-love. Self-love is not the same as vanity; rather it enhances our ability to love others. And although we may not be able to love all of life or love others as much as we love ourselves, we can accept others as possible objects of our love. As everything loves itself, inasmuch as they do what they can to preserve themselves, there is love in everything. We can try to love the love that is in everything. As Singer puts it:

> Those who love the love in everything, who care about this bestowal and devote themselves to it, experience an authentic love of life. It is a love that yields its own kind of happiness and affords many opportunities for joyfulness. Can anything in nature or reality be better than that?[69]

Summary – We give meaning to life by loving the good in everything.

17. E. D. Klemke: Living without Appeal

E.D. Klemke (1926-2000) taught for more than twenty years at Iowa State University. He was a prolific editor and one of his best known collections is *The Meaning of Life,* first published in 1981. (Almost all of the articles of every edition of that text have been summarized in this book.) The following summary is of his 1981 essay: "Living Without Appeal: An Affirmative Philosophy of Life."

Klemke begins by stating that the topics of interest to professional philosophers are abstruse and esoteric. This is in large part justified as we need to be careful and precise in our thinking if we are to make progress in solving problems; but there are times when a philosopher ought to "speak as a man among other men."[70] In short a philosopher must bring his analytical tools to a problem such as the meaning of life. Klemke argues that the essence of the problem for him was captured by Camus in the phrase: "Knowing whether or not one can live without appeal is all that interests me."[71]

Many writers in the late 20th century had a negative view of civilization characterized by the notion that society was in decay. While the problem has been expressed variously, the basic theme was that some ultimate, transcendent principle or reality was lacking. This transcendent ultimate (TU), whatever it may be, is what gives meaning to life. Those who reject this TU are left to accept meaninglessness or exalt natural reality; but either way this hope is futile because without this TU there is no meaning.

Klemke calls this view *transcendentalism*, and it is composed of three theses: 1) a TU exists and one can have a relationship with it; 2) without a TU (or faith in one) there is no meaning to life; and 3) without meaning human life is worthless. Klemke comments upon each in turn.

1. Regarding the *first* thesis, Klemke assumes that believers are making a cognitive claim when they say that a TU exists, that it exists in reality. But neither religious texts, unusual persons in history or the fact that large numbers of persons believe this provide evidence for a TU—and the traditional arguments are not thought convincing by most experts. Moreover, religious experience is not convincing since the source of the experience is always in doubt. In fact there is no evidence for the existence of a TU and those who think it a matter of faith agree; there is thus no reason to accept the claim that a TU exists. The believer could counter that one should employ faith to which Klemke responds: a) we normally think of faith as implying reasons and evidence; and b) even if faith is something different in this context Klemke claims he does not need it. To this the transcendentalist responds that such faith is needed for there to be a meaning of life which leads to the *second* thesis:

2. The transcendentalist claims that without faith in a TU there is no meaning, purpose, or integration.

    a. Klemke firsts considers whether meaning may only exist if a TU exists. Here one might mean subjective or objective meaning. If we are referring to objective meaning Klemke replies that: i) there is nothing inconsistent about holding that objective meaning exists without a TU; and ii) there is no evidence that objective meaning exists. We find many things when we look at the universe, stars in motion for example, but meaning is not one of them. We do not discover values we create, invent, or impose them on the world. Thus there is no more reason to believe in the existence of objective meaning than there is to believe in the reality of a TU.

        i. The transcendentalist might reply by agreeing that there is no objective meaning in the universe but argue that subjective meaning is not possible without a TU. Klemke replies: 1) this is false, there is subjective meaning; and 2) what the transcendentalists are talking about is not subjective meaning but rather objective meaning since it relies on a TU.

        ii. The transcendentalist might reply instead that one cannot find meaning unless one has faith in a TU. Klemke replies: 1) this is false; and 2) even if it were true he would reject such faith because: "If I am to find any meaning in life, I must attempt to find it without the aid of crutches, illusory hopes, and incredulous beliefs and aspirations."[72] Klemke admits he may not find meaning, but he must try to find it on his own in something comprehensible to humans, not in some incomprehensible mystery. He simply cannot rationally accept meaning connected with things for which there is no evidence and, if this makes him less happy, then so be it. In this context he quotes George Bernard Shaw: "The fact that a believer is happier than a skeptic is no more to the point than the fact that a drunken man is happier than a sober one. The happiness of credulity is a cheap and dangerous quality."[73]

b. Klemke next considers the claim that without the TU life is purposeless. He replies that objective purpose is not found in the universe anymore than objective meaning is and hence all of his previous criticisms regarding objective meaning apply to the notion of objective purpose.

c. Klemke now turns to the idea that there is no integration with a TU. He replies:

    i. This is false; many persons are psychologically integrated or healthy without supernaturalism.

    ii. Perhaps the believer means metaphysical rather than psychological integration—the idea is that humans are at home in the universe. He answers that he does not understand what this is or if anyone has achieved it, assuming it is real. Some may have claimed to be one with the universe, or something like that, but that is a subjective experience only and not evidence for any objective claim about reality. But even if there are such experiences only a few seem to have had them, hence the need for faith; so faith does not imply integration and integration does not need faith. Finally, even if faith does achieve integration for some, it does not work for Klemke since the TU is incomprehensible. So how then does Klemke live without appeal?

3. He now turns to the third thesis that without meaning (which one cannot have without the existence of or belief in a TU) life is worthless. It is true that life has no objective meaning—which can only be derived from the nature of the universe or some external agency—but that does not mean life is subjectively worthless. Klemke argues that even if there were an objective meaning "It would not be mine."[74] In fact he is glad there is not such a meaning since this allows him the freedom to create his own meaning. Some may find life worthless if they must create their own meaning, especially if they lack a rich interior life in which to find the meaning absent in the world. Klemke says that: "I have found subjective meaning through such things as knowledge, art, love, and work."[75] There is no objective meaning but this opens us the possibility of endowing meaning onto things through my consciousness of them—rocks become mountains to climb, strings make music, symbols make logic, wood makes treasures. "Thus there is a sense in which it is true … that everything begins with my consciousness, and nothing has any worth except through my consciousness."[76]

Klemke concludes by revisiting the story told by Tolstoy of the man hanging on to a plant in a pit, with dragon below and mice eating the roots of the plant, yet unable to enjoy the beauty and fragrance of a rose. Yes, we all hang by a thread over the abyss of death, but still we possess the ability to give meaning to our lives. Klemke says that if he cannot do this—find subjective meaning against the backdrop of objective meaninglessness—then he ought to curse life. But if he can give life subjective meaning to life despite the inevitability of death, if he can respond to roses, philosophical arguments, music, and human touch, "if I can so respond and can thereby transform an external and fatal event into a moment of conscious insight and significance, then I shall go down without hope or appeal yet passionately triumphant and with joy."[77]

Summary – The meaning of life is found in the unique way consciousness projects meaning onto an otherwise tragic reality

18. Commentary On Subjective Meaning

Baier's arguments against the religious conception of objective meaning are convincing, as is his claim that life can have subjective meaning nonetheless. Edwards expands on this theme, arguing that life can have terrestrial meaning even if we cannot show that existence itself is ultimately worthwhile. Edwards also claims that subjective meaning is enough for most people, but this argument is problematic. I do not think that ordinary people are content with subjective meaning. To the contrary nearly the entire edifice of human culture—art, science, religion, philosophy—emanates from the desire to have our lives mean something in the cosmic sense. Those content with meaning in the terrestrial sense are the exception; those searching for the meaning of their lives in the cosmic context don't have special standards as Edwards claims.

Flew makes the same basic claim, meaning is found *in* life even if there is no meaning *of* life, but he asks us to forego our dreams of immortality and make a better world. Barnes asks us to grow up and create meaning in a world without gods, comforted by the fact that there is some small immortality in the repercussions that emanate from our lives. For Barnes we create the rules of the game. In the end neither Flew nor Barnes satisfies our desire for meaning anymore than Baier or Edwards. They all counsel us to accept that meaning *in* life is all we can get. But we want more than subjective meaning even if that's all we can have.

In Martin's analysis we find despair—a fast car and a good woman cannot satisfy for long. The only comfort in his analysis is that death is a welcome relief from our insatiable appetites. Kekes moves the argument further along, detaching meaning from anything objective, including morality. He thus brings us back to active engagement in our lives without moral limitations as the source of meaning. For Schmidt finding meaning in whatever we are engage—such as coaching little league football—is about the best we can do, while Solomon suggests we choose a vision of life without telling us how to do this or whether some vision is better than others. Lund recommends that we give our lives meaning by searching for what we will probably never find, but that the searching is as close to meaning as we will probably ever come. These are all brave words from brave men, and their poignancy is felt deeply. Baggini's account is the most uplifting, we can give our lives meaning by loving, but even love has its limits, is fragile, and exists without transcendental support.

Russell argued that persons free of metaphysical narratives can find some meaning in the beauty they create and the truth they find; Taylor argued that our labors are precisely what give our lives meaning, since they are motivated by our inner nature; Hare claimed that we bestow mattering on the world; Singer that we create meaning by creating and loving; and Klemke claimed that we can live without appeal by finding subjective meaning in art, work and love. All these thinkers maintain that creating meaning is all we have left once objective meaning is lost. Still, something important is missing from all of these accounts. Something we deeply long for—that our labors matter not just to us but to the cosmos, and that we are part of something bigger than the attachment to our will. What such lives lack is objective meaning. Is loving computers, golf, sunsets, or children really enough?

Consider for example Hare's response to his young guest. The reason that Meursault was relevant for the boy was because he identified with Meursault. True he was not facing execution, but the boy recognized that we all die. In fact at the end of the novel Meursault is comforted by the fact that everyone dies sooner or later. So the boy was moved because he saw his own life revealed in a new way by the novel. Yes, the young man later admitted that things did matter to him, but suppose that when asked if anything mattered to him the boy had replied that nothing did? What would Hare have said then? Would he have screamed: "No, some things do matter to you!" If the boy demurred then they would have been at an impasse, and that is why Hare counsels that some things really are objectively valuable. But what if the young man denied this?

In the same way the beauty, perfection, work, art, and love that Russell and Taylor and Klemke appeal to seems tainted, not because they are not worthwhile and not because we might not care about them, but because they are not worthwhile enough to satisfy us. The foregoing discussion reveals the basic problem with creating your own meaning—such a requirement asks too much. How is a lone individual to make their lives meaningful by themselves against the backdrop of the infinity of space and time? Is it really something we can create, all by ourselves? Yes, we can collect baseball cards and find that meaningful, but surely that is not enough and we are right to be dissatisfied if there is nothing more to life than that. And even if we can shake our fist at the world, create some momentary perfection, have relationships or coach little league, how can we resist asking: is that all there is?

If transcendental support for meaning is absent, and subjective meaning is not enough, then we must turn to objective meanings and values inherent in human experience, ones that exist in the natural world. It is to such considerations that we now turn.

CHAPTER 6 – NATURALISTS: OBJECTIVE MEANING

There is a pleasure in philosophy, and a lure even in the mirages of metaphysics, which every student feels until the coarse necessities of physical existence drag him from the heights of thought into the mart of economic strife and gain. Most of us have known some golden days in the June of life when philosophy was in fact what Plato calls it, "that dear delight;" when the love of a modestly elusive truth seemed more glorious – incomparably – than the lust for the ways of the flesh and the dross of the world. And there is always some wistful remnant in us of that early wooing of wisdom. "Life has meaning," we feel with Browning. "To find its meaning is my meat and drink."

So much of our lives is meaningless, a self-canceling vacillation and futility. We strive with the chaos about and within, but we should believe all the while that there is something vital and significant in us, could we but decipher our own souls. We want to understand. "Life means for us constantly to transform into light and flame all that we are or meet with!" We are like Mitya in The Brothers Karamazov – "one of those who don't want millions, but an answer to their questions." We want to seize the value and perspective of passing things and so to pull ourselves up out of the maelstrom of daily circumstance.

We want to know that the little things are little, and the things big, before it is too late. We want to see things now as they will seem forever – "in the light of eternity."
~ Will Durant

*For age is opportunity no less
Than youth itself, though in another dress,
And as the evening twilight fades away
The sky is filled with stars, invisible by day.*
~ Henry Wadsworth Longfellow

1. Naturalism and Objective Meaning

If one finds both the supernatural and subjective answers unsatisfying, then perhaps meaning is objective and found in the natural world. Objectivists believe that (at least some) meaning is independent of their desires, attitudes, interests, wants, and preferences; that there are invariant standards of meaning independent of human minds. Such meaning is *not* derived from a supernatural realm, but from objective elements in the natural world. However, this does not mean that value or meaning is *exclusively* objective, as the following thinkers recognize. Effort on the part of the subject is necessary to derive or discover the objective meaning in the world.

2. Joseph Ellin: Morality Gives Life Meaning

Joseph Ellin, professor emeritus at Western Michigan University, received his PhD from Yale University. He concludes his 1995 book, *Morality and the Meaning of Life*, with a discussion of how meaning in life is found in objective values.

How the Question of the Meaning of Life Arises - The question might arise because we are depressed or unhappy with our careers, love life, or health; or from the realization that we will be forgotten after we die. It might also arise because of the subjectivity of value. If values are subjective then what we do may not matter, since nothing then would be objectively right or wrong. And if nothing matters then why do anything or care about anything? A final reason the question arises is that thoughtful human beings ask: Why are we here? What does it mean? Is life going somewhere or just perpetuating itself? We want answers, hence the popularity of philosophies and religions that provide them.

Is the Meaning of Life a Kind of Knowledge? - Can the meaning of life be stated as a proposition, as knowledge or information to be passed along to others? If so is this knowledge interesting, like physics or biology, or is it useful, like plumbing or carpentry? This knowledge should not be merely interesting, since it is supposedly so important, so it should be useful. Its usefulness derives not because it makes one rich or helps someone achieve a goal; it would be useful because its intrinsically valuable, it enhance one's life, it allows one to live it differently or see why life really is worth living. And there can be knowledge like this. If you worried that you had no friends and found out that you did, you would feel better, you would see your life differently. Now if you worried that life had no meaning what knowledge would remove that anxiety? Would knowledge that god loves you or that Buddha was your personal savior do it for you? It is not clear whether any fact or piece of information could be the meaning of life, thereby dispelling your doubts about life's meaning.

Instead Ellin suggests that the meaning of life might be ineffable. Perhaps it is a kind of wisdom—knowing how to live well—that cannot be verbalized but when possessed makes self-evident both how one should live and the meaning of life. But even supposing there is knowledge capable of being grasped by the mind that cannot be stated, and which also reveals the meaning of life, how can one be sure they have such knowledge? How do they know—or how do *we* know—that they are not mistaken about possessing this knowledge? So it is hard to see how the meaning of life can be a piece of knowledge because either it can be stated propositionally—in which case it is hard to see how any fact could be the meaning of life—or it cannot be so stated—in which case one wonders if one has found it.

Moreover, even if one knew that the meaning of life was x, knowing that fact by itself does not make life meaningful. To make life meaningful you must act on your knowledge by loving god, making friends, seeking knowledge or whatever you are supposed to do. But these are not facts; they are prescriptions or injunctions concerning action.

Is the Meaning of Life Happiness? - Perhaps what is missing in a meaningless life is happiness. If you think life has no meaning maybe you are unhappy. What is the relationship between meaning and happiness? Meaning may be a *necessary* condition for happiness—you cannot be happy without meaning—but people differ in what makes them happy and what they think is meaningful. Or meaning may be a *sufficient* condition for happiness—if you have meaning, you have happiness. For instance if you do noble work that gives your life meaning you would be happy, even if you lack all other elements of happiness. Maybe then happiness and meaning occur together, if you have one you have the other. Of course this does not mean that they are the same thing, and it does not tell us what meaning is.

Nevertheless, we do have reason to think that having meaning and being happy are *not* the same, for we can be unhappy for many reason, lack of meaning is just one of them. So even if meaning is a necessary condition for happiness, it is not sufficient. Having meaning does not guarantee happiness, although it does prevent a certain kind of unhappiness, the kind that follows from lack of meaning.

The Death Argument - So what is lost when we lose meaning? What does life not have when meaning is lost? A good way to understand this is to look again at Tolstoy, for whom death undermined meaning. But does death take the meaning out of life? Tolstoy's argument is:

Life is good;
Death ends this goodness; thus
Death is bad; thus
Life is meaningless.

As Ellin points out this argument does show that death is bad, but it does *not* show that death removes meaning. In fact the badness of death reveals the goodness of life. Most persons fear death precisely because they want to live. Still, some argue that death is not bad because it is nothing and cannot harm you. Ellin agrees that death cannot harm you but it is still bad because your annihilation is harmful to you, it is the greatest harm that can befall you. Other reasons for thinking death is not evil include the idea that eternity would be boring or that the prospect of death forces us to do things we would otherwise put off.

Despite these arguments Ellin concludes that death is bad. It is something that we want to avoid but which is inevitable. The best we can do is to be as unconcerned about our not being alive in the future, as we are now about our not being alive in the past. Still, the evil of death does not show that life is meaningless.

Repetitive Pointlessness, Ultimate Insignificance, and Absurdity - What other considerations might lead then to the conclusion that life is meaningless? Ellen notes three. First there are Camus' ideas about the *repetitiveness and pointlessness* of Sisyphus' labor. Ellin responds that most lives are not like this, containing at least some variation as well as goals that give those lives a point. He also wants to know what would count as a meaningful life. Either you can state what makes life meaningful or you cannot. If you can state this but claim that no one can achieve it—you must win a noble prize and be immortal—why should we accept your high standards for a meaningful life? If you cannot state what counts as a meaningful life but say that life cannot have a point by definition—you beg the question. To show that life is meaningless you have to show that what most people think gives life meaning does not. To do this Camus would have to show that every life is like Sisyphus'. Needless to say this would be nearly impossible.

A second consideration that might lead to the conclusion that life is meaningless is our *ultimate insignificance*. Russell thought that the vast expanses of space and time discovered by science reveals the insignificance of our lives. For Russell cherishing perfection, mathematics, art, love, and truth is the best attitude to adopt in an uncaring universe. In this way we preserve our ideals without wishful thinking. Ellin responds that the presence or absence of the universe has nothing to do with meaning. If the rest of the universe was absent, if only earth existed, why would that add to meaning? And if it does not, then why does the presence of a vast universe destroy meaning?

A final consideration that might lead to thinking that life is meaningless results from the notion of *absurdity*. The idea that life is absurd, irrational, and pointless is common to many modern thinkers, especially existentialists like Jean Paul Sartre, who responded that individuals must create their own values and meaning. Still, others maintain that life is not a tragedy but a farce, and the appropriate response accepts that we are ridiculous. Although there are many responses to the supposed meaninglessness of life—Tolstoy's leap of faith, Camus' defiance, Russell's upholding ideals, Sartre's terror—Ellin doubts that we must accept life's meaningless in the first place.

"Big Picture" Meaning and Faith - Is your life meaningful if it is part of a larger scheme? How does a big picture view give something meaning? Ellin gives the examples of a shortstop in baseball or a soldier in an army. In both cases their actions appear unimportant, pointless, and meaningless unless you understand the big picture of which they are a part. We often understand the

meaning of activity in precisely this way. Ellin argues that we want a big picture to explain: 1) the purpose of all life; 2) our individual lives by reference to that purpose; 3) how suffering and death are necessary for that purpose; and 4) how life is good.

The big picture is usually explained by a story, but not any story will do—being food for a super race making an intergalactic journey will not do. Such a story satisfies the first three criteria, but not the fourth. Religious stories typically fulfill all four criteria but they may not be true. Note that we do not need to believe all the details of the story, we only need to believe that there is a big picture. After all life may be like a movie of which we have only seen fragments. We do not know the meaning of the movie, but we can believe there is one anyway; we can have faith that if we saw the entire movie, we would understand its meaning. True we do not know this with certainty but deep truths are often beyond are grasp. Believing in a big picture is thus a reasonable option; and it is reasonable to believe that life makes sense after all. But why believe in something for which there is little or no evidence? How do we believe in something when we don't know what that something is? And how does such a belief differ from no belief, since it tells you nothing about what to do or value?

Is the Question of Meaning Meaningful? – Ellin now adumbrates the typical objections of the logical positivist. Words, sentences, and actions refer to things but life refers only to itself, hence it cannot be the kind of thing that has meaning. Thus the question does not make sense. To put the point another way, a question only makes sense if we have some idea of the range of answers to the question. With the meaning of life question, we do not know what would count as an answer. The upshot of all this is that we feel even less secure of proposed solutions.

If Life Has No Meaning, What Then? – In summary Ellin claims that the meaning of life is not a piece of knowledge, not the same as happiness, but not ruled out by death. The arguments from repetitive pointlessness, ultimate insignificance, and absurdity are *not* entirely convincing, but neither are the arguments that there is a big picture from which to derive meaning. This all suggest that life may have no meaning, or that if there is meaning it is beyond us, or that the question makes no sense. Some, like Tolstoy, respond to this situation with an optimistic belief that the big picture is good;

others, like Camus and Russell, respond with heroic pessimism toward an ultimately meaningless cosmos.

Both the optimists and pessimists agree that life must have meaning to be worthwhile. Could it be that this is mistaken? Ellin suggests that while life as a whole may have no meaning, individuals lives still can. You can have friends and knowledge and love and all the rest; you can say of a life that the world is better because that person lived. But the universe cannot give you meaning, you must give meaning to your life: "…meaning is not a kind of knowledge at all … but at bottom a feeling, a sense of well-being from having made a difference."[1]

So it appears Ellin agrees with the subjectivists, but not quite. He now asks: Will any activity suffice in giving one's life meaning? No he argues. Finding things you are good at and developing those talents is not sufficient, inasmuch as being a wonderful child torturer or crime boss would satisfy those requirements. Lives better off not lived; those that did not make useful contributions to the world are not meaningful. Immoral lives are not meaningful: "… a truly valuable life is one of which more people than not have reason to be glad that the life was lived."[2]Although there is no ultimate justification for our lives; we can still give them meaning. But to have the most meaning possible, morality must be part of our lives—it is the means to the objective values of love, friendship, loyalty and trust that make life worth living.

Summary – The meaning of life is not a kind of knowledge, not the same as happiness, not completely undermined by death, not made obvious by religious stories, and, if actual, possibly unknowable. Still, nothing compels us to accept that life is meaningless for we can derive meaning from life by discovering objective moral goods and leading live in accord with them.

3. Garrett Thomson: Meaning is Found in Transcendent Values

Garrett Thomson, who received his PhD from Oxford University in 1984, is the Elias Compton Professor of Philosophy at the College of Wooster in Ohio. His 2003 book, *On the Meaning of Life*, begins by contrasting the medieval worldview with the modern scientific one. The medieval worldview is more easily reconciled with the belief that life is meaningful because the modern one implies that "because everything is made of matter, we have no immaterial soul and so, very soon, each one of us shall die. There is probably no God … just inert matter."[3] The question of the meaning of life is now an urgent one "partly because the modern scientific view has largely replaced the medieval view…"[4]

The main point of his first chapter is to clarify the meaning of the question. He carefully distinguishes, as we did in our opening chapter, between unanswerable questions, unknowable answers, and there being no universal answers to the question. In sorting out the various ways to understand the question he comes to one basic conclusion "An understanding of the meaning of life must have some practical implications for the way that we conduct our lives."[5] The question of meaning is not asking for a piece of information but for some guidance in living and, if it cannot give such guidance, the advice is basically useless.

Thomson proceeds to investigate nine different mistakes that people make in thinking about the meaning of life. The *first* assumes that meaning depends upon the existence of and our relationship with a god. He replies that the mere fact that a god has a purpose for human life does not entail that we honor that purpose. The *second* is that the meaning of life is some goal or purpose, whether it was planted in us by a god or evolution, or whether it refers to our spiritual development. But if we regard our lives as meaningful merely as a means to some end or goal, we invariably miss life's intrinsic meaning. The *third* is that meaning is the same as pleasure or desire. This is contradicted by the fact that something would be lacking in a pleasure machine. The *fourth* mistake is that meaning must be invented or is subjective. In contrast he argues that activities are meaningful because of the real value associated with them. The *fifth* is that there can be no meaning given materialism. Thomson replies that values may be properties of material things; that material things may give rise to values; or that material things can be described as valuable. The *sixth* is that the value judgments are nothing more than reasons for actions. Thomson argues that there are values and meanings of which we are unaware, just like we are ignorant of some facts, and these have nothing to do with guiding actions. This implies the *seventh* mistake; that meaning cannot extend beyond our experiences. The *eighth* mistake is to assume only linguistic items can have meaning, and a *ninth*, that meaning is living in accord with a self-determined plan.

What all this leads to are the positive lessons of Thomson's book. Foremost among these is that meaning is found in everyday life because that is where we reside. Individuals have intrinsic value as do the processes that constitute those lives. These processes are themselves comprised of experiences and activities that constitute a life, hence meaningful lives consist of the most valuable and meaningful activities. Life can be made more meaningful by increasing our attention and appreciation of these valuable activities, as well as becoming more aware of values in the world that we have previously not appreciated.

However, we should try to make the world and our lives better. How do we do this? Not by acting in accord with every want or desire we have but by acting in accord with our interests, with what is intrinsically good for us. This leads to a conception of value that is neither absolute nor relative. The appreciation of value implies they can be recognized, they are in some sense out there, but values are not absolute since they depend on our interests. The meanings of life are determined by our interest in valuable things like beauty and friendship. This latter value is especially important, since our meaning depends on recognizing the non-instrumental value of other persons. When we do recognize the value of others we transcend the limitations of our own lives.

We can also find meaning by connecting to values like goodness, beauty, and truth. Part of the value of our lives is found in things beyond ourselves so that the search for meaning attempts to transcend particular actions. If life has what is called spiritual significance, it is not because there is a transcendent state which denies the immanent meaning of life, but because we can appreciate the immanent values in life. Thomson's states his conclusion as follows:

> It must consist in the process of development, not according to an externally imposed divine plan or purpose, nor as a personally invented one, but rather in accordance with the fundamental nature of our interests. It should be conceived, in part, as the process of our reaching out to values beyond ourselves with our attention and actions.[6]

Summary – The meanings of life are found in everyday life in objective values that include friendship, goodness, beauty, and truth, all of which both appeal to our nature and allow us to go beyond ourselves.

4. Karl Britton: It is Objectively True That Life Has Meaning

Karl William Britton (1909-83) was Professor of Philosophy at the University of Newcastle upon Tyne. He graduated from the University of Cambridge (Clare College) where he was President of the Union and a personal friend of Ludwig Wittgenstein. He did postgraduate work at Harvard University, and then held lectureships at Aberystwyth and Swansea before being appointed in 1951 to the chair of philosophy at King's College, Newcastle upon Tyne.

In the first chapter of his 1969 book *Philosophy and the Meaning of Life,* Britton claims that the question of the meaning of life is comprised of two related and interconnected questions: 1) why does the universe exist, does it have meaning? And 2) why do I exist, what gives my life meaning? These queries lead to Britton's first conclusion: "that for life to have a meaning it is necessary that there should be some things worth doing for their own sakes."[7] For some, intrinsically worthwhile values are sufficient, but others claim that this is not enough; they need goals outside of themselves set by a god or nature to make life fully meaningful. Britton suggests that the reasons people seek more than just intrinsic values and goals in life are: 1) they do not agree on what the intrinsically valuable things are; 2) they are driven to think they were born for something; and 3) it is hard to live without believing there is some goal for their lives outside of themselves. Britton concludes that if one finds an intrinsically valuable goal in life, as well as a goal set by a god or nature, one can be said to have lived a meaningful life. The problem is whether the latter goal exists.

The first kinds of answers that Britton explores to the question of meaning are authoritative answers—particularly Western religious answers. The basic problem with such answers is that they assume problematic concepts like the existence of gods and an afterlife. He then turns to what he calls a metaphysical answer—Aristotelian contemplation. While contemplation is worthwhile, it leads to theoretical knowledge and does not fully answer the question of meaning. There are also some informal or common sense answers—meaning is to be found in service to church, country, other people, or in work, family, or self-realization. The problems here are: a) to say there is a list of meaningful things does not tell us what the list is comprised of; and b) while all of these may be necessary for a meaningful life they hardly seem sufficient; we can imagine having all of them and still wondering whether our lives are meaningful.

All of this brings Britton back to his original questions. As for his first question—w hat is the meaning, cause, or explanation of the universe—this is a theoretical question best answered by science, although people often try to answer it in non-scientific ways. The second question—what is the meaning of my life—is a practical question about how one should live and what one should value. An answer to this question must assert both facts and principles of conduct, and can be criticized because it is mistaken about either.

Britton states that for a person's life to be meaningful it must be true that: 1) persons are guided by their convictions; 2) persons matters to themselves and others; 3) the relationships between persons matter intrinsically; and 4) persons detect a pattern in their life. Britton concludes that the possibility of these conditions being met is enough for life to be meaningful. And since it is possible for these conditions to be met then life has meaning by virtue of this possibility, whether or not that possibility is actualized.

Regarding whether there is meaning to the whole thing, Britton reminds us that this requires some teleology that is external to us. However, we could be mistaken that such teleology is real or good. In the end it is not gods or the creation of meaning that gives life meaning. Instead it is "that life has a meaning and that this arises from the possibilities which remain in the fact of all actualities. I am not merely saying that the lives of some people have meaning: I am saying that the life of any man does have meaning."[8]

Summary – Life has meaning because the facts of the world are such that a person's life does matter both to themselves and to others.

5. Terry Eagleton: Agapeistic Love is the Answer

Terence Francis Eagleton (1943 -) is a British literary theorist widely regarded as Britain's most influential living literary critic. He currently serves as Distinguished Professor of English Literature at the University of Lancaster. Formerly he was Thomas Warton Professor of English Literature at the University of Oxford (1992–2001) and John Edward Taylor Professor of English Literature at the University of Manchester until 2008. His 2007 book, *The Meaning of Life*, begins with this perceptive comment:

If you were to ask what provides some meaning in life nowadays for a great many people, especially men, you could do worse than reply 'football.' Not many of them perhaps would be willing to admit as much; but sport stands in for all those noble causes—religious faith, national sovereignty, personal honor, ethnic identity—for which, over the centuries, people have been prepared to go to their deaths. It is sport, not religion, which is now the opium of the people.[9]

Eagleton continues by probing much deeper. He answers the question of the meaning of life without appealing to either gods or subjective meaning but to certain objective values in the natural world. He notes the false dichotomy of arguing that either there are gods that give meaning or life is meaningless:

> The cosmos may not have been consciously designed, and is almost certainly not struggling to say something, but it is not just chaotic, either. On the contrary, its underlying laws reveal a beauty, symmetry, and economy that are capable of moving scientists to tears. The idea that the world is either given meaning by God, or is utterly random and absurd, is a false antithesis.[10]

But he rejects the claims of postmodernists and constructivists who say the meaning of life is subjective—that life means whatever we say it means. "Meaning, to be sure, is something people do; but they do it in dialogue with a determinate world whose laws they did not invent, and if their meanings are to be valid, they must respect this world's grain and texture."[11]

When it comes time for Eagleton to answer his question he turns to the idea of happiness as the end and purpose of human life. "The meaning of life is not a solution to a problem, but a matter of living in a certain way. It is not metaphysical, but ethical."[12] But how should we act in order to achieve meaning and happiness? The key is to disconnect happiness from selfishness and ally it with a love of humanity—agapeistic love is the central notion of a meaningful life. When we support each other in this manner we find the key to our own fulfillment: "For love means creating for another the space in which he might flourish, at the same time as he does this for you. The fulfillment of each becomes the ground for the fulfillment of the other. When we realize our nature in this way, we are at our best."[13]

In the end then happiness and love coincide. "If happiness is seen in the Aristotelian terms as the free flourishing of our faculties, and if love is the kind of reciprocity that allows this to happen, there is no final conflict between them."[14] Interestingly, true reciprocity is only possible among equals, so societies with great inequality are ultimately in nobody's self-interest. Eagleton's final metaphor compares the good and meaningful life to a jazz ensemble. The musicians improvise and do their own thing, but they also are inspired and cooperate with the other members to form a greater whole. The meaning of life consists of individuals collectively engaged in finding happiness through love and concern for each other. It turns out for Eagleton, as for Aristotle, that individual and collective well-being, happiness, and meaning are closely related.

Summary – Happiness and love are the meaning of life. We should create a world where they can thrive.

6. Morris Schlick: The Meaning of Life is Found in Play

Mortiz Schlick (1882– 1936) was a German philosopher and the founding father of logical positivism and the Vienna Circle. He was shot to death at the University of Vienna by a former student.

According to Schlick the innocent or childlike never ask the question of the meaning of life; others, the weary, no longer ask the question because they have concluded that there is none. *"In between are ourselves, the seekers."*[15] While some lament that they have not fulfilled the goals of youth and accept that their lives are meaningless, they nevertheless believe that life is meaningful for those who have fulfilled their goals. Others achieve their goals, only to find that this achievement has not provided meaning. So it is hard to see the meaning of life. We set goals and head toward them with hope, but their achievement does not bring meaning. The goals are reached but the desire for new goals follows. There is never satisfaction, and all this longing ends in death. How then to escape all this?

Nietzsche sought to escape this pessimism thru art and then through knowledge, but neither led to meaning. He concluded that if we think of the meaning of life as a purpose, we will never find meaning. If we ask people about their purpose, most persons would say that they are working to maintain life or to stay alive, but pure existence is valueless without content. So we are caught in a circle, working to stay alive, and staying alive to keep working. Work is generally a means to an end, never an end in itself; and though some activities are intrinsically meaningful, like pleasurable ones, they are too fleeting to give life meaning.

In response Schlick argues that meaning is to be found in activities that are intrinsically valuable—where the means and the ends are united; where the means is the end. He quotes Schiller that *play* is the activity that carries its own purpose. Only when we have no purpose except to play will there be meaning. Work can be play, if it is doing what you want to do; that is, play and creative work may coincide. Creative play is found clearly in the work of the artist or in the search for scientific or philosophical knowledge. Almost any activity can be turned into art and Schlick wants work to become artistic; he longs for a world in which individuals engage in meaningful, joyful, playful, work. But would such an idyllic life reduce humans to an animal existence, since humans would be living for the moment rather than contemplating eternity as self-conscious beings should? Schlick says we do not sacrifice by playing; life becomes meaningful if we do what we want to do. The result is joy, which is more than mere pleasure.

We should then be like children who are capable of joy in play (work). This passionate enthusiasm of youth, unconcerned with goals, devoted to the intrinsic nature of the play is true play. But doesn't it seem strange that youth, the preparation for adulthood, is where the meaning of life is found? Not at all says Schlick. Humans tend to think of every imperfect state as the mere prelude to another state, in the same way they often think of this life as having completion in another. But the meaning of life, if it is to be found at all, must be found in this world. Meaning may be found in youth or adulthood or old age, if one is engaged in creative play. "The more youth is realized in life, the more valuable it is, and if a person dies young, however long he may have lived, his life has had meaning."[16]

Summary – The meaning of life is found in joyfully playing, in doing what one really wants to do.

7. Susan R. Wolf: Active Engagement with Objective Values

Susan R. Wolf (1952 -) is a moral philosopher who has written extensively on the meaning in human life. She is currently the Edna J. Koury Professor of Philosophy at the University of North Carolina at Chapel Hill.

Wolf maintains that meaningful lives have within them the possibility of answering one's need for meaning. These needs center on questions of whether life is worth living, has any point, or provides sufficient reason to go on. Paradigms of meaningful lives include lives of moral or intellectual accomplishment, whereas meaningless lives include those lived in quiet desperation or in futile labor. In short, Wolf claims that: "... meaningful lives are lives of active engagement in projects of worth."[17]

Active engagement refers to being griped or excited by something. Active engagement relates to being passionate rather than alienated about something, whereas being engaged is not always pleasant since it may involve hard work. *Projects of worth* suggests that some objective value exists, and Wolf argues that meaning and objective value are linked. While Wolf doesn't offer a philosophical defense of objective value she claims that "there can be no sense to the idea of meaningfulness without a distinction between more and less worthwhile ways to spend one's time, where the test of worth is at least partly independent of a subject's ungrounded preferences or enjoyment."[18]

To see this point, first consider that people's longings for meaning are independent of whether they find their lives enjoyable. They may have a fun life but might come to think it lacks meaning. Second, why do we seem to have an intuitive sense of meaningful and meaningless lives? Most of us would agree that certain kinds of lives are or are not meaningful. Both of the above suggest that objective values are related to meaning.

This leads Wolf to reiterate that meaningful lives are ones actively engaged in worthwhile projects. If one is engaged in life, then it has a point; looking for meaning is looking for worthwhile projects. In addition, this view shows us why some projects are thought of as meaningful and others are not. Some projects are meaningful but boring (like writing checks to the ACLU), whereas others are pleasurable (like riding roller coasters) but do not seem to give meaning to life. In this context, Wolf notes Bernard Williams' distinction between categorical desires, whose objects are worthwhile independent of our desires; and all other desires, whose objects worthiness, presumably, depends on our desires. In short, she is saying some values are objective.

To reiterate, meaningful lives link active engagement with objectively worthwhile projects. Lives lived without engagement lack meaning, even if what they are doing is meaningful, since the person living such a life is bored or alienated. However, lives lived with engagement are not necessarily meaningful, if the objects of the engagement are worthless, since those objects lack objective value. Wolf summaries her view as follows: "Meaning arises when subjective attraction meets objective attractiveness…meaning arises when a subject discovers or develops an affinity for one or typically several of the more worthwhile things…"[19]

Summary – Meaningful lives consist of one's active engagement with objectively worthwhile things.

8. Steven Cahn: Subjectivist Reply to Wolf

Steven Cahn is Professor of Philosophy at CUNY Graduate Center and the author or editor of many philosophical textbooks. Cahn rejects Wolf's distinction between meaningful and meaningless lives, arguing that it does not make sense to judge a life meaningful or meaningless. While Wolf does not offer a theory of objective value, she does give examples of activities that are meaningful, some that are meaningless and some that she is uncertain about. Her examples are:

1. Meaningful activities include: moral or intellectual accomplishments, personal relationships, religious practices, mountain climbing, training for a marathon, and helping a friend.
2. Meaningless activities include: collecting rubber bands, memorizing the dictionary, making handwritten copies of great novels, riding roller coasters, meeting movie stars, watching sitcoms, playing computer games, solving crossword puzzles, recycling, or writing checks to Oxfam and the ACLU.
3. Uncertain cases include: a life obsessed with corporate law, being devoted to a religious cult, or being a pig farmer who buys more land to grow more corn to feed more pigs...[20]

Cahn seizes on how controversial these cases are. Why are some meaningful and some not? What about all the other cases she mentions? Is golf a useful way to spend your time? Some think so, others do not. And even if some activity is mindless and futile, does that mean it is meaningless? Weightlifting may be mindless and futile, but does that make it meaningless? Many might think it meaningless to read articles about the meaning of life, and then write articles about the meaning of life which are in turn read by others. Cahn concludes that lives that do not harm others should be appreciated as relatively meaningful.

Summary – Meaningful lives consist of finding happiness without doing harm to others.

9. Susan R. Wolf: The Importance of Objective Values

Wolf elaborated on her ideas about meaning in two lectures delivered at Princeton in 2007. There she claimed that meaning is not reducible to either happiness or morality. While philosophers often argue that individual happiness or impersonal duty motivate why people act, Wolf maintains that meaning also motivates action. She thus seeks a middle way between recommendations to "follow your bliss" or "do your duty."

To explain this she differentiates between the Fulfillment view—that meaning is found in whatever fulfills you—and the

Larger-Than-Oneself view—that meaning if found in dedicating yourself to something larger than yourself. The fulfillment view satisfies subjectively but may lack objective value; whereas the larger-than-oneself view suffers from the reverse, it may be objectively meaningful but not subjectively fulfilling. The solution combines the best features of both. Meaningfulness in life thus comes from engaging in, being fulfilled by, and ultimately loving things objectively worthy of love. (The subjective attraction and objective attractiveness she spoke of earlier.) Furthermore, she argues that subjective fulfillment depends on being engaged in the objectively worthwhile—counting cracks on the sidewalk will not do, but pursuing medical research could. Therefore the subjective and objective elements are inextricable linked.

This leads Wolf back to the question of objective meaning. How does one answer Cahn's objection that meaning is subjective? While Wolf does not provide a theory of objective value, she does claim that there are subject-independent values, since at least some things are valuable to everyone. If this is true then the truth or falsity of whether a life is meaningful is subject-independent, although Wolf defers from assessing the meaningfulness of other's lives.

The question of meaning is not merely academic then, since answers to it inform individuals about themselves and others. The concept of meaning also has explanatory value, explaining why people do thing for reasons other than self-interest or duty. In short, meaningfulness matters. It may not be the only value, but it is valuable nonetheless. Moreover, the concept of meaning is unintelligible without some notion of objective value, despite the fact that we cannot specify this value with much precision.

Summary – Meaning is a value distinct from both happiness and morality, but it relies on the reality of some objective value, however non-specifically that is defined.

10. James Rachels: Good Things Make Life Worth Living

James Rachels (1941- 2003) was a distinguished American moral philosopher and best-selling textbook author. He taught at the University of Richmond, New York University, the University of Miami, Duke University, and the University of Alabama at

Birmingham, where he spent the last twenty-six years of his career.

The final chapter of his book, *Problems from Philosophy*, explores the question of the meaning of life. Although Rachels admits the question of the meaning of life does come up when one is depressed, and hence can be a symptom of mental illness, it also arises when we are not depressed, and thus mental illness is not a prerequisite for asking the question. He agrees with Nagel that the questions typically results from recognizing the clash between the subjective or personal point of view—from which things matter—and the objective or impersonal view—from which they do not.

Regarding the relationship between happiness and meaning, Rachel notes that happiness is not well correlated with material wealth, but with personal control over one's life, good relationships with family and friends, and satisfying work. In Rachels view happiness is not found by seeking it directly, but as a by-product of intrinsic values like autonomy, friendship, and satisfying work. Nonetheless, a happy life may still be meaningless because we die, and in times of reflection we may find our happiness undermined by the thought of our annihilation.

What attitude should we take toward our death? For those who believe they do not die, death is good because they will live forever in a hereafter. For them death "is like moving to a better address."[21] But for those who believe that death is their final end, death may or may not be a good thing. What attitude should these people take toward death? Epicurus thought that death was the end but that we should not fear it, since we will be nothing when dead and nothingness cannot harm us. He thought that such an attitude would make us happier while alive. On the contrary, Rachels thinks that death is bad because it deprives us of, and puts an end to, all the good things in life. (This is a version of the deprivation argument that will be discussed in detail in Chapter 7.)

Although death is bad it does necessarily make life meaningless, inasmuch as the value of something is different than how long it lasts. A thing can be valuable even if it is fleeting; or worthless even if it lasts a forever. So the fact that something ends does not, by itself, negate its value.

There is yet another reason that a happy life might be meaningless—and that reason is that the universe may be indifferent. The earth is but a speck in the inconceivable vastness of the universe, and a human lifetime but an instant of the immensity of time. The universe does not seem to care much for us. One way to avoid this problem is with a religious answer—that the universe and a god do cares for us. But how does this help, even if it is true? As we have seen, being a part of another's plan does not seem to help, nor does being a recipient of the god's love, or living forever. It is simply not clear how positing gods gives our lives meaning.

Rachels suggest that if we add the notion of commitment to the above, we can see how religion provides meaning to believer's lives. Believers voluntarily commit themselves to various religious values and get their meaning from those values. But while you can get meaning from religious values, you can also get them from other things—from artistic, musical, or scholarly achievement for example. Still, the religious answer has a benefit that these other ways of finding meaning do not; it assumes that the universe is not indifferent. The drawback of the religious view is that it assumes the religious story is true. If it is not, then we are basing our lives on a lie.

But even if life does not have a meaning, particular lives can. We give our lives meaning by finding things worth living for. These differ between individuals somewhat, yet there are many things worth living for about which people generally agree—good personal relationships, accomplishments, knowledge, playful activities, aesthetic enjoyment, physical pleasure, and helping others. Could it nonetheless be that all of this amounts to nothing, that life is meaningless after all? From the objective, impartial view we may always be haunted by the suspicion that life is meaningless. The only answer is to explain why our list of good things is really good.

> Such reasoning may not show that our lives are 'important to the universe,' but it will accomplish something similar. It will show that we have good, objective reasons to live in some ways rather than others. When we step outside our personal perspective and consider humanity from an impersonal standpoint, we still find that human beings are the kinds of creatures who can enjoy life best by devoting themselves to such things as family and friends, work, music, mountain climbing, and all the rest. It would be foolish, then, for creatures like us to live in any other way.[22]

Summary - Happiness is not the same as meaning and is undermined by death. Death is bad unless religious stories are true, but they probably are not true. Thus, while there is probably no objective meaning to life, there are good things in life. We should pursue those good things that most people think worthwhile—love, friendship, knowledge, and all the rest.

11. Owen Flanagan: Self-Expression Gives Life Meaning

Owen Flanagan (1949 -) is the James B. Duke Professor of Philosophy and Professor of Neurobiology at Duke University. He has done work in philosophy of mind, philosophy of psychology, philosophy of social science, ethics, moral psychology, as well as Buddhist and Hindu conceptions of the self.

Flanagan does not assume "that life is or can be worth living."[23] Perhaps we are just biologically driven to live worthless lives. So he begins by asking: "Is life worth living?" And if it is then "…what sorts of things make it so?"[24] He notes that reflecting on this question may be a waste of time, as life might be better for the non-reflective. Reflection may lead to despair, if one determines that life is worthless, or to joy, if one concluded to the contrary. The question of whether life is worth living and what makes it so is connected with another bewildering question: "Do we live our lives?"[25] In one sense the answer is obvious—we spend time not dead—but Flanagan wants to know if we act freely or are merely controlled like puppets. So questions about the value of living involve issues about who we are and what kinds of things are true about us.

Flanagan argues that even happiness is not enough to guarantee that life is worthwhile, inasmuch as a life may contain much happiness and still be meaningless. Happiness is not sufficient for meaning, since one might derive happiness from evil things, and it may not be necessary either, since a meaningful life may be devoid of happiness. But even if happiness is a component of a worthwhile life, he argues that identity and self-expression are more crucial. "Wherever one looks, or so I claim, humans seek, and sometimes find worth in possessing an identity and expressing it."[26] Identity and self-expression are necessary but not sufficient conditions for worthwhile living, since we need to clarify what forms of identity and expressions of it are valuable.

But what if there is no self to find meaning through self-expression? There are three standard arguments supporting the idea that we are not selves. First, maybe I am just a location where things happen from a universal perspective. Second, I may simply be the roles I play in various social niches, with self just a name for this apparent unity. Third, my apparent unity may be just various stages which change as we age. Regarding this last argument, Flanagan concedes that there is no same self continuing over time, but that this does not show there is no self, just that it changes over time. Even granting the second argument that I am a social construction; I am still something, so the death of self does not follow. The first argument suggests determinism; but even if I am determined, I am still an agent who does things. So these death-of-subject arguments, while deflating our view of self, do not destroy it. Flanagan agrees that humans are contingent and do not posses eternal souls—but this does not mean they are not subjects.

But why is there anything at all? And why am I one of the things that is? Such questions invite answers such as: 1) the gods decided that the universe and creatures should exist and I have the chance to join them if I follow their commands; or 2) we don't know why there is anything except to say that the big bang and subsequent cosmic and biological evolution led to me. Flanagan notes that neither answer is satisfactory, because both posit something eternal—gods or physical facts. But that does not answer why there is something rather than nothing. (Reminiscent of earlier claims that we can't answer ultimate why questions.)

And yet many find the first story comforting, presumably because it links us with transcendent meaning. The second story has less appeal to most since it raises questions about one's significance, moral objectivity, concept of self, and ultimate meaning. But is the first story really more comforting than the second? How do the gods' plans make my life meaningful? And if the gods are the origin of all things are they really good? Thus it does not seem that either the theological or scientific story about origins can ground meaning in our lives.

Thus Flanagan suggests that we look elsewhere for meaning. Perhaps a person's meaning comes from relationships with others, or with work, or from nature—from things we can relate to in this life. After all, the scientific story never says that life does not

188

matter. In fact a lot of things matter to me, from mundane things that I love to do—hiking and travel—to more long term projects that matter even more—learning, loving, and working creatively. This means that we are creatures that thrive on self-expression and, to the extent that we are not thwarted in this desire, can ameliorate the human condition and diminish the tragedy of our demise by this expression. As Flanagan concludes:

> This is a kind of naturalistic transcendence, a way each of us, if we are lucky, can leave good-making traces beyond the time between our birth and death. To believe this sort of transcendence is possible is, I guess, to have a kind of religion. It involves believing that there are selves, that we can in self-expression make a difference, and if we use our truth detectors and good detectors well, that difference might be positive, a contribution to the cosmos.[27]

Summary – We find meaning through self expression in our work and in our relationships.

12. Victor Frankl: The Search for Meaning

Viktor Emil Frankl M.D., PhD. (1905 - 1997) was an Austrian neurologist and psychiatrist as well as a Holocaust survivor. Frankl was the founder of logo-therapy, a form of Existential Analysis, and best-selling book author of, *Man's Search For Meaning,* which belongs on any list of the most influential books in last half-century. It has sold over 12 million copies. The first part of the book tells the story of his life in the concentration camps—needless to say it is not for the faint of heart. Although Frankl survived, his parents, brother, and pregnant wife all perished. (There is no good substitute for a close reading of the book to convey the unrelenting misery of the situation, or to appreciate Frankl's reflections on it.) The record of his personal experience and observation is a priceless cultural legacy.

Frankl's philosophical views that emanate from his experience begin with his quoting Nietzsche: "He who has a why to live can bear with almost any how." If we live to return to our loved ones or to finish our book, if we have a why to live for, if we have a meaning to live for, then we have a reason to survive, no matter how miserable the conditions of our lives. This desire to live, what Frankl calls "the will to meaning," is the primary motive of human life. Putting these ideas together we are driven by the desires to survive, exist, and find meaning.

Frankl believes that a large part of meaning is subjective. It is not what we expect from life but what it expects from us that will provide meaning. We are free and we are responsible for how we live our lives. In this way Frankl sounds like an existentialist and subjectivist, extolling us to create our own meaning. But we classify him as an objectivist, for in the end there are objective values, there are things in this world that can provide meaning for anyone. The three objective sources of meaning are: 1) the experience of goodness or beauty, or of loving others; 2) creative deeds or work; and 3) the attitude we take toward unavoidable suffering. It is easy to see that love or work could give life meaning. If others whom we love depend upon us, or if we have some noble work to finish, we have a meaning for our lives; we have a why for which to bear any how.

But how is the attitude we take toward suffering a potential source of meaning? Frankl says first that we reveal our inner freedom in the attitude we take toward unavoidable suffering; and second, like the Stoics, we can see our suffering as a task to be borne nobly. Thus our suffering can be an achievement in which tragedy is transformed into triumph. Frankl observed that prisoners who changed their attitudes toward suffering in this way were the ones who had the best chance of surviving. In the end Frankl makes a case for tragic optimism. Life may be tragic, but we should remain optimistic that it meaningful nonetheless—life even in its most tragic manifestations provides ways to make life meaningful.

Summary – Meaning in life is found in productive work, loving relationships, and enduring suffering nobly.

13. Christopher Belshaw: Relationships and Projects

Christopher Belshaw is a Senior Lecturer in philosophy at the Open University. He received his PhD from the University of California-Santa Barbara. His 2005 book, *10 Good Questions about Life and Death*, devotes a chapter to the question "Is It All Meaningless?"

Belshaw argues that those who seek meaning are concerned that life does not have one. They think either that their own life or all life lacks a point, purpose or significance. Some reasons we might think life meaningless include: a) the brevity of our lives; b) the smallness of life compared with the vastness of the universe; c) the pain and suffering of life; or d) that there are no gods with a master plan.

But are these good reasons to think life meaningless? Belshaw thinks not. The last argument only follows if there are no gods, and lots of people believe the opposite. As for the claim that life is full of suffering, we might retort that it is full of satisfaction as well. It is hard to challenge the fact that we are small and the universe vast, but is that really significant? Why would life be more meaningful if the universe were smaller or we were bigger? And why would it make a difference for meaning that humans continue to exist forever? These replies lead Belshaw to believe that we do not want meaning per se, such as fitting into something else's scheme, but our *own* meaning and purpose. He suggests we change the focus of our question from the meaning of life in general to that of our individual lives. And he rejects a singular answer in favor of considering various things as giving life meaning. In this way we can make progress in answering our question.

Now the first suggestion is that meaning is up to you; meaning is entirely subjective. Belshaw dismisses this with a thought experiment. If someone claims they live a meaningful life by trying to make their plants sing then, though they may be happy, they are living a pointless and foolish life. You cannot make a life meaningful simply by believing it to be. After all plants don't sing! Or you might be happy as a drug addict, but we would still judge your life to be a waste.

If the subjective approach doesn't work, what about the objective approach? Belshaw says that the things that matter are relationships, projects, and morally good living. If we really love others, share their pleasures and pains, their hopes and aspirations, it is hard to believe that our lives are insignificant. If we have a project that means something to us—to build a house, write a book, see the world—this fits poorly with the notion that our lives are meaningless. And if we seek to help others and make the world a better place, such a life such will not seem meaningless. Moreover, these points are connected. Involvement with others gives rise to projects, and projects involve you with other people. Living a moral life does something similar. All of these activities are held together by giving our temporal lives a constructive, creative, and ultimately meaningful dimension.

But on reflection the objective approach doesn't seem to work either. Our moral lives and our projects don't seem to be meaningful if we are not engaged in them. So your attitude, although not sufficient to meaning, does seem necessary.

But even if there are ways to live which are better than others, does it matter in the end? Belshaw counters that the fate of the universe is independent of whether it matters that people suffer, and likewise for the more mundane matters in our lives. Things matter to us and the fate of the universe is irrelevant. You might object that such things don't *really* matter but this is no different than plain mattering. If something matters, then it does. The idea of ultimately mattering does not really make sense. Once you ask for the meaning of the meaning, you are involved in an infinite regress—there will be no way to end the search for the ultimate meaning. And yet, although we can view our lives as meaningful from the inside, the external perspective continually reappears. Should we just accept our lives as absurd then? Belshaw says no. The ordinary things in our lives are important even if they do not change the history of the universe, and there is no inconsistency in this recognition. Life is not absurd.

Should we then be concerned with meaning? Many in the past have not been concerned about it, and Belshaw argues that our current concern emanates from the twentieth century existentialists. The question is not necessarily one of perennial concern. If we consider the life of a typical person that works, gets married, raises a family, and has a little fun, it is not especially meaningful but it is not meaningless either. Such a person may not be very moral, or have any satisfying relationships or work, but if they find their lives worth living we should let the matter rest there. After all too much about life may not be much help, and a simple life of limited meaning and contemplation is probably best.

Our lives differ by degree in terms of their meaning. The meaning of a life differs depending on what the life is like and what the subject living it thinks about it. As for the meaning of the universe we can say that it probably has no meaning, but Belshaw says this does not matter, since we cannot imagine how the universe could have meaning. Thus we don't lack anything real when we lack ultimate meaning. Belshaw concludes: "Even if we decide that we can see that, really, there is nothing that it's all about, that's alright as well."[28]

Summary – Relationships, projects, and moral lives are the objectively good things that give our subjective lives meaning. And that is enough, as concerns about the ultimate meaning of everything are unfounded.

14. Raymond Belliotti: Leaving a Legacy

Raymond Angelo Belliotti is Distinguished Teaching Professor of Philosophy SUNY Fredonia. He holds a PhD in philosophy from the University of Miami and a J.D. from Harvard University.

Belliotti's book *What is the Meaning of Human Life* (2001) advances an objective naturalist approach to meaning. He begins by addressing the bearing of theistic belief for meaning and concludes that for those who truly believe doubts vanish and the meaning of life is clear. "Charitably interpreted, theism can fulfill the deepest human yearnings."[29] The problem is that belief is hard to maintain and doubt hard to swallow. In short, belief requires a leap of faith that many will resist. Yet he finds nihilism even less compelling. It is just not true that life is pointless. Meaning is possible, and the process of creating it satisfies most of us at least some of the time. Still, the question of life's meaning continually intrudes, becoming most acute in times of psychological crisis. As for subjective accounts of meaning, they are deflationary, providing a starting point in the search for meaning but not the robust meaning that most desire. Believing one's life has meaning does not make it so.

These considerations lead to a kind of philosophical paralysis, especially when our lives our viewed from the cosmic perspective. Adopting the cosmic perspective we might conclude that the cosmos and our lives lack meaning, that we are limited, insignificant, and impermanent. In response numerous strategies are available. One would be to accept that meaningful lives do not require significance from a cosmic perspective but only from a human perspective. One could lower the bar that needs to be reached in order to call a life meaningful. Another might use the cosmic perspective to help put things in perspective, to take ourselves less seriously, and to view our sufferings as less grave. Used creatively the cosmic perspective can help us. Thus we should oscillate between perspectives, using whichever one aided us at the moment. If we want to feel vibrant in the moment, savoring our current achievements, we could adopt the personal perspective. If we want to reflect on our situation from afar, we could adopt the cosmic perspective. So we can maximize happiness and minimize suffering by deftly switching perspectives.

This discussion of perspectives shows that meaning is connected with consciousness, freedom, and creativity. The more these attributes adhere to a being, the greater the possibility of meaning. Thus meaning is not out there waiting to be discovered, the individual must contribute to its creation. Still, we cannot create meaning out of nothing, but only from our interaction with objects of value. This takes us back to the familiar discussion of objective values. Belliotti argues that engaged lives concerned with freely chosen trivial values count as minimally meaningful. Thus a meaningful life does not have to be significant or important, but fully meaningful lives are both—significant because they influence other people, and important because they made a difference in the world. And to be valuable a life must produce moral, intellectual, aesthetic, or religious value. Value is the most important attribute of meaningful lives. Of course most of us do not live robustly meaningful lives because our lives are not valuable as thus defined, but they can be meaningful to a lesser extent by being important or significant.

Talk of valuable lives leads Belliotti to the idea of leaving historical footprints or legacies. For example, we think of Picasso's life as valuable and robustly meaningful for the reason that it left a legacy of artwork independent of whatever moral shortcoming he may had. A legacy does not grant us immortality but it does give meaning to our lives by tying us to something beyond ourselves. Dedicated service to our community or commitment to rearing children are classic examples of intense labor that points beyond ourselves and gives so many lives meaning. We can always bemoan our insignificance from a cosmic perspective, but why should we? Meaning is found by standing in relationship to things and people of value, importance, and significance. In simple terms by having fulfilling relationships and appreciating music, literature, and philosophy, as opposed to watching television or engaging in small talk.

In the end we must love life and the world; we must love the valuable things of this world to find meaning in it. Often our habits and the diversions of life obscure our search for meaning, but we can come back to it. With joyous engagement in and relationship to valuable things and people of this world, we can live meaningful lives, and leave some trace of that encounter as our legacy.

Summary – We find meaning in relationship with persons and the objective values of this world, and leaving a legacy if possible.

15. Paul Thagard: Brain Science and the Meaning of Life

Paul Thagard (1950 -) is professor of philosophy, psychology, and computer science and director of the cognitive science program at the University of Waterloo in Canada. His recent book, *The Brain and the Meaning of Life* (2010), is the first book length study of the implications of brain science for the philosophical question of the meaning of life.

Thagard admits that he long ago lost faith in his childhood Catholicism, but that he still finds life meaningful. Like most of us, love, work, and play provide him with reasons to live. Moreover, he supports the claim that persons find meaning this way with evidence from psychology and neuroscience. (He is our first writer to do this explicitly.) Thus his approach is naturalistic and empirical as opposed to a priori and rationalistic. He defends his approach by noting that thousands of years of philosophizing have not yielded undisputed rational truths, and thus we must seek empirical evidence to ground our beliefs.

While neurophysiology does not tell us what to value, it does explain how we value—we value things if our brains associate them with positive feelings. Love, work, and play fit this bill because they are the source of the goals that give us satisfaction and meaning. To support these claims, Thagard notes that evidence supports the claim that personal relationships are a major source of well-being and are also brain changing. Similarly work also provides satisfaction for many, not merely because of income and status, but for reasons related to the neural activity of problem solving. Finally, play arouses the pleasures centers of the brain thereby providing immense psychological satisfaction. Sports, reading, humor, exercise, and music all stimulate the brain in positive ways and provide meaning.

Thagard summarizes his findings as follows: "People's lives have meaning to the extent that love, work, and play provide coherent and valuable goals that they can strive for and at least partially accomplish, yielding brain-based emotional consciousness of satisfaction and happiness."[30]

To further explain why love, work, and play provide meaning, Thagard shows how they are connected with psychological needs for competence, autonomy, and relatedness. Our need for *competence* explains why work provides meaning, and why menial work generally provides less of it. It also explains why skillful playing gives meaning. The love of friends and family is the major way to satisfy our need for *relatedness*, but play and work may do so as well. As for *autonomy*, work, play, and relationships are more satisfying when self-chosen. Thus our most vital psychological needs are fulfilled by precisely the things that give us the most meaning—precisely what we would expect.

Thagard believes he has connected his empirical claim the people do value love, work, and play with the normative claim that people should value them because these activities fulfill basic psychological needs for competence, autonomy, and relatedness. Our psychological needs when fulfilled are experienced as meaning.

Summary – Love, work, and play are our brains way of satisfying our basic needs for competence, autonomy, and relatedness. In the process of engaging in these activities, we find meaning.

16. Thaddeus Metz: The Good, the True, and the Beautiful

Thaddeus Metz is Head of the Department of Philosophy at the University of Johannesburg in South Africa. He grew up in Iowa and received his PhD from Cornell University in 1997. After teaching at the University of Missouri-St. Louis for a number of years, he relocated to South Africa in 2004. He is probably the most prolific and thoughtful scholar working today on an analytic approach to the meaning of life, publishing more than a dozen articles on the subject including the entry on the meaning of life in the Stanford Encyclopedia of Philosophy.

Metz most recent and summative statement on the topic is found in his 2010 essay: "The good, the true, and the beautiful: toward a unified account of great meaning in life." Of the good, true, and beautiful, Metz begins by asserting: "I aim to make headway on the grand Enlightenment project of ascertaining what, if anything, they have in common."[31] Metz asks if there is some single property which makes the moral, the intellectual, and the aesthetic worth admiring or striving for. Put as a question: is there something that the lives of a Gandhi, Darwin, or Beethoven might share that are admirable and worthwhile and which thereby confer great meaning to their lives?

In his search for "a unification of moral achievement, intellectual reflection, and aesthetic creation,"[32] Metz does not explore that a god's purposes unify the triad or that the long term consequences of the triad give meaning to life for a simple reason—we are more justified in thinking that one of the triad gives life meaning that we are in thinking that a god exists or that moral, intellectual or aesthetic activity will have good long-term consequences. Given this disparity in our epistemic confidence, we should not hold that our triad is grounded in the gods or consequences.

Instead Metz focuses on a "non-consequentialist naturalism, the view that the good, the true, and the beautiful confer great meaning on life (at least partly) insofar as they are physical properties that have a superlative final value obtaining independently of their long-term results."[33] In other words, ethical, intellectual, and aesthetic actions leading to certain accomplishments are intrinsically worthwhile. And the reason is that such actions make it possible for individuals to transcend themselves. But how do moral, intellectual, and artistic activities allow for self-transcendence and, simultaneously, give meaning? Metz answers by distinguishing seven consequentialist, naturalistic theories of self-transcendence that account for how it is that moral achievement, intellectual reflection, and aesthetic creation provide meaning. He lists them from weakest to strongest and explains why each fails. He then proceeds to present his own account.

The *first* and weakest self-transcendent account of meaning is *captivation by an object.* The good, true and the beautiful confer meaning by shifting the focus from ourselves to something else. One's total absorption in artistic feeling, moral goodness, or intellectual inquiry is self-transcendence. Yet this account fails for it is not necessary to be absorbed or captivated by an activity for it to be one of moral achievement—working in a soup kitchen—nor is it sufficient since one may be captivated by something trivial or imaginary—like video games.

This leads to *second* form of self-transcendence, *close attention to the real.* The good, true and the beautiful confer meaning by shifting the focus from ourselves to some real natural object. The essence of the good, true, and beautiful is found in captivation by the real, physical, and natural. Metz objects citing that absorption on the navel does not provide meaning. Perhaps then we need to be absorbed with real objects which are also valuable.

This consideration leads to *third* form of self-transcendence, *connection with organic unity.* The good, true and the beautiful confer meaning by shifting the focus from ourselves to a relationship with a whole that is beyond us. Metz thinks this partially explains the value of helping others, and of having children and relationships, because persons are valuable insofar as they are organic unities. Art also unifies content, form, and technique into a single object. But this account does not explain much of the true. The importance of metaphysics and the natural sciences are not well explained this way. For example, developing a theory of quarks may give meaning to one's life, but so could developing a theory about anything trivial. Intrinsic value, the conditions constitutive of meaning, does not seem to reduce to organic unity.

This consideration leads to *fourth* form of self-transcendence, *advancement of valuable open-ended goals.* The good, true and the beautiful confer meaning to the extent we make progress toward worthwhile states of affair that cannot be otherwise be realized because our knowledge of these states changes as we try to achieve them. The ends of meaningful activities cannot ultimately be achieved precisely because, as the activities evolve, so too do the ends.

Metz is willing to grant that the pursuit of truth, beauty, and goodness are open-ended, but he rejects that this open-endedness confers meaning upon them. Ending racial discrimination, painting the Mona Lisa, or discovering evolution confers meaning not because they are open-ended pursuits, but because they are closed-ended as it were. They each accomplished something even though justice, beauty, and truth are still open-ended pursuits. Furthermore, to say that moral achievement, intellectual reflection, or aesthetic creation confer meaning because they progress toward valuable goals begs the question. We want to know what makes such things meaningful, so it does no good to simply state that they are valuable. We want to know *how* the good, true, and beautiful confer meaning.

These considerations lead to the *fifth* form of self-transcendence, *using reason to meet standards of excellence*. The good, the true, and the beautiful confer meaning in life when we transcend our animal nature with our rational nature to meet certain objective criteria. And we must exercise our reason in exemplary ways to gain meaning. But what are these standards of excellence? What rational activities using reason satisfy the criteria? Why not exercise reason for fiendish ends, as in criminal pursuits?

These questions lead to the *sixth* form of self-transcendence, *using reason in creative ways*. The good, the true, and the beautiful confer meaning in life insofar as we transcend our animal nature with our rational nature in creative ways. Life is redeemed through the creative power of artists and thinkers who bring new values into the world. Yet this theory still has trouble accounting for the apparent meaninglessness of the creative criminal. It also cannot account for moral virtue, which often has nothing to do with creativity.

These questions lead to the *seventh* form of self-transcendence, *using reason according to a universal perspective*. The good, the true, and the beautiful give meaning to life when we transcend our animal nature by using our rational nature to realize states of affairs that would be appreciated from a universal perspective. Art, scientific theories, and moral deeds all satisfy this criterion. Great art reveals universal themes; great science discovers universal laws; and great moral deeds take everyone's interests into account and are approved of from an impartial perspective. Metz considers this the best account of a self-transcendent theory of meaning. Yet it is inadequate because much that could be approved of from this universal perspective would be trivial and not the source of great meaning—writing a novel about dust or distributing implements for toenail cutting.

Having surveyed various naturalistic and non-consequentialist theories that tried to capture how the good, true, and beautiful give meaning to life, and having found them wanting, Metz proposes his own theory of self-transcendence: "The good, the true, and the beautiful confer great meaning on life insofar as we transcend our animal nature by positively orienting our rational nature in a substantial way toward conditions of human existence that are largely responsible for many of its other conditions."[34]

Metz explains this focus on fundamental conditions by considering the difference between a well-planned crime and moral achievements such as providing medical care or freeing persons from tyranny. The latter actions respect personal autonomy, support other's choices and confer meaning. Intellectual reflection that gives meaning explains many other facts and conditions about human nature or reality. Knowledge of human nature tells us about aspects of ourselves, as scientific knowledge about the world explains reality. Similarly great art is about facets of human experience—love, death, war, peace—which are themselves responsible for so much else about us. In each case meaning derives when the true, good, and beautiful address fundamental issues.

One might object that reading trashy fiction or pondering that $2 + 2 = 4$ involve reason and focus on fundamental conditions, but do not confer meaning. Metz replies that substantial effort is necessary to fully meet his standard, and that is missing in the above examples. In addition we might add that significant advancement over the past is also necessary for meaning. Not simply doing, knowing, or making what was done, known, or made before, but the bringing forth of something new. All of this leads to his conclusion: that we can transcend ourselves and obtain great meaning in the good, the true, and the beautiful "by substantially orienting one's rational nature in a positive way toward fundamental objects and perhaps thereby making an advancement."[35]

Summary – Meaning is found by transcending oneself through moral achievement, intellectual reflection, and artistic creation.

17. Commentary on Objective Meaning

Ellin's suggestion that the moral life provides meaning is fruitful, as is Thomson's suggestion that we add intellectual and aesthetic value for fully meaningful lives. But Britton's comment that all these values may be necessary for meaning but not sufficient is telling. We could live virtuous lives and still question life's meaningfulness. Yet Britton affirms that life is meaningful because there are meaningful relationships, and Eagleton furthers that claim with his emphasis on love of our fellows and the subsequent happiness derived as the meaning of life. Schlick's emphasis on play adds greatly to our conception of the meaningful life. Such a life does not have to be infused with undo profundity, but with the playful attitude of the child. So truth, goodness, beauty, love, and play provide a nice list of the objective goods that provide meaning.

Wolf combines subjective engagement with the objective values of the moral, intellectual, and artistic domains. It is not enough that there are valuable things in life; one must be engaged in and passionate about their pursuit to fully achieve meaning. Cahn offers a subjectivist account of value against Wolf, but hedges his bet by introducing an objective value—bringing no harm. We might combine Cahn's view with Wolf's and say that meaningful lives consist of active engagement in projects that do no harm. Wolf then could grant the no harm clause as a minimum, but add that lives are even more meaningful if engaged in worthwhile projects that help others. To resolve this issue we probably need a resolution to the problem of the objectivity of value, and Wolf admits as much in her follow up lecture. Meaning itself must be some kind of objective value.

Rachels is confident that there are objective values. These values give us reasons to live in certain ways and provide limited meaning and consolation in a universe where we are always haunted by the specter of death and meaninglessness. Flanagan evokes a similar theme, focusing specifically on self-expression and self-transcendence that follow from things like our work and relationships. Frankl's emphasizes objective ways to find meaning that are becoming familiar—relationships and work. His addition of bearing suffering is a unique contribution to ways of finding meaning in the world. Belshaw reiterates the theme that we find meaning in our lives in objective goods; and we should not ask what meaning objectively good things have, for that involves us in an infinite regress. To all of the above, Belliotti adds that leaving a legacy of our encounter with the meaning-providers of life contributes greatly to our search for meaning. Thagard takes us into new territory, connecting the objective values of love, work, and play to psychology and neurophysiology in order to explain why we experience meaning in these ways. Finally, Metz clarifies the essence of the ideas of most of these thinkers. Life is meaningful because there are good, true, and beautiful things in the world.

When considering these thinkers together we should note the consistency of thinking about the issue of meaning. There is great unanimity that personal relationships, productive work, and enjoyable play are meaningful activities. They are meaningful precisely because in each we may discover or create goodness, beauty, and truth. Enduring suffering nobly, self-expression, and leaving a legacy also exemplify specific activities that allow us to participate in truth, beauty, and goodness Together these thinkers disclose a universal theme. *People find meaning in life by their involvement with, connection to, and engagement in, the good, the true, and the beautiful.* We should be satisfied.

Yet we are not. There is another voice within, another perspective that cannot be stilled. After Gandhi, after Beethoven, after Einstein; after helping the unfortunate, playing our games, loving our family, bearing our suffering, and leaving our legacy—it still asks: is that all there is? Perhaps this is a voice that should be silenced, but if these meaningful things are themselves ephemeral, we cannot help but wonder if they really give meaning. The voice within cannot and should not be quieted. We can accept that these good things exist—and want more. There may be good things in the world, and we may add to that value by our creation, but that is not enough. And the reason that these good things are not enough is that there is a specter that accompanies us always. Everywhere we go, every thought we have, every happiness, every joy, every triumph—it is always with us. There to intrude on every meaningful moment, tainting the truth, the beauty, and the goodness that we experience. It is to the specter of death that we now turn.

CHAPTER 7 – DEATH AND THE MEANING OF LIFE

This is a special way of being afraid
No trick dispels. Religion used to try,
That vast, moth-eaten musical brocade
Created to pretend we never die,
And specious stuff that says No rational being
Can fear a thing it will not feel, not seeing
That this is what we fear - no sight, no sound,
No touch or taste or smell, nothing to think with,
Nothing to love or link with,
The anesthetic from which none come round.

And so it stays just on the edge of vision,
A small, unfocused blur, a standing chill
That slows each impulse down to indecision.
Most things may never happen: this one will,
And realization of it rages out
In furnace-fear when we are caught without
People or drink. Courage is no good:
It means not scaring others. Being brave
Lets no one off the grave.
Death is no different whined at than withstood.
~ Philip Larkin

After I die, human history will continue, but I won't get to be
part of it. I will see no more movies, read no more books, make
no more friends, and take no more trips. If my wife survives me, I
will not get to be with her. I will not know my grandchildren's
children. New inventions will appear and new discoveries will be
made about the universe, but I won't ever know what they are.
New music will be composed, but I won't hear it. Perhaps we
will make contact with intelligent beings from other worlds, but I
won't know about it. That is why I don't want to die, and
Epicurus' argument is beside the point.
~ James Rachels

1. The Death of Ivan Ilyich

The subject of death has been with us since the beginning of our inquiry. Tolstoy's novel, The Death of Ivan Ilyich, provides a great introduction to connection between death and meaning. It tells the story of a forty-five year old lawyer who is self-interested, opportunistic, and busy with mundane affairs. He has never considered his own death until disease strikes. Now, as he confronts his mortality, he wonders what his life has meant, whether he has made the right choices, and what will become of him. For the first time he is becoming … conscious.

The novel begins a few moments after Ivan's death, as family members and acquaintances have gathered to mark his passing. These people do not understand death, because they cannot really comprehend their own deaths. For them death is something objective which is not happening to them. They see death as Ivan did all his life, as an objective event rather than a subjective existential experience. "Well isn't that something—he's dead, but I'm not, was what each of them thought or felt."[1] They only praise God that they are not dying, and immediately consider how his death might be to their advantage in terms of money or position.

The novel then takes us back thirty years to the prime of Ivan's life. He lives a life of mediocrity, studies law, and becomes a judge. Along the way he expels all personal emotions from his life, doing his work objectively and coldly. He is a strict disciplinarian and father figure, the quintessential Russian head of the household. Jealous and obsessed with social status, he is happy to get a job in the city where he buys and decorates a large house. While decorating he falls and hits his side, an accident that will facilitate the illness that eventually kills him. He becomes bad tempered and bitter, refusing to come to terms with his own death. As his illness progresses a peasant named Gerasim stays by his bedside, becoming his friend and confidant.

Only Gerasim shows sympathy for Ivan's torment—offering him kindness and honesty—while his family thinks that Ivan is a bitter old man. Through his friendship with Gerasim Ivan begins to look at his life anew, realizing that the more successful he became, the less happy he was. He wonders whether he has done the right thing, and comprehends that by living as others expected him to, he may not have lived as he should. His reflection brings agony. He cannot escape the belief that the kind of man he became was not the kind of man he should have been. He is finally experiencing the existential phenomenon of death.

Gradually he becomes more contented and begins to feel sorry for those around him, realizing that they are too involved in the life he is leaving to understand that it is artificial and ephemeral. He dies in a moment of exquisite happiness. On his deathbed: " It occurred to him that his scarcely perceptible attempts to struggle against what was considered good by the most highly placed people, those scarcely noticeable impulses which he had immediately suppressed, might have been the real thing, and all the rest false."[2]

Tolstoy's story forces us to consider how painful it is to reflect on a life lived without meaning, and how the finality of death seals any possibility of future meaning. If, when we approach the end of our lives, we find that they were not meaningful—there will be nothing we can do to rectify the situation. What an awful realization that must be. It was as if Kierkegaard had Ilyich in mind when he said:

> This is what is sad when one contemplates human life, that so many live out their lives in quiet lostness … they live, as it were, away from themselves and vanish like shadows. Their immoral souls are blown away, and they are not disquieted by the question of its immortality, because they are already disintegrated before they die.[3]

Now consider an even more chilling question: what difference would it make if the life one lived had been meaningful? Wouldn't death erase most if not all of its meaning anyway? Wouldn't it be even more painful to leave a life of meaningful work and family? Perhaps we should live a meaningless life to reduce the pain we will feel when leaving it?

Summary – When truly confronted, the reality of death forces us to reflect on the meaning of life.

2. Is There an Afterlife?

The literature on death is voluminous and deserving of its own book length study. What we can do here is *briefly* discuss a few of the issues involved. Belief in immorality is widespread, as anthropological studies reveal, but most people regard death as the ultimate tragedy and crave continued existence. Yet there is little if any evidence for immortality; and we do not personally know anyone who came back from the dead to tell us about an afterlife. Still, many people cling to any indirect evidence they can—near death experiences, belief in reincarnation, ghost stories, communication with the dead, and the like. The problem is that none of this so-called evidence stands up well to critical scrutiny. It is so much more likely that the propensity of individuals to deceive or be deceived explains such beliefs, than that these phenomena are real. Those who accept such evidence are most likely grasping at straws—engaging in wishful thinking.

Modern science generally ignores this so-called evidence for an afterlife for a number of reasons. First, the soul which is thought immortal plays no explanatory or predictive role in the modern scientific study of human beings. Second, overwhelming evidence supports the view that consciousness ceases when brain functioning does. If ghosts or disembodied spirits exist, then we would be forced to rethink much of modern science—such as the belief that consciousness cannot exist without matter!

Of course this cursory treatment of the issue does not establish that an afterlife is impossible, especially since that possibility depends on answers to complicated philosophical questions about personal identity and the mind-body problem. But suffice it to say that explaining either the dualistic theory of life after death—where the soul separates from the body at death and lives forever—or the monist theory—where a new glorified body related to the earthly body lives on forever—is extraordinarily difficult. In the first case substance dualism must be defended, and in the second case the miraculous idea of the new body must be explained. Either way the philosophical task is enormous. Clearly the scientific winds are blowing against these ancient beliefs.

Given these considerations, we will proceed as if death is the end of human existence; we will advance without philosophically problematic assumptions about the existence of an afterlife. This has the advantage that if we find meaning without introducing such assumptions, we will be more assured of our results. And if it miraculously turns out that when we die we really do move to a better neighborhood ... so much the better.

Summary – We will assume there is no afterlife.

3. Vincent Barry: Does Death Make Life More or Less Meaningful?

Vincent Barry is Professor Emeritus of Philosophy at Bakersfield College, having taught there for thirty-four years. He received his M.A. in philosophy from Fordham University and has been a successful textbook author. In his 2007 textbook, *Philosophical Thinking About Death and Dying*, Barry carefully considers the question of the relationship between life, death, and meaning.

Is Death Bad? - One of Barry's main concerns is whether death is or is not bad for us. As he notes, the argument that death is not bad derives from Epicurus' aphorism: "When I am, death is not; and when death is, I am not." Epicurus taught that fear in general, and fear of the gods and death in particular, was evil. Consequently, using reason to rid ourselves of these fears was a primary goal of his speculative thinking. A basic assumptions of his thought was a materialistic psychology in which mind was composed of atoms, and death the dispersal of those atoms. Thus death is not then bad for us since something can be bad only if we are affected by it; but we have no sensation after death and thus being dead cannot be bad for us. Note that this does not imply that the process or the prospect of dying cannot be bad for us—they can—nor does Epicurus deny that we might prefer life to death. *His argument is that being dead is not bad for the one who has died.*

Epicurus' argument relies on two separate assumptions—the experience requirement and the existence requirement.[4] The experience requirement can be summarized thus:

1. A harm to someone is something that is bad for them.
2. For something to be bad for someone it must be experienced by them.

3. Death is a state of no experience.
4. Therefore death cannot be bad for someone.

The existence requirement can be summarized thus:

1. A person can be harmed only if they exist.
2. A dead person does not exist.
3. Therefore a dead person cannot be harmed.

As we will see, counter arguments attack one of the two requirements. Either they try to show that someone can be harmed without experiencing the harm, or that someone who is dead can still be harmed.

One noted philosopher who attacks the Epicurean view is Thomas Nagel. In his essay "Death," Nagel argues that death is bad for someone who dies even if that person does not consciously survive death. According to *this deprivation theory*, death is bad for persons who die because of the good things their deaths deprive them of. However, if death is bad because it limits the possibility of future goods, is death not then good in limiting the possibility of future evils? So the possibility of future goods does not by itself show that death is bad; to show that one would have to show that a future life would be worth living, that is, that it would contain more good than bad. But how can any deprivation theory explain how it is bad for us to be deprived of something if we do not *experience* that deprivation? How can what we don't know hurt us?

In reply Nagel argues that we can be harmed without being aware of it. An intelligent man reduced to the state of infancy by a brain injury has suffered a great misfortune, even if unaware of, and contented in, his injurious state. Nagel argues that many states that we do not experience can be bad for us—the betrayal of a friend, the loss of reputation, or the unfaithfulness of a spouse. And just as an adult reduced to infancy is the subject of a misfortune, so too is one who is dead. But critics wonder *who* it is that is the subject of this harm? Even if it is bad to be deprived of certain goods, who is it that is deprived? How can the dead be harmed? There apparently no answer to this question.

And there is another problem. While the deprivation argument may explain why death is bad for us, it follows from it that being denied prenatal existence would also be bad. Yet we do not ordinarily consider ourselves harmed by not having been born sooner. How can we explain this asymmetry?

Epicurus argued that this asymmetry could not be explained, and we should feel indifferent to death just as we do to prenatal existence. This sentiment was echoed by Mark Twain:

> Annihilation has no terrors for me, because I have already tried it before I was born—a hundred million years—and I have suffered more in an hour, in this life, than I remember to have suffered in the whole hundred million years put together. There was a peace, a serenity, an absence of all sense of responsibility, an absence of worry, an absence of care, grief, perplexity; and the presence of a deep content and unbroken satisfaction in that hundred million years of holiday which I look back upon with a tender longing and with a grateful desire to resume when the opportunity comes.[5]

In reply, deprivationists argue that we do not have to hold symmetrical views about prenatal and postnatal experience—claiming instead that asymmetrical views are consistent with ordinary experience. To see why consider the following. Would you rather have suffered a long surgical operation last year or undergo a short one tomorrow? Would you rather have had pleasure yesterday, or pleasure tomorrow? In both cases we have more concern with the future than the past; we are less interested in past events than in future ones. Death in the future deprives us of future goods, whereas prenatal nonexistence deprived us of past goods about which we are now indifferent. For all these reason Barry concludes that *death is probably bad and a fear of death rational.* But does death undermine meaning?

The Connection Between Death and Meaning - Tolstoy and Schopenhauer claimed that *death makes life meaningless*; Russell and Taylor believe that death detracts greatly from the meaning of life, and Buddha argued that death undermines the good things of life. All thought death conflicts with meaning in some sense. Opponents argue that *death makes life meaningful.* No matter what side they are on, all these thinkers believe that death is the crucial element for determining the extent to which life is, or is not, meaningful.

While there are many arguments that death makes life meaningless, there are also many philosophical arguments, in addition to religious ones, that death makes life meaningful. These latter arguments all coalesce around the idea that death is necessary for a life to be truly human. They take a variety of forms.

a) *Death as necessary for life* – There is no development in life without death. Death is happening to you because the universe is happening to you; while you live you are slowly being destroyed. The universe produces life through death so that, while death may be bad for you individually, it is good for the whole.

b) *Death as part of the life cycle* – Without the life cycle our experience of being human would be altered. Death is the goal of life, we are programmed to die; it is part of the continuum of life.

c) *Death as ultimate affirmation* – Facing death we realize the ultimate value of life; so death has meaning in revealing this value. In addition life is valuable because it is fleeting, fragile, and temporary.

d) *Death as motive to commitment and engagement* – Without the finitude of life we would be less motivated to do worthwhile things, and besides immortality may be boring.

e) *Death as stimulus to creativity* – Some argue that the nearness of death focuses them to be creative as never before. Others argue that death literally promotes creativity, which emanates from our desire to overcome mortality.

f) *Death as socially useful* – Death is necessary to limit overpopulation. Many disagree, arguing that if we lived longer or were immortal we would worry more and be more concerned about the world we live in.

In opposition to all those who think death does or does not give meaning to life are those who argue that life has or lacks meaning independent of death. In other words, they argue that life gives or does not give meaning to death, thereby turning all our previous considerations upside down. But how does a life give or not give death a meaning?

Death and the Meaning of Life - Barry argues that things close to us provide clear answers about meaning—caring for our families, our work, or some cause that is important to us. But when we move to the larger picture and ask about the meaning of everything, we are perplexed. Some speculate that individuals are related to something larger, like a god or a universal plan of which they are part, and that this gives their lives meaning; others that they create or discover meaning in the world without positing a supernatural realm. Such views, as we have seen, are divided between theistic and non-theistic positions. The main problem with the former position is that most contemporary philosophers doubt religious stories are true; the basic problem with the latter is that we are probably mistaken when we imbue an indifferent universe with meaning. Even the notion of progress is insufficient to ground meaning. Such concerns lead Barry to re-examine nihilism.

As we saw previously there are multiple responses to nihilism—we can reject, accept, or affirm it. Yet none of these responses appear adequate; the challenge of nihilism cannot be fully met. Where does this leave us? Barry concludes that though life has no meaning in the objective sense, it still can be meaningful subjectively; it still can be worth living. While persons differ as to how to give their lives meaning and value, Barry maintains that all meaningful lives are examined ones. And that is why the life of Ivan Ilyich lacked meaning—he had not examined his life or his death. Meaningful lives are those that include deep thinking about death and dying. So it seems that death is at least good in this regard. As Barry puts it:

> Yes, an individual life can be worthwhile even though life itself may have no ultimate meaning. *But only if that life is examined*, still resonates the venerable admonition of Socrates borne on the face of the dead Ivan Ilyich—which is to say, *only if that life includes philosophical thinking about death and dying.*[6]

Summary – It is uncertain if death is a good or bad thing. The connection between death and meaning is that thinking about death can make a life subjectively meaningful.

4. Stephen Rosenbaum: Death is Not Bad; A Defense of Epicurus

Stephen Rosenbaum is Dean of the honors college at the University of Nevada-Las Vegas and Emeritus Professor of Philosophy. He received his PhD in philosophy from the University of Illinois. In his 1986 piece, "How to Be Dead and Not Care: A Defense of Epicurus," he rejects the view that death is bad for the person that dies, undertaking a systematic defense of the Epicurean position.[7] As we have seen, while we ordinarily think that death is bad for the person that dies, Epicurus argued that this is mistaken. And, since fear of something that is not bad is groundless, it is irrational to fear death.

Rosenbaum begins by differentiating between: 1) dying—the process that leads to death; 2) death—the time at which a person becomes dead; and 3) being dead—the state after death. The Epicurean argument does not deny that dying or death can be bad, but argues that being dead cannot be bad for the one who is dead. Just as a totally deaf person cannot experience a Mozart symphony, a dead person cannot have positive or negative experiences. The purpose of Epicurus' argument, according to Rosenbaum, was to help us achieve inner peace and to free us from unnecessary fear and worry. It also was a meant to revise common sense in light of philosophical reflection. Rosenbaum reconstructs that argument as follows:

a) A state of affairs is bad for a person P only if they can experience it; thus
b) P's being dead is bad for P only if it is a state P can experience;
c) P can experience a state of affairs only if it begins before P's death;
d) P's being dead is not a state of affairs that begins before P's death; thus
e) P's being dead is not a state of affairs that P can experience; thus P's being dead is not bad for P.

Since B and E are logical deductions, only A, C, and D are premises. Since D is true by definition, only premises A and C are possibly controversial, but Rosenbaum argues that both stand up to critical scrutiny. The only way to attack the argument then is if it misses the entire point. Perhaps death is bad because we anticipate not having experiences, opportunities, and satisfactions. Rosenbaum responds that such anticipations occur only while we are alive; they cannot be experienced after we are dead. That is why anticipating death is not like anticipating going to the dentist. In the latter both the anticipation and the actual experience of the dental chair are bad, while in the former there is only the anticipation. In fact Epicurus thought the anticipation pointless, since there would be no badness after death. But if Epicurus' argument is sound, why do many fear death?

Lucretius offered an explanation. Since we have a hard time thinking of ourselves as separate from our bodies, we think that bad things happening to our bodies are happening to us. We think of the decaying body as somehow us, but it is not. Another possible explanation is that we believe death takes us to some other realm that will be highly unpleasant. But Epicurus can apply a salve to our concerns—being dead is nothing to the dead person.

Summary – The Epicurean argument that death is not bad and nothing to fear is sound. Being dead is not bad for the dead person.

5. Oswald Hanfling: Agnosticism Regarding Death and Meaning

Hanfling accepts as obvious the claim that meaning is affected by our knowledge of death, and agrees that "death casts a negative shadow over our lives."[8] Moreover, while the naturalness of death may provide some consolation from our anxiety, it does not show that our apprehension about death is misplaced. Still, Epicurus' sound argument should mitigate our worries and provide consolation. *Death is not totally bad.*

But are there any overriding reasons to regard death as mostly evil? Hanfling does not think such reasons are convincing. For while I may wish to fulfill some goal and regret that I cannot, I will not be harmed after my death by the fact that I didn't fulfill that goal. Or though one might argue that death is bad because life is good, it is unclear whether life in general is good. Similarly one might argue that merely having experiences is a good in itself, but this does not hold up either, as we are not comforted in times of misfortune by being said to have the benefit of existence. Even the fact that we generally desire life does not show that it is good. Hanfling concludes that arguments from the goodness of life to the badness of death are unsound—there are no convincing reasons to think that death is primarily bad. But none of this shows that a life *without* death would be meaningful; they do not show that death is necessary for meaning. *Death is not necessarily good either.*

In the end death is a somber prospect and not something we look forward to, but it is neither a definitive blessing nor a curse. Death makes a great difference to us, but we cannot come to any simple conclusions about the meaning of death. "Death, like life itself, is not amenable to such conclusions."[9]

Summary – The thought of death is unpleasant, but we cannot determine the implications of death for meaning.

6. George Pitcher: It is a Misfortune To Be Dead

George Pitcher is emeritus professor of philosophy at Princeton where he was a member of the department from 1956-1981. His 1984 article "The Misfortunes of the Dead," addresses the question of whether the dead can be harmed.

Pitcher begins by assuming that death is the end of our consciousness. It has benefits—no pain, suffering, or anxiety—but does death harm the dead person? On the one hand, it doesn't seem so. If after my death my college closes down that doesn't hurt me. On the other hand, if I've given a lot of my life to my college and it was important to me, it might seem bad for me. In this article Pitcher defends the claim (claim 1) that the dead can be harmed. But first he defends the claim (claim 2) that the dead can be wronged. If your son promises to bury you but sells your body for spare parts, or you won a gold medal at the Olympics and it is now unjustly taken away, you have been wronged even though you are now dead. In both cases an injustice has been done to you, or so Pitcher argues. So it seems the dead can be wronged.

Pitcher distinguished two ways to describe a dead person: 1) as they were when alive—*ante-mortem*; or 2) as they are dead, as a rotting corpse or pile of ashes—*post-mortem*. He argues that we can be wronged ante-mortem, but not post-mortem. For instance, if one is slandered after death, one is slandering the ante-mortem person but not the post-mortem person. Or when you break a promise, you break it to the ante-mortem person, since you cannot break (or make I suppose) a promise to a post-mortem person.

Pitcher now turns back to claim 1, his strongest claim, that the dead can be harmed. (In Pitcher's hierarchy being harmed is worse than being wronged, and being wronged worse than being the victim of hostility.) Now Pitcher asks: "is it possible for something to happen after a person's death that harms the living person he was before he died?"[10] He answers in the affirmative.

By definition harms are events or states of affairs contrary to your desires or interests. Of course we cannot be killed or experience pain after death—the post mortem person can't be harmed—but we can have desires thwarted after death—the ante mortem person can be harmed. If I desire to be remembered after I die with a statue on campus and you destroy the statue, then you have defeated my desire and harmed the ante-mortem person I was. To better understand this nuance, compare two worlds. In World 1 I had discovered the absolute truth about reality, disseminated my work, and after my death proclaimed the world greatest philosopher; in World 2 my neighbor destroyed all my works the day after I died and nobody knows of my philosophy and I'm forgotten. If World 2 came about we would feel I was harmed—all my work obliterated and my name forgotten even though I was the greatest philosopher of all time. This suggests the (ante-mortem) dead can be harmed.

Pitcher notes that the idea that the dead can be at least *slightly* harmed goes back to at least Aristotle. But how is a living person affected by something that happens after they die? We have seen that ante-mortems can be *wronged*—by being slandered for example—but how can they be *harmed*? How can something that happens now, at a later time after the person is dead, affect the person at an earlier time, when they were alive? If this is true, we have a case of backward causation—of the present causing the past.

Pitcher doesn't think he needs to invoke backward causation to make his argument work. All he needs to show is that being harmed does not entail knowing about the harm. Of course most of the time you are harmed you know about it, but you don't have to know about it to be harmed. You are harmed if you contract a terminal illness, or if everyone ridicules you behind your back, even if you don't know about either. So a person can be harmed after their death even though they won't know about it then. For example, if I know my child will die young this is a misfortune for me, but it is not the *only* harm that befalls me. The other harm is that my child will actually die young. And even if I didn't know my child would die, there was still some harm being done to me *before* my child died. And that harm was that my child was going to die. This is a harm for me whether I know of it or not.

"So the shadow of harm that an event casts can reach back across the chasm even of a person's death and darken his ante-mortem life."[11] While I do not suffer my son's death when I'm (post-mortem) dead, I do suffer it understood as (ante-mortem) death. Thus it is not that after I'm dead I now suffer for the first time and my ante-mortem person is harmed retroactively. Rather the ante-mortem person is harmed by events that occur after one's death because: "the occurrence of the event makes it true that during the time before the person's death, he was harmed—harmed in that the unfortunate event was going to happen."[12]

Summary – We are harmed by death because while alive the knowledge of death harmed us.

7. Steven Luper: Annihilation is a Terrible Misfortune

Steven Luper is Professor of Philosophy at Trinity University in San Antonio Texas. He received his PhD from Harvard in 1982. In his essay "Annihilation," he argues that death is a terrible thing and that Epicurus' indifference to death is badly mistaken.[13]

Luper begins by noting that while there may be fates worse than death, death is still a terrible fate. We may prefer death to eternal torture or boredom, but few would reject the offer to live as long as they want, and Epicurus' argument is beside the point. Can we really believe that death is nothing to us? Luper thinks not.

Death is a misfortune for us primarily because it thwarts our desires. If we have a desire we want fulfilled, then death may prevent its fulfillment; if we enjoy living, then dying prevents us from continuing to do so; if we have hopes and aspirations; then they will be frustrated by our deaths; if we have reasons to live, then we have reasons not to want to die. For all these reasons death is a grave misfortune.

Moreover, we should care about dying, for to be indifferent to this calamity is to be hard-hearted and dispassionate. What kind of person is indifferent to their desires, or their deaths, or their children? Would our lives not be poorer if we were detached from the cares, concerns, and relationships that bind us to life? To the extent we tolerate death, we give up on life. Better to think that dying is bad than that life is no longer worth living.

Still, if we must die, we can soften the blow somewhat. We can live passionately and have realistic goals that can be accomplished in a lifetime. If we live accordingly, accomplishing what we set out to do, then dying will be less bad. But it will still be a great misfortune unless we can honestly say that we could have done no more had we been granted more time. But who could honestly say that?

Summary – Death is a misfortune because it thwarts our desires.

8. David Benatar: Why It Is Better Never to Have Been

David Benatar is professor of philosophy and head of the Department of Philosophy at the University of Cape Town in Cape Town, South Africa. He is best known for his advocacy of antinatalism. His article, "Why It Is Better Never to Come into Existence," espouses the view that it is always a harm to be born.

It is commonly assumed that we do nothing wrong bringing future people into existence if their lives will, on balance, be good. This assumes that being brought into existence is generally beneficial. In contrast Benatar argues that: "Being brought into existence is not a benefit but always a harm."[14] While most maintain that living is beneficial as long as the benefits of life outweigh the evil, Benatar argues that this conclusion does not follow because: 1) pain is bad, and 2) pleasure good; but 3) the absence of pain is always good whether people exist or not, whereas 4) the absence of pleasure is only bad if people exist to be denied it.

To support this asymmetry between 3 & 4 Benatar presents *three* arguments. The first is that: 1) while there is a duty not to bring people who will suffer into the world (supports 3), there is no duty to bring people who will be happy into the world (supports 4). Thus a lack of suffering is always good, whether or not someone enjoys this absence; whereas a lack of happiness is not always bad, unless people exist to be denied it.

His second argument is that though we think it strange to say we have children so they will benefit, we think it normal to say we should not have children because they will be harmed. We don't think people should have as many children as they can to benefit those children, but we do think people should refrain from having children if this will cause them suffering.

His third argument to support the asymmetry is that while not having children may be bad or good for the living, not having been born cannot deprive those who have never been born of anything.

This fundamental asymmetry—suffering is an intrinsic harm, but the absence of pleasure is not—allows Benatar to draw his nihilistic conclusions. In other words, the measure by which the absence of pain is better than its presence is itself greater than the measure by which the presence of pleasure is better than its absence. This means that not existing is either a lot better than existing, in the case of pain, or a little worse, in the case of pleasure. Or to think of it another way, the absence of pain and the presence of pleasure are both good, but the presence of pain is much worse than the absence of pleasure. (Here is my own thought experiment that might help. Suppose that before you were born the gods were trying to decide whether to create you. If they decide to create you, you will suffer much if you have a bad life or a gain greatly if you have a good life. If they decide not to create you, you will gain greatly by avoiding a bad life, but suffer only *slightly* if at all by not existing—as you wouldn't know what you had been deprived of.)

To further his argument, Benatar notes that most persons underestimate how much suffering they will endure. If their lives are going better than most, they count themselves lucky. Consider death. It is a tragedy at any age, and only seems acceptable at ninety because of our expectations about life-spans. But is lamenting death inconsistent with his anitnatalism? Benatar thinks not. While non-existence does not harm a possible person, death is another harm that will come to those in existence. In response you could say that you can't be mistaken about whether you prefer existence to non-existence. Benatar grants that you may not be mistaken if you claim that you are *currently* glad to have been born, but you could still be mistaken that it was better to have been born at all. You might now be glad you were born, and then suffer so badly latter that you change your mind. (I might wish I hadn't been born, after I find out what's in store for me.)

What follows from all this? That we shouldn't have children? That no one should have children? Benatar claims that to answer yes to these questions goes against a basic drive to reproduce, so we must be careful not to let such drives bias our analysis. Having children satisfies many needs of those who bring children into existence, but this does not mean it serves the interests of the children—in fact it causes them great harm. One could reply that the harm is not that great to the children, since the benefits of existing may outweigh the harm, and, at any rate, we cannot ask future persons if they want to be born. Since we enjoy our lives we assume they will too, thus providing the justification for satisfying our procreational needs. Most people do not regret their existence, and if some do we could not have foreseen it.

But might we be deceiving ourselves about how good life is? Most of us assume life would be unbearable if we were in certain situations. But often, when we find ourselves in these situations, we adapt. Could it be that we have adapted to a relatively unbearable life now? Benatar says that a superior species might look at our species with sympathy for our sorry state. And the reason we deceive ourselves is that we have been wired by evolution to think this way—it aids our survival. Benatar views people's claims about the benefits of life skeptically, just as he would the ruminations of the slave who claims to prefer slavery.

Benatar concludes by saying: "One implication of my view is that it would be preferable for our species to die out."[15] He claims that it would be heroic if people quit having children so that no one would suffer in the future. You may think it tragic to allow the human race to die out, but it would be hard to explain this by appealing to the interests of potential people.

Summary – It is better never to come into existence as being born is always a harm.

9. John Leslie: We Should Not Let Life Go Extinct

John Leslie (1940 -) is currently Professor emeritus at the University of Guelph, in Ontario, Canada. In his essay "Why Not Let Life Become Extinct?" he argues that we ought not to embrace the view that extinction would be best.

Some argue that it would not be sad or a pity if humans went extinct because: 1) there would be nobody left to be sad; or 2) life is so bad that extinction is preferable. Leslie maintains that this issue has practical implications since someone with power might decide that life is not worth it, and press the nuclear button (or bring about some other extinction scenario.) Fortunately most do not reason this way, but if they do there is a paucity of philosophical arguments to dissuade them. Moreover, philosophers often advance arguments that we should improve the lives of the worst off and, since so many people live wretched lives, it is easy to see that a solution might entail killing a lot of people.

But what of letting all life go extinct? Some philosophers argue that we have no duty to prevent this, that even if life is a good we have no duty to propagate it, or if someone is about to lose their life we have no obligation to save it. The principle behind such thinking is that though we ought not to hurt people, we have no duty to help them. Other lines of thinking may lead to similar conclusions. A utilitarian might argue that life should go extinct if it is sufficiently unhappy now or will be so in the future. Other argue that we have no duties to produce future people no matter how happy they might be, for the simple reason that these possible people cannot be deprived of anything, as they do not yet exist. Leslie counters that deciding whether to produce a situation should be influenced by what the situation will be like, by its consequences. If one is deciding whether to produce a certain future, the most relevant fact is whether that future will be good.

He now makes some concessions. First, it is morally good to want to make the lives of the worst off better, but not if this entails destroying the entire human race. Second, actual people are not obligated to make all sacrifices for possible people, anymore than you are obliged to give food to others when your own family is starving. Third, given overpopulation, we are not obligated to have children.

And since ethics is imprecise, we cannot be sure that we have duties to future generations. Still, the universe has value despite the evil it contains, leading Leslie to speculate that there might be an "ethical requirement that it exist..."[16] In other words a thing's nature, if it has intrinsic value, makes its existence ethically required. But how can the description of a thing's nature lead to the prescription that it ought to exist? Leslie argues that we cannot derive that a thing should exist from a description of its nature. Perhaps it *would* be better if no life existed. But suppose we agree that life is intrinsically good, would we then have an obligation to perpetuate it? Leslie answers no. A thing's intrinsic goodness only implies *some* obligation that it exist, since other ethical considerations might overrule that obligation. For instance a moral person might think it better that life ended then have a world with so much suffering. The upshot of all this is that there are no knockdown arguments either way. Competent philosophers who argue that it is better for there to be no life probably are equal footing with those who argue the opposite. Leslie continues: "Still, pause before joining such people."[17]

In the end, we cannot show conclusively that we should not let life become extinct because we can never go from saying that something is—even happiness or pleasure—to saying that something should be. And it is also not clear that maximizing happiness is the proper moral goal. Perhaps instead we should try to prevent misery—which may entail allowing life to go extinct. Philosophers do not generally advocate such a position, but their reluctance to do so suggests that they are willing to tolerate the suffering of some for the happiness of others.

Summary – There are strong arguments for letting life go extinct, although Leslie suggests we generally reject them because life has intrinsic goodness.

10. James Lenman: Immortality Would Not Be Pleasant

James Lenman a Professor in the Department of Philosophy at the University of Sheffield. He did his undergraduate work at Oxford University and received his PhD from St. Andrews University.

Lenman's article, "Immortality: A Letter," (1995) concerns a letter from a fictional philosopher to her fictitious biological friend in which she presents arguments against taking his immortality drug. She worries that if only some people get the drug, those who don't will regret it; while if everyone gets the drug, overpopulation will ensue unless people stop having children. But this will lead to more unhappiness, as people want to have children.

Most importantly immortality would undermine our humanity by transforming us into different kinds of beings. Just as an angel who gives up immortality to become human would transform into a human, so too would a human who accepts immortality give up their humanity. To be granted immortality is to become a different kind of being. In addition an immortal life might become boring. And finally the value of life derives in large part from its fragility, which would be undermined by immortality. Lenman's letter concludes:

> The problem with your discovery is that … it precisely wouldn't be a *human* good that was advanced because so much of what makes us *human* would then be obsolete. And *human* good … is the only sort of good we can make much sense of or coherently view as intrinsically worth our wanting. Nothing … is intrinsically worth *anybody's* wanting and what is worth our wanting can only be *our* good. There is no such thing as the good. Our proper concern being rather with … the good for *man*.[18]

Summary – More value will be lost than gained if we become immortal.

11. Nick Bostrom: The Fable of the Dragon-Tyrant

Nick Bostrom (1973 -) holds a PhD from the London School of Economics (2000). He is a co-founder of the World Transhumanist Association (now called Humanity+) and co–founder of the Institute for Ethics and Emerging Technologies. He was on the faculty of Yale University until 2005, when he was appointed Director of the newly created Future of Humanity Institute at Oxford University. He is currently Professor, Faculty of Philosophy & Oxford Martin School; Director, Future of Humanity Institute;

and Director, Program on the Impacts of Future Technology; all at Oxford University.

Bostrom's article, "The Fable of the Dragon-Tyrant," tells the story of a planet ravaged by a dragon (death) that demands a tribute which is satisfied only by consuming thousands of people each day. Neither priests with curses, warriors with weapons, or chemists with concoctions could defeat the dragon. The elders were selected to be sacrificed, although they were often wiser than the young, because they had at least lived longer than the youth. Here is a description of their situation:

> Spiritual men sought to comfort those who were afraid of being eaten by the dragon (which included almost everyone, although many denied it in public) by promising another life after death, a life that would be free from the dragon-scourge. Other orators argued that the dragon has its place in the natural order and a moral right to be fed. They said that it was part of the very meaning of being human to end up in the dragon's stomach. Others still maintained that the dragon was good for the human species because it kept the population size down. To what extent these arguments convinced the worried souls is not known. Most people tried to cope by not thinking about the grim end that awaited them.[19]

Given the ceaselessness of the dragon's consumption, most people did not fight it and accepted the inevitable. A whole industry grew up to study and delay the process of being eaten by the dragon, and a large portion of the society's wealth was used for these purposes. As their technology grew, some suggested that they would one day build flying machines, communicate over great distances without wires, or even be able to slay the dragon. Most dismissed these ideas.

Finally, a group of iconoclastic scientists figured out that a projectile could be built to pierce the dragon's scales. However, to build this technology would cost vast sums of money and they would need the king's support. (Unfortunately, the king was busy raging war killing tigers, which cost the society vast sums of wealth and accomplished little.) The scientists then began to educate the public about their proposals and the people became excited about the prospect of killing the dragon. In response the king convened a conference to discuss the options.

First to speak was a scientist who explained carefully how research should yield a solution to the problem of killing the dragon in about twenty years. But the king's moral advisors said that it is presumptuous to think you have a right not to be eaten by the dragon; they said that finitude is a blessing and removing it would remove human dignity and debase life. Nature decries, they said, that dragons eat people and people should be eaten. Next to speak was a spiritual sage who told the people not to be afraid of the dragon, but a little boy crying about his grandma's death moved most toward the anti-dragon position.

However, when the people realized that millions would die before the research was completed, they frantically sought out financing for anti-dragon research and the king complied. This started a technological race to kill the dragon, although the process was painstakingly slow, and filled with many mishaps. Finally, after twelve years of research the king launch a successful dragon-killing missile. The people were happy but the king saddened that they had not started their research years earlier—millions had died unnecessarily. As to what was next for his civilization, the king proclaimed: "Today we are like children again. The future lies open before us. We shall go into this future and try to do better than we have done in the past. We have time now—time to get things right, time to grow up, time to learn from our mistakes, time for the slow process of building a better world..."[20]

Summary – We should try to overcome the tyranny of death with technology.

12. Michaelis Michael & Peter Caldwell: Optimism is Rational

Michaelis Michael is a senior lecturer of the University of New South Wales in Sydney Australia, and Peter Caldwell is a lecturer at the University of Technology in Sydney. In their insightful piece, "The Consolations of Optimism" (2004), they argue for adopting an attitude of optimism regarding the meaning of life.

The optimist and pessimist may agree on the facts, but not on their attitude toward those facts. "This nicely sketches what our thesis is: optimism is an attitude, not a theoretical position; moreover, there are reasons why one ought to be an optimist."[21]

The reasons for preferring optimism have nothing to do with how the world is—optimism is not a better description of reality. Instead it is that a reasonable optimism is best for ourselves and those around us. To better understand reasonable optimism, the authors turn to the Stoics.

The Happiness of the Stoic Sage - Stoics are often characterized as emotionless, indifferent, individuals who simply put up with their fate, accepting that life is bad. Such a picture is uninspiring. While resignation toward the dreadfulness of life is cynical and pessimistic, this is not how the authors interpret Stoicism. The Stoics counsels us to embrace that which we cannot change rather than fight against it and, in the process, embrace reality. Thus Stoicism is realistic, not cynical.

For the Stoics emotions follow from beliefs. For example, if we believe that death is bad then the emotion of fear or dread may follow. In this case, Stoics generally holds that the belief that death is bad is unjustified and hence negative emotions should *not* follow. Now consider cheerfulness. There are good reasons to be cheerful and happy—it feels better than being unhappy. This is the reason to be cheerfully optimistic. But can we adopt this optimistic attitude, is it psychologically feasible? The authors think it is both feasible and reasonable to adopt optimism. While the pessimist might object that optimism provides little consolation, optimism contributes to a happier existence and that is a reason to adopt it. Optimism is more than a small consolation.

But optimism is not a set of beliefs about how reality is; rather it is a response to reality. A stoical attitude does not mean not caring or being indifferent to unpleasant things, rather it doesn't add lamenting to one's caring. Stoics do not deny that pain and suffering exist—because that is to deny reality—but accept such evils without resenting them. The Stoics reject responding to situations with strong, irrational emotions that would cloud judgment, counseling instead to remain calm and optimistic. "This way of experiencing pains without losing equanimity is the key to stoical optimism."[22] Optimism leads to happiness and is therefore reasonable.

The Rationality of Beliefs - Beliefs represent how things are to us. If we find beliefs do not adequately do this, we ought to reject them; if they do represent the world well, then we ought to keep them. In addition to believing things about the world, we might desire, expect, hope, fear, or want things about the world. If we expect things about the world, we believe those things will happen. If we hope, desire, want, or fear things, we might not believe those things will happen, instead believing only that they *might* happen. In all of these cases beliefs are about possibilities that are rational to entertain. But what counts as making a belief rational? Here we can distinguish between strongly rational—the evidence is nearly irrefutable—or weakly rational—as a practical necessity we must believe some things that are not certain but necessary for us to act in the world. So the test of a belief system may be whether it is practical in this way.

Optimism & Pessimism - Again optimists and pessimists do not necessarily disagree about how the world is, although they could, but instead project differing attitudes toward it. Since optimism is an attitude, it does not assume any cluster of beliefs and thus cannot be undermined for being irrational like a belief can. Pessimism is an attitude which demands things from reality and resent that reality does not conform to their wishes. Optimists are typically more accepting of the limitations of the world. Of course optimists may lose their optimism when bad fortune strikes, but we are all happier when we are optimistic and less happy when we are pessimistic—this is the rational ground for optimism.

Yet optimism is not wishful thinking. Wishful thinking involves beliefs that are false, whereas optimism is an attitude that does not necessarily involve false beliefs. Furthermore, optimism has positive results, as the case of Hume's attitude toward his impending death shows. Diagnosed with a fatal disease Hume begins his ruminations on his situation thus: "I was ever more disposed to see the favorable than unfavorable side of things: a turn of mind which it is more happy to possess, than to be born to an estate of ten thousand a year... It is difficult to be more detached from life than I am at the present."[23] While many fear death or react variously in ways that disturb tranquility "Hume's calm and sanguine resignation stands like a beacon of reasonableness, calling out for emulation."[24] Optimism is a reasonable and beneficial response to the human condition.

Summary – We do not know if life is meaningful or not. For now we might as well be optimistic, especially when facing death.

13. Conclusion: Death is an Ultimate Evil

The story of Ivan Ilyich indicates an inseparable connection between death and meaning. The precise connection is unclear, but surely it depends in large part on whether death is the end of our consciousness. While beliefs in immortality have been widespread among humans, such beliefs are extremely difficult to defend rationally.

If death is the end of an individual human life, the question naturally arises whether this is a good, bad, or indifferent thing. The argument of Epicurus states that being dead cannot be bad for someone, and thus the fear of death is misplaced. Deprivationists argue that we can be harmed by things we don't experience, but it is hard to see how someone can be harmed if that someone is non-existent. But even if the deprivationists are correct, their view implies the counter-intuitive conclusion that we should regret that we did not exist before birth. In reply, deprivationists try to explain this asymmetry by pointing out that most of us do care more about the future than the past. After considering the arguments, Barry says that death probably is bad for us and nihilism a real possibility. Nonetheless he concludes that we give life subjective meaning by reflecting about our life and death.

Rosenbaum replies that being dead cannot be bad for the dead person—the Epicurean arguments is sound—and fears about death, while explainable, are unfounded. Hanfling stakes out the middle ground, acknowledging the pall that death casts over life while accepting the Epicurean view as palliative. In the end we just do not know the role death plays regarding the meaning of life. Pitcher defends the claim that a dead person can be wronged and harmed, with the caveat that this harm is to be understood as affecting the ante-mortem rather than post-mortem individual. However, it is not clear that this undercuts the Epicurean argument since it is addressed to the post-mortem individual. Luper defends the badness of death by the simple observations that few would reject the offer to live longer, and most believe they could accomplish more if they had more time. These observations make it clear that almost everyone does think that death is an unmitigated disaster, and the Epicurean argument is of limited value.

Benatar relies on an asymmetry to claim that it is better never to have been born, and it would be a good thing if the human race became extinct. Despite its philosophical subtlety, it is hard to believe that Benatar believes his own argument. Can one really prefer eternal nothingness to the possibility of a good life? If I prefer to remain alive, I am not implicitly accepting that life is better than non-life? Does it really make sense to dedicate a book to the parents who harmed you by bringing you into existence? Still, Benatar's arguments are persuasive enough that Leslie cannot find any knock-down arguments against them, although he cautions us against accepting philosophical prescriptions that, if followed, will result in the death of the species. Surely we ought to tread carefully here despite the power of Benatar's claims.

These considerations lead to another question. If life is worth something, as most of us generally believe, then why not have as much of it as we like? Lenman rejects immortality for multiple reasons, primarily because immortals would no longer be human. It is easy to see how young philosophers would advocate such a view, thinking that they have enough time to do what they want, but few older, healthy persons could think such a thing. (Lenman wrote this piece when quite young.) For them aging causes the smell of death to be more real, powerful and putrid. As for losing our humanity, that was gained in the course of our long evolutionary history and we will, hopefully, transcend it.

Bostrom picks up the argument here, arguing forcefully that death is evil. Some tell us we will be born again or that death is good or natural, but all such explanations are cases of *adaptive preferences*. If we cannot do anything about death, we adapt and say we prefer it; but when we can do something about it, almost everyone will rejoice. When the elixir is real, you can be sure it will be used. At the moment we do not know how to prevent death, but we have some scientific insights that could lead in that direction. If some individuals still want to die when death is preventable, we should respect their autonomy, but for those of us who do not want to die, our autonomy should be honored as well. Thus we agree with Bostrom; we should rid ourselves of the dragon—*death should be optional.*

At the moment, however, death is not optional. Given our predicament—the problem of life that we discussed in the introduction—we have little choice then but to face death stoically, bravely, optimistically. The optimistic attitude prescribed by Michael and Caldwell violates no principles of reason and is practical to boot. A similar kind of optimism was captured in a famous passage from William James essay "The Will To Believe,"

> We stand on a mountain pass in the midst of whirling snow and blinding mist, through which we get glimpses now and then of paths which may be deceptive. If we stand still we shall be frozen to death. If we take the wrong road we shall be dashed to pieces. We do not certainly know whether there is any right one. What must we do? 'Be strong and of a good courage.' Act for the best, hope for the best, and take what comes. ... If death ends all, we cannot meet death better.[25]

A comparable viewpoint was relayed to me in a hand-written letter (remember those?) in the mid 1990s from my friend and graduate school mentor, Richard J. Blackwell. Replying to my queries about the meaning of life he wrote:

> As to your "what does it all mean" questions, you do not really think that I have strong clear replies when no one else since Plato has had much success! It may be more fruitful to ask about what degree of confidence one can expect from attempted answers, since too high expectations are bound to be dashed. It's a case of Aristotle's advice not to look for more confidence than the subject matter permits. At any rate, if I am right about there being a strong volitional factor here, why not favor an optimistic over a pessimistic attitude, which is something one can control to some degree? This is not an answer, but a way to live.

This seems right. We really have nothing to lose by being optimistic and, given the current reality of death, this is a wise option. *But that does not change the fact that death is bad.* Bad because it puts an end to something which at its best is beautiful; bad because all the knowledge and insight and wisdom of that person is lost; bad because of the harm it does to the living; bad because it causes people to be unconcerned about the future beyond their short lifespan; and bad because we know in our bones, that if we had the choice, and if our lives were going well, we would choose to on. That death is generally bad—especially so for the physically, morally, and intellectually vigorous—is nearly self-evident.

But most of all, death is bad because it renders completely meaningful lives impossible. It is true that longer lives do not guarantee meaningful ones, but all other things being equal, longer lives are more meaningful than shorter ones. (Both the quality and the quantity of a life are relevant to its meaning; both are necessary though not sufficient conditions for meaning.) An infinite life can be without meaning, but a life with no duration must be meaningless. Thus the possibility of greater meaning increases proportionately with the length of a lifetime.

Yes, there are indeed fates worse than death, and in some circumstances death may be welcomed even if it extinguishes the further possibility of meaning. Nevertheless, death is one of the worst fates that can befall us, despite the consolations offered by the *deathists*—the lovers of death. We may become bored with eternal consciousness, but as long as we can end our lives if we want, as long as we can opt out of immortality, who wouldn't want the option to live forever?

Only if we can choose whether to live or die are we really free. Our lives are not our own if they can be taken from us without our consent, and, to the extent death can be delayed or prevented, further possibilities for meaning ensue. Perhaps with our hard-earned knowledge we can slay the dragon tyrant, thereby opening up the possibility for more meaningful lives. This is perhaps the fundamental imperative for our species. For now the best we can do is to remain optimistic in the face of the great tragedy that is death.

CHAPTER 8 – HOW SCIENCE CAN DEFEAT DEATH AND WHY IT SHOULD

Humanity looks to me like a magnificent beginning but not the final word.
~ Freeman Dyson

I and many other scientists now believe that in around twenty years we will have the means to reprogram our bodies' stone-age software so we can halt, then reverse, aging. Then nanotechnology will let us live forever.
~ Ray Kurzweil

I believe in transhumanism": once there are enough people who can truly say that, the human species will be on the threshold of a new kind of existence, as different from ours as ours is from that of Peking man. It will at last be consciously fulfilling its real destiny.
~ Julian Huxley

… transhumanism, a nascent philosophical and political movement that epitomizes the most daring, courageous, imaginative, and idealistic aspirations of humanity.
~ Ronald Bailey

1. Can Science Give Us Immortality?

As we have seen, if death is the end of us our best response to that grave tragedy is hope and optimism. *But perhaps we don't have to die!* Although we previously rejected the reality of a spiritual afterlife as a fanciful solution to the disaster of death, many respectable scientists and futurists suggest that humans can overcome death through the use of future technologies. By immortality in this sense we refer roughly to the uninterrupted, eternal continuation of an individual consciousness—let us call this physical immortality in contrast to religious immortality. And we all might be immortal if technology develops fast enough, which may entail any number of technologies in any number of combinations.

The first way we might achieve physical immortality is by conquering our biological limitations—we age, become diseased, and suffer trauma. Aging research, while woefully underfunded, has yielded positive results. Average life expectancies have tripled since ancient times, increased by more than fifty percent in the industrial world in the last hundred years, and most scientists think we will continue to extend our life spans. We know that we can further increase our life span by restricting calories, and we increasingly understand the role that telomeres play in the aging process. We also know that certain jellyfish and bacteria are essentially immortal, and the bristlecone pine may be as well. There is no thermodynamic necessity for senescence—aging is presumed to be a byproduct of evolution —although why mortality should be selected for remains a mystery. There are even reputable scientists who believe we can conquer aging altogether—in the next few decades with sufficient investment—most notably the Cambridge researcher Aubrey de Grey.[11] Still, not all researchers are convinced that our biological limitations will be eliminated.

If we do unlock the secrets of aging, we will simultaneously defeat many other diseases as well, since so many of them are symptoms of aging. (Many researches now consider aging itself to be a disease; as you age, the disease progresses.) There are also a number of strategies that could render disease mostly inconsequential. Nanotechnology may give us nanobot cell-repair machines and robotic blood cells; biotechnology may supply replacement tissues and organs; genetics may offer genetic medicine and engineering; and full-fledge genetic engineering could produce beings impervious to disease. Trauma is a more intransigent problem from the biological perspective, although it too could be defeated through some combination of cloning, regenerative medicine, and genetic engineering. We can even imagine that your physicality could be recreated from a bit of your DNA, and other technologies could then fast forward your regenerated body to the age of your traumatic death, where a backup file with all your experiences and memories would be implanted in your brain. Even the dead may be eventually resuscitated if they have undergone the process of cryonics— preserving organisms at very low temperatures in glass-like states. Ideally these clinically dead would be brought back to life when future technology was sufficiently advanced. This is a long shot, but if nanotechnology fulfills its promise, there is a reasonably good chance that cryonics may be successful.

In addition to biological strategies for eliminating death, there are a number of technological scenarios for immortality which would utilize advanced brain scanning techniques, artificial intelligence, and robotics. The most prominent scenarios have been advanced by the renowned futurist Ray Kurzweil and Carnegie-Mellon roboticist Hans Moravec. Both have argued that the exponential growth of computing power in combination with other technologies will make it possible to upload the contents of one's consciousness into a virtual reality. This could be accomplished by cybernetics, whereby hardware would be gradually installed in the brain until the entire brain was running on that hardware, or via scanning the brain and simulating or transferring its contents to a computer with sufficient artificial intelligence. Either way we would no longer be living in a physical world. (We will discuss both of these scenarios in detail in a moment.)

In fact we may already be living in a computer simulation! Nick Bostrom has argued that it is possible that advanced civilizations have created computer simulations containing individuals with artificial intelligence, and, if they have, we might unknowingly be in the simulation.[2] He then asks which is more likely: that we are the one civilization not in a simulation or that we are one of billions of simulations being run? Needless to say he thinks the latter more likely. So either civilizations never have the technology to run simulations, they have the technology but decided not to use it, or we almost certainly live in a simulation. Think of it this way. If the human race could develop and use simulation technology then they would likely run ancestor simulations to study their past which would lead to sub-simulations ad infinitum. And, since we cannot know if we live in the original universe or one of the multitudes of simulations, it is more likely we live in a simulation.

If one doesn't like the idea of being immortal in a virtual reality—or one doesn't like the idea that they may already be in one now—one could upload one's brain to a genetically engineered body, if they liked the feel of flesh, or to a robotic body, if they liked the feel of silicon or whatever materials comprised the robotic body. MIT's Rodney Brooks envisions the merger of human flesh and machines, wherein humans slowly incorporate technology into their bodies, thus becoming more machine-like and indestructible.[3] So it seems a cyborg future may await us.

The rationale underlying most of these speculative scenarios has to do with adopting an evolutionary perspective. Once one embraces that perspective, *it is not difficult to imagine that our descendants will resemble us about as much as we do the amino acids from which we sprang.* Our knowledge is growing exponentially and, given eons of time for future innovation, it easy to envisage that humans will defeat death and evolve in unimaginable ways. For the skeptical, remember that our evolution is no longer moved be the painstakingly slow process of Darwinian evolution—where bodies exchange information through genes—but by cultural evolution—where brains exchange information through memes. The most prominent feature of the cultural evolution driving change is the exponentially increasing pace of technological evolution—an evolution that may soon culminate in a *technological singularity.*

The technological singularity, an idea first proposed by the mathematician Vernor Vinge, refers to the hypothetical future emergence of greater than human intelligence. (A number of futurists, in particular Ray Kurzweil, predict that the singularity will happen in our lifetimes.) Since the capabilities of such an intelligence would be difficult for our minds to comprehend, the singularity is seen as an event horizon beyond which the future becomes nearly impossible to understand or predict. Nevertheless, we may surmise that this intelligence explosion will lead to increasingly powerful minds for which the problem of death will be solvable. Science may well vanquish death—quit possibly in the lifetime of some of my readers. Let us now turn to some serious thinkers who believe this.

Summary – There are good reasons to think that science will conquer death in the foreseeable future.

2. Ray Kurzweil: Uploading Our Minds Into Computers

Ray Kurzweil (1948 -) is an author, inventor and futurist. He is involved in fields such as optical character recognition, text-to-speech synthesis, speech recognition technology, and electronic keyboard instruments; he is the author of several books on health, artificial intelligence, transhumanism, the technological singularity, and futurism; and he may be the most prominent spokesman in the world today for advocating the use of technology to transform humanity.

In his 1999 book, *The Age of Spiritual Machines: When Computers Exceed Human Intelligence*, Kurzweil argues that in the next one hundred years machines will surpass human intelligence. Computers already surpass humans in playing chess, diagnosing certain medical conditions, buying and selling stocks, guiding missiles, and solving complex mathematical problems. However, unlike human intelligence, machine intelligence cannot describe objects on a table, write a term paper, tie shoes, distinguish a dog from a cat, or appreciate humor. One reason for this is that computers are simpler than the human brain, about a million times simpler. However, this difference will go away as computers continue to double in speed every twelve months, achieving the memory capacity and computing speed of the human brain around 2020.

Still, this won't allow computers to match the flexibility of human intelligence because the software of intelligence is as important as the hardware. One way to mirror the brain's software is by reverse engineering—scanning a human brain and copying its neural circuitry into a neural computer of sufficient capacity. If computers reach a human level of intelligence through such technologies, they will then go beyond it. They already remember and process information better than we do, remembering trillions of facts perfectly while we have a tough time with a few phone numbers. The combination of human-level intelligence along with greater speed, accuracy, and memory capabilities will push computers beyond human intelligence. A main reason for this is that our neurons are slow compared with electronic circuits, and most of their complexity supports life processes, not computation and information analysis. Thus, while many of us think of evolution as a billion-year drama that leads to human intelligence, the creation of greater than human intelligence will quickly dispel that notion.

Kurzweil supports his case with a number of observations about cosmic evolution and human history. Consider that for most of the history of the universe, cosmologically significant events took eons of time—the interval between significant events was quite long for most of cosmic evolution. But as the universe aged the interval between significant events grew shorter, and cosmically significant events now happen at increasingly shorter intervals. We can see this in the pace of cosmic evolution: ten billion years until the earth's formation; a few billion more for life to evolve, hundreds of millions of years till the emergence of primates, millions of years till the emergence of humanoids, and the emergence of homo sapiens a mere 200 thousand years ago. In short, transformation is speeding up; the interval between salient events is shrinking.

Now technology is moving this process. Technology— fashioning and using ever more sophisticated tools—is simply another means of evolution which expedites the process of change considerably. Consider that Homo sapiens sapiens appeared only 90 thousand years ago, and become the lone hominoids a mere 30 thousand years ago. Still, it took tens of thousands of years to figure out how to sharpen both ends of stones to make them effective! Needless to say, the pace of technological change has accelerated remarkably since then. For example, the 19th century saw technology increase at a dramatic rate compared to the 18th century, and increased unbelievably fast compared to the 12th century. In the 20th century major shifts in technology began to happen in decades or in some cases in a few years. A little more than a hundred years ago there was no flight or radio; and a mere fifty years ago there were no wireless phones or personal computers, much less cell phones or the internet. Today it seems your phone and computer are obsolete in a matter of months.

Technology has enabled our species to dominate the earth, exercise some control over our environment, and survive. Perhaps the most important of these technological innovations has been computation, the ability of machines to remember, compute, and solve problems. So far computers have been governed by Moore's law: every two years or so the surface area of a transistor is reduced by fifty percent, putting twice as many transistors on an integrated circuit. The implication is that every two years you get twice the computing power for the same amount of money. This trend should continue for another fifteen years or so after which it will break down when transistor insulators will be but a few atoms wide. (At that point quantum computing may move the process forward in fantastic ways.) To really understand what will happen in the 21st century and beyond, we need to look at the *exponential growth* of the technology that will bring about vast changes in the near future.

Crucial to Kurzweil's analysis is what he calls "the law of time and chaos." He asks why some processes begin fast and then slow down—salient events in cosmic evolution or in the biological development of an organism—and why others start slowly and then speed up—the evolution of life forms or technology. The law of time and chaos explains this relationship. If there is a lot of chaos or disorder in a system, the time between salient events is great; as the chaos decreases and the order increases, the time between salient events gets smaller. The "law of accelerating returns" describes the latter phenomenon and is essential to Kurzweil's argument. (You might say that his entire philosophy is a meditation on accelerating returns or exponential growth.) He argues that though the universe as a whole increases in disorder or entropy, evolution leads to increasing pockets of order (information for the purpose of survival) and complexity. Technology evolution is evolution by means other than biology, and it constantly speeds up as it builds upon itself.

We might reconstruct his basic argument as follows: a) evolution builds on itself, thus; b) in an evolutionary process order increases exponentially, thus; c) the returns accelerate. This law of accelerating returns drives cultural and technological evolution forward, with the returns building on themselves to create higher returns. Thus the entire process changes and grows exponentially, meaning that the near future will be radically different than the present.

> ... evolution has found a way around the computational limitations of neural circuitry. Cleverly, it has created organisms that in turn invented a computational technology a million times faster than carbon-based neurons ... Ultimately, the computing conducted on extremely slow mammalian neural circuits will be ported to a far more versatile and speedier electronic (and photonic) equivalent.[4] This will eventually lead to reverse engineering the human brain by scanning it, mapping it, and eventually *downloading our minds into computers*. This means that your mind (software) would

no longer be dependent on your body (hardware). Moreover, your evolving mind file will not be stuck with the circuitry of the brain, making it capable of being transferred from one medium to another, just as files are transferred from one computer to another. Then "our immortality will be a matter of being sufficiently careful to make frequent backups. If we're careless about this, we'll have to load an old backup copy and be doomed to repeat our recent past."[5]

We could download our personal evolving mind files into our original bodies, upgraded bodies, nanoengineered bodies, or virtual bodies. As we are currently further along with body transformation than with brain transformation—titanium devices, artificial skin, heart values, pacemakers—we might want to first completely rebuild our bodies using genetic therapies. But this will only go so far because of the limitations of DNA-based cells that depend on protein synthesis. No matter how well we enhance our bodies, they would still just be second-rate robots.

Instead Kurzweil suggests we use nanotechnology to rebuild the world atom by atom. The holy grail of nanotechnology would be intelligent self-replicating nanomachines capable of manipulating things at the nanolevel. (The great physicist Richard Feynman originally explained the possibility of nanotechnology in the 1950s. Today, important theorists like Eric Drexler and Ralph Merkle have shown the feasibility of self-replicating nanobots.) The possibilities for nanotechnology to transform the world are extraordinary. It could build inexpensive solar cells to replace fossil fuels, or be launched in our bloodstream to improve the immune system, destroy pathogens, eradicate cancer cells, and reconstruct bodily organs and systems. It even has the potential to reverse engineer human neurons or any cell in the human body. Will people use this technology?

> There is a clear incentive to go down this path. Given a choice, people will prefer to keep their bones from crumbling, their skin supple, and their life systems strong and vital. Improving our lives through neural implants on the mental level, and nanotech enhance bodies on the physical level, will be popular and compelling. It is another one of those slippery slopes— there is no obvious place to stop this progression until the

human race has largely replaced the brains and bodies that evolution first provided.[6]

Kurzweil also argues that Law of Accelerating Returns applies to the entire universe. He conjectures that life may exist elsewhere in the universe and proceed through various thresholds: the evolution of life forms; of intelligence; of technology; of computation; and finally the merging of a species with its technology—all driven by accelerating returns. Of course there are many things that can go wrong—nuclear war, climate change, asteroids, bacteria, self-replicating nanobots, and software viruses. Still, he remains optimistic.

Kurzweil ends by arguing that intelligence is *not* impotent against the forces of the universe. Intelligence thwarts gravity and manipulates other physical phenomena despite its density being vanishingly small in a vast cosmos. If intelligence increases exponentially with time, then it will become a worthy competitor for big universal forces. He concludes: "The laws of physics are not repealed by intelligence, but they effectively evaporate in its presence... the fate of the Universe is a decision yet to be made, one which we will intelligently consider when the time is right."[7]

3. John Searle: Critique of Kurzweil

John Searle (1932 -) is currently the Slusser Professor of Philosophy at the University of California, Berkeley. He received his PhD from Oxford University. He is a prolific author and one of the most important living philosophers.

According to Searle, Kurzweil's book is an extensive reflection on the implications of Moore's law.[8] The essence of that argument is that smarter than human computers will arrive, we will download ourselves into this smart hardware, thereby guaranteeing our immortality. Searle attacks this fantasy by focusing on the chess playing computer "Deep Blue," (DB) which defeated world chess champion Gary Kasparov in 1997.

Kurzweil thinks DB is a good example of the way that computers have begun to exceed human intelligence. But DB's brute force method of searching through possible moves differs dramatically from the how human brains play chess. To clarify Searle offers his famous Chinese Room Argument. If I'm in a room with a program that answers questions in Chinese even though I do not understand Chinese, the fact that I can output the answer in Chinese does not mean I understand the language. Similarly DB does not understand chess, and Kasparov was playing a team of programmers, not a machine. Thus Kurzweil is mistaken if he believes that DB was thinking.

According to Searle, Kurzweil confuses a computers seeming to be conscious with it actually being conscious, something we should worry about if we are proposing to download ourselves into it! Just as a computer simulation of digestion cannot eat pizza, so too a computer simulation of consciousness is not conscious. Computers manipulate symbols or simulate brains through neural nets—but this is not the same as duplicating what the brain is doing. To duplicate what the brain does the artificial system would have to act like the brain. Thus Kurzweil confuses simulation with duplication.

Another confusion is between observer-independent (OI) features of the world, and observer-dependent (OD) features of the world. The former include features of the world studied by, for example, physics and chemistry; while the latter are things like money, property, governments and all things that exist only because there are conscious observers of them. (Paper has objective physical properties, but paper is money only because persons relate to it that way.)

Searle says that he is more intelligent than his dog and his computer in some absolute, OI sense because he can do things his dog and computer cannot. It is only in the OD sense that you could say that computers and calculators are more intelligent than we are. You can use intelligence in the OD sense provided that you remember it does not mean that a computer is more intelligent in the OI sense. The same goes for *computation*. Machines compute analogously to the way we do, but they don't computer intrinsically at all—they know nothing of human computation.

The basic problem with Kurzweil's book is its assumption that increased computational power leads to consciousness. Searle says that increased computational power of machines gives us no reason to believe machines are duplicating consciousness. The only way to build conscious machines would be to duplicate the way brains work and we don't know how they work. In sum, behaving like one is conscious is not the same as actually being conscious.

Summary – Computers cannot be conscious.

4. Daniel Dennett: In Defense of Robotic Consciousness

Daniel Dennett (1942 -) is an American philosopher, writer and cognitive scientist whose research is in the philosophy of mind, philosophy of science and philosophy of biology, particularly as those fields relate to evolutionary biology and cognitive science. He is currently the Co-director of the Center for Cognitive Studies, the Austin B. Fletcher Professor of Philosophy, and a University Professor at Tufts University. He received his PhD from Oxford University in 1965 where he studied under the eminent philosopher Gilbert Ryle.

In his 1995 book, *Darwin's Dangerous Idea: Evolution And The Meaning of Life*, Dennett present a thought experiment that defends strong artificial intelligence (SAI)—one that matches or exceeds human intelligence.[9] Dennett asks you to suppose that you want to live in the 25th century and the only available technology for that purpose involves putting your body in a cryonic chamber where you will be frozen in a deep coma and later awakened. In addition you must design some supersystem to protect and supply energy to your capsule. You would now face a choice. You could find an ideal fixed location that will supply whatever your capsule will need, but the drawback would be that you would die if some harm came to that site. Better then to have a mobile facility to house your capsule that could move in the event harm came your way—better to place yourself inside a giant robot. Dennett claims that these two strategies correspond roughly to nature's distinction between stationary plants and moving animals.

If you put your capsule inside a robot, then you would want the robot to choose strategies that further your interests. This does not mean the robot has free will, but that it executes branching instructions so that when options confront the program, it chooses those that best serve your interests. Given these circumstances you would design the hardware and software to preserve yourself, and equip it with the appropriate sensory systems and self-monitory capabilities for that purpose. The supersystem must also be designed to formulate plans to respond to changing conditions and seek out new energy sources.

What complicated the issue further is that, while you are in cold storage, other robots and who knows what else are running around in the external world. So you would need to design your robot to determine when to cooperative, form alliances, or fight with other creatures. A simple strategy like always cooperating would likely get you killed, but never cooperating may not serve your self-interests either, and the situation may be so precarious that your robot would have to make many quick decisions. The result will be a robot capable of self-control, an autonomous agent which derives its own goals based on your original goal of survival; the preferences with which it was originally endowed. But you cannot be sure it will act in your self-interest. It will be out of your control, acting partly on its own desires.

Now opponents of SAI claim that this robot does not have its own desires or intentions, those are simply derivative of its designer's desires. Dennett calls this "client centrism." I am the original source of the meaning within my robot, it is just a machine preserving me, even though it acts in ways that I could not have imagined and which may be antithetical to my interests. Of course it follows, according to the client centrists, that the robot is not conscious. Dennett rejects this centrism, primarily because if you follow this argument to its logical conclusion you have to conclude the same thing about yourself! You would have to conclude that you are a survival machine built to preserve your genes and your goals and your intentions derive from them. You are not really conscious. To avoid these unpalatable conclusions, why not acknowledge that sufficiently complex robots have motives, intentions, goals, and consciousness? They are like you; owing their existence to being a survival machine that has evolved into something autonomous by its encounter with the world.

Critics like Searle admit that such a robot is possible, but deny that it is conscious. Dennett responds that such robots would experience meaning as real as your meaning; they would have transcended their programming just as you have gone beyond the programming of your selfish genes. He concludes that this view reconciles thinking of yourself as a locus of meaning, while at the same time being a member of a species with a long evolutionary history. We are artifacts of evolution, but our consciousness is no less real because of that. The same would hold true of our robots.

Summary – Sufficiently complex robots would be conscious.

5. Hans Moravec: Becoming Robots

Hans Moravec (1948 -) is a faculty member at the Robotics Institute of Carnegie Mellon University and the chief scientist at Seegrid Corporation. He received his PhD in computer science from Stanford in 1980, and is known for his work on robotics, artificial intelligence, and writings on the impact of technology, as well as his many of publications and predictions focusing on transhumanism.

Moravec set forth his futuristic ideas most clearly in his 1998 book *Robot: Mere Machine To Transcendent Mind.* He notes that by almost any measure society is changing faster than ever before, primarily because the products of technology keep speeding up the process. The radical future that awaits us can be understood by thinking of technology as soon reaching an escape velocity. In the same way that rubbing sticks together in the proper manner will produce ignition, or powering a rocket correctly will allow it to escape the earth's gravity, our machines will soon escape their previous boundaries. At that time the old rules will no longer apply; robots will have achieved their own escape velocity.

For many of us this is hard to imagine because we are like riders in an elevator who forget how high we are until we get an occasional glimpse of the ground—as when we meet cultures frozen in time. Then we see how different the world we live in today is compared to the one we adapted to biologically. For all of human history culture was secondary to biology, but about five thousand years ago things changed, as cultural evolution became the most important means of human evolution. It is the technology created by culture that is exponentially speeding up the process of change. Today we are reaching the escape velocity from our biology.

Not that building intelligent machines will be easy—Moravec constantly reminds us how difficult robotics is. He outlines the history of cybernetics, from its beginnings with Alan Turing and John von Neumann, to the first working artificial intelligence programs which proved many mathematical theorems. He admits that most of these programs were not very good and proved theorems no better or faster than a college freshman. So reaching escape velocity will require hard work.

One of the most difficult issues in robotics/artificial intelligence is the disparity between programs that calculate and reason, versus programs that interact with the world. Robots still don't perform as well behaviorally as infants or non-human animals but play chess superbly. So the order of difficulty for machines from easier to harder is: calculating; reasoning; perceiving; and acting. For humans the order is exactly the reverse. The explanation for this probably lays in the fact that perceiving and acting were beneficial for survival in a way that calculation and abstract reasoning was not. Machines are way behind in many areas yet catching up, and Moravec predicts that in less than fifty years inexpensive computers will exceed the processing power of a human brain. Can we then program them to intuit and perceive like humans? Moravec thinks there is reason to answer in the affirmative, and much of his book cites the evolution of robotics as evidence for this claim.

He also supports his case with a clever analogy to topography. The human landscape of consciousness has high mountains like hand-eye coordination, locomotion and social interaction; foothills like theorem proving and chess playing; and lowlands like arithmetic and memorization. Computers/robots are analogous to a flood which has drowned the lowlands; has just reached the foothills, and well eventually submerge the peaks.

Robots will advance through generational change as technology advances: from lizard-like robots, to mouse-like, primate-like, and human-like ones. Eventually they will be smart enough to design their own successors —without help from us! So a few generations of robots will mimic the four hundred million year evolution marked by the brain stem, cerebellum, mid-brain, and neo-cortex. Will our machines be conscious? Moravec says yes. Just as the terrestrial and celestial was once a sacred distinction, so today is the animate/inanimate distinction. Of course if the animating principle is a supernatural soul, then the distinction remains, but our current knowledge suggests that complex organization provides animation. This means that our technology is doing what it took evolution billions of years to do—animating dead matter.

Moravec argues that robots will slowly come to have a conscious, internal life as they advance. Fear, shame, and joy may be emotions valuable to robots to help them retreat from danger, reduce the probability of bad decisions, or reinforce good ones. He even thinks there would be good reasons for robots to care about their owners or get angry, but surmises that generally they will be nicer than humans, since robots don't have to be selfish to guarantee their survival. He recognizes that many reject the view that dead matter can give rise to consciousness. The philosopher Herbert Dreyfus has argued that computers cannot experience subjective consciousness, his colleague John Searle says, as we have already seen, that computers will never think, and the mathematician Roger Penrose argues that consciousness is achieved through certain quantum phenomena in the brain, something unavailable to robots. But Moravec points to the accumulating evidence from neuroscience to disagree. Mind is something that runs of a physical substrate and we will eventually accept sufficiently complex robots as conscious.

Moravec sees these developments as the natural consequence of humans using one of their two channels of heredity. Not the slower biological means utilizing DNA, but the faster culture channel utilizing books, language, databases, and machines. For most of human history there was more info in our genes than in our culture, but now libraries alone hold thousands of times more information than genes. "Given fully intelligent robots, culture becomes completely independent of biology. Intelligent machines, which will grow from us, learn our skills, and initially share our goals and values, will be the children of our minds."[10]

To get a better understanding of the coming age of robots consider our history as it relates to technology. A hundred thousand years ago, our ancestors were supported by, what Moravec calls, a fully automated nature. With agriculture we increased production but added work and, until recently, production of food was the chief occupation of humankind. Farmers lost their jobs to machines and moved to manufacturing, but more advanced machines displaced farmers out of factories and into offices—where machines have put them out of work again. Soon machines will do all the work. Tractors and combines amplify farmers; computer workstations amplify engineers; layers of management and clerical help slowly disappear; and the scribe, priest, seer and chief are no longer repositories of wisdom—printing and mass communication ended that. Automation and robots will displace gradually replace labor as never before; just consider how much physical and mental labor has already been replaced by machines. In the short run this will cause panic and the scramble to earn a living in new ways. In the medium run it will provide the opportunity to have a more leisurely lifestyle. In the long run, "it marks the end of the dominance of biological humans and the beginning of the age of robots."[11]

Moravec is optimistic that robotic labor will make life more pleasant for humanity, but inevitably evolution will lead beyond humans to a world of "ex-humans" or "exes." These post-biological beings will populate a galaxy which is as benign for them as it is hostile for biological beings. "We marvel at the Earth's biodiversity ... but the diversity and range of the post-biological world will be astronomically greater. Imagination balks at the challenge of guessing what it could be like."[12] Still, he is willing to hazard a guess: "...Exes trapped in neutron stars may become the most powerful minds in the galaxy ... But, in the fast-evolving world of superminds, nothing lasts forever .... Exes, [will] become obsolete."[13]

In that far future, Moravec speculates that exes will "be transformed into intelligence-boosting computing elements ... physical activity will gradually transform itself into a web of increasingly pure thought, here every smallest interaction represents a meaningful computation."[14] Exes may learn to arrange space-time and energy into forms of computation, with the result that "the inhabited portions of the universe will be rapidly transformed into a cyberspace, where overt physical activity is imperceptible, but the world inside the computation is astronomically rich."[15] Beings won't be defined by physical location but will be patterns of information in cyberspace. Minds, pure software, will interact with other minds. The wave of physical migration into space will have long given way to "a bubble of Mind expanding at near lightspeed."[16] Eventually, the expanding bubble of cyberspace will recreate all it encounters "memorizing the old universe as it consumes it."[17]

For the moment our small minds cannot give meaning to the universe, but a future universal mind might be able to do so, when that cosmic mind is infinitely subjective, self-conscious, and powerful. At that point our descendents will be capable of traversing in and through other possible worlds. Unfortunately, those of us alive today are governed by the laws of the universe, at least until we die when our ties to physical reality will be cut. It is possible we will then be reconstituted in the minds of our super intelligent successors or in simulated realities. But for the moment this is still fantasy, all we have for now is Shakespeare's lament:

To die, to sleep;
To sleep: perchance to dream: ay there's the rub;
For in that sleep of death what dreams may come
When we have shuffled off this mortal coil …

Summary – Our robotic descendents will be our mind children and they will live in unimaginable worlds. For now though, we die.

6. Charles T. Rubin: Rejecting Technological Extinction

Charles T. Rubin is a professor of political science at Duquesne University. His 2003 article, "Artificial Intelligence and Human Nature," is a systematic attack on the thinking of Kurzweil and Moravec.[18]

Rubin finds nearly everything about the futurism of Kurzweil and Moravec problematic. It involves metaphysical speculation about evolution, complexity, and the universe; technical speculation about what may be possible; and philosophical speculation about the nature of consciousness, personal identity, and the mind-body problem. Yet Rubin avoids attacking the futurists, whom he calls "extinctionists," on the issue of what is possible, focusing instead on their claim that a future robotic-type state is necessary or desirable.

The argument that there is an evolutionary necessity for our extinction seems thin. Why should we expedite our own extinction? Why not destroy the machines instead? And the argument for the desirability of this vision raises another question. What is so desirable about a post-human life? The answer to this question, for Kurzweil and Moravec, is the power over human limitations that would ensue. The rationale that underlies this desire is the belief that we are but an evolutionary accident to be improved upon, transformed, and remade.

But this leads to another question: will we preserve ourselves after uploading into our technology? Rubin objects that there is a disjunction between us and the robots we want to become. Robots will bear little resemblance to us, especially after we have shed the bodies so crucial to our identities, making the preservation of a self all the more tenuous. Given this discontinuity, how can we know we would want to be in this new world, or whether it would be better, anymore than one of our primate ancestors could have imagined what a good human life would be like. Those primates would be as uncomfortable in our world, as we might be in the post-human world. We really have no reason to think we can understand what a post-humans life would be like, but it is not out of the question that the situation will be nightmarish.

Yet Rubin acknowledges that technology will evolve, moved by military, medical, commercial, and intellectual incentives, hence it is unrealistic to limit technological development. The key in stopping or at least slowing the trend is to educate individuals as to the unique characteristics of being human which surpass machine life in so many ways. Love, courage, charity, and a host of other human virtues may themselves be inseparable from our finitude. Evolution may hasten our extinction, but even if it did not there is no need to pursue the process, because there is no reason to think the post-human world will be better than our present one. If we pursue such Promethean visions, we may end up worse off than before.

Summary – We should reject transhumanist ideals and accept our finitude.

7. Marshall Brain: We Will Discard Our Bodies

Marshall Brain (1961 -) is an author, public speaker, and entrepreneur. He earned an MS in computer science from North Carolina State University where he taught for many years, and is the founder of the website HowStuffWorks, which was sold in 2007 to Discovery Communications for $250,000,000. He also maintains a website where his essays on transhumanism, robotics, and naturalism can be found. His essay, "The Day We Discard Our Bodies," presents a compelling case that sometime in this century the technology will be available to discard our bodies.[19] And when the time comes, most of us will do so.

Why would we want to discard our bodies? The answer is that by doing so we would achieve an unimaginable level of freedom and longevity. Consider how vulnerable your body is. If you fall off a horse or dive into a too-shallow pool of water, your body will become completely useless. If this happened to you, you would gladly discard your body. But this happens to all of us as we age—our bodies generally kill our brains—creating a tragic loss of knowledge and experience. Our brains die because our bodies do.

Consider also how few of us are judged to have beautiful bodies, and how the beauty we do have declines with age. If you could have a more beautiful body, you would gladly discard your body. Additionally, your body has to go to the bathroom, it smells, it becomes obese easily, it takes time for it to travel through space, it cannot fly or swim underwater for long, and it cannot perform telekinesis. As for the aging of our bodies, most would happily dispense with it, discarding their bodies if they could.

Why would the healthy discard their bodies? Consider that healthy people play video games in staggering numbers. As these games become more realistic, we can imagine people wanting to live and be immersed in them. Eventually you would want to connect your biological brain to your virtual body inside the virtual reality. And your virtual body could be so much better than your biological body—it could be perfect. Your girlfriend or boyfriend who made the jump to the virtual world would have a perfect body. They would ask you to join them. All you would have to do is undergo a painless surgery to connect your brain to its new body in the virtual reality. There you could see anything in the world without having to take the plane ride (or go through security.) You could visit the Rome or Greece of two thousand years ago, fight in the battle of Stalingrad, talk to Charles Darwin, or live the life of Superman. You could be at any time and any place, you can overcome all limitations, you could have great sex! When your virtual body would be better in every respect from your biological body, you would discard the latter.

Initially your natural brain may still be housed in your natural body, but eventually your brain will be disconnected from your body and housed in a safe brain storage facility. Your transfer will be complete—you will live in a perfect virtual reality without your cumbersome physical body, and the limitations it imposes.

Summary – We will be able to discard our bodies and live in a much better virtual reality relatively soon. We should do so.

8. Michio Kaku: An Overall Vision of the Future

Michio Kaku (1947 -) is the Henry Semat Professor of Theoretical Physics at the City College of New York of City University of New York. He is the co-founder of string field theory and a popularizer of science. He earned his PhD in physics from the University of California-Berkeley in 1972.

In his 1997 book *Visions: How Science Will Revolutionize the 21st Century* Kaku sets out an overall picture of what is happening in science today that will revolutionize our future.[20] He begins by noting the three great themes of 20th century science—the atom, the computer, and the gene. *The revolutions associated with these themes ultimately aim at a complete understanding of matter, mind, and life.* Progress toward reaching our goals has been stunning—in just the past few years more scientific knowledge has been created than in all previous human history. We no longer need to be passive observers of nature, we can be its active directors; we are moving from discover of nature's laws to their masters.

The quantum revolution spawned the other two revolutions. Until 1925 no one understood the world of the atom; now we have an almost complete description of matter. The basic postulates of that understanding are: 1) energy is not continuous but occurs in discrete bundles called "quanta;" 2) sub-atomic particles have both wave and particle characteristics; and 3) these wave/particles obey Schrodinger's wave equation which determines the probability that certain events will occur. With the standard model we can predict the properties of things from quarks to supernovas. *We now understand matter and we may be able to manipulate it almost at will in this century.*

The computer revolution began in the 1940s. At that time computers were crude but subsequent development of the laser in the next decade started an exponential growth. Today there are tens of millions of transistors in the area the size of a fingernail. As microchips become ubiquitous, life will change dramatically. *We used to marvel at intelligence; in the future we may create and control it.*

The bio-molecular revolution began with the unraveling of the double helix in the 1950s. We found that our genetic code was written on the molecules within the cells—DNA. The techniques of molecular biology allow us to read the code of life like a book. With the owner's manual for human beings, science and medicine will be irrevocably altered. *Instead of watching life we will be able to direct it almost at will.*

Hence we are moving from the unraveling stage to the mastery stage in our understanding of nature. We are like aliens from outer space who land and view a chess game. It takes a long time to unravel the rules and merely knowing the rules doesn't make one a grand master. We are like that. We have learned the rules of matter, life, and mind but are not yet their masters. Soon we will be.

What really moves these revolutions is their interconnectivity, the way they propel each other. Quantum theory gave birth to the computer revolution via transistors and lasers; it gave birth to the bio-molecular revolution via x-ray crystallography and the theory of chemical bonding. While reductionism and specialization paid great dividends for these disciplines, intractable problems in each have forced them back together, calling for synergy of the three. Now computers decipher genes, while DNA research makes possible new computer architecture using organic molecules. Kaku calls this cross-fertilization—advances in one science boost the others along—and it keeps the pace of scientific advance accelerating.

In the next decade Kaku expects to see an explosion in scientific activity that will include growing organs and curing cancer. By the middle of the 21st century he expects to see progress in slowing aging, as well as huge advances in nanotechnology, interstellar travel, and nuclear fusion. By the end of the century we will create new organisms, and colonize space. Beyond that we will see the visions of Kurzweil and Moravec come to pass—we will extend life by growing new organs and bodies, manipulating genes, or by merging with computers.

Where is all this leading? One way to answer is by looking at the labels astrophysicists attach to hypothetical civilizations based on ways they utilize energy—labeled Type I, II, and III civilizations. Type I civilizations control terrestrial energy, modify weather, mine oceans, and extract energy from planet's core. Type

II civilizations have mastered stellar energy, use their sun to drive machines and explore other stars. Type III – manage interstellar energy, since they have exhausted their stars energy. Energy is available on a planet, its star and in its galaxy, while the type of civilization corresponds to that civilizations power over those resources.

Based on a growth rate of about 3% a year in our ability to control resources, Kaku estimates that we might expect to become a Type I civilization in a century or two, a type II civilization in about 800 years, and a type III civilization in about ten thousand years. At the moment, however, we are a Type 0 civilization which uses the remains of dead plants and animals to power our civilization. (And change our climate dramatically.) By the end of the 22nd century Kaku predicts we will be close to becoming a Type 1 civilization, and take our first steps into space. Agreeing with Kurzweil and Moravec, Kaku believes this will lead to a form of immortality when our technology replaces our brains, preserving them in robotic bodies or virtual realities. Evolution will have replaced us, just as we replaced all that died in the evolutionary struggle so that we could live. Our job is to push evolution forward.

Summary – Knowledge of the atom, the gene, and the computer will lead to a mastery of matter, life, and mind.

9. Jaron Lanier: Against Cybernetic Totalism

Jaron Lanier (1960 -) is a pioneer in the field of virtual reality who left Atari in 1985 to found VPL Research, Inc., the first company to sell VR goggles and gloves. In the late 1990s Lanier worked on applications for Internet2, and in the 2000s he was a visiting scholar at Silicon Graphics and various universities. More recently he has acted as an advisor to Linden Lab on their virtual world product Second Life, and as "scholar-at-large" at Microsoft Research where he has worked on the Kinect device for Xbox 360.

Lanier's "One Half A Manifesto" opposes what he calls "cybernetic totalism," the view of Kurzweil and others which proposes to transform the human condition more than any previous ideology. The following beliefs characterize cybernetic totalism.

1. That cybernetic patterns of information provide the ultimate and best way to understand reality.
2. That people are no more than cybernetic patterns.
3. That subjective experience either doesn't exist, or is unimportant because it is some sort of peripheral effect.
4. That what Darwin described in biology, or something like it, is in fact also the singular, superior description of all creativity and culture.
5. That qualitative as well as quantitative aspects of information systems will be accelerated by Moore's Law. And
6. That biology and physics will merge with computer science (becoming biotechnology and nanotechnology), resulting in life and the physical universe becoming mercurial; achieving the supposed nature of computer software. Furthermore, all of this will happen very soon! Since computers are improving so quickly they will overwhelm all the other cybernetic processes, like people, and fundamentally change the nature of what's going on in the familiar neighborhood of Earth at some moment when a new "criticality" is achieved—maybe in about the year 2020. To be a human after that moment will be either impossible or something very different than we now can know.[21]

Lanier responds to each belief in detail. A summary of those responses are as follows:

1. Culture cannot be reduced to memes, and people cannot be reduced to cybernetic patterns.
2. Artificial intelligence is a belief system, not a technology.
3. Subjective experience exists, and it separates humans from machines.
4. Darwin provides the "algorithm for creativity" which explains how computers will become smarter than humans. However, that nature didn't require anything "extra" to create people doesn't mean that computers will evolve on their own.

5. There is little reason to think that software is getting better, and no reason at all to think it will get better at a rate like hardware.

The sixth belief, the heart of the cybernetic totalism, terrifies Lanier. Yes, computers might kill us, preserve us in a matrix, or be used by evil humans to do harm to the rest of us. It is deviations of this latter scenario that most frightens Lanier for it is easy to imagine that a wealthy few would become a near godlike species, while the rest of us remain relatively the same. And Lanier expects immortality to be very expensive, unless software gets much better. For example, if you were to use biotechnology to try to make your flesh into a computer, you would need excellent software without glitches to achieve such a thing. But this would be extraordinarily costly.

Lanier grants that there will indeed be changes in the future, but they should be brought about by humans not by machines. To do otherwise is to abdicate our responsibility. Cybernetic totalism, if left unchecked, may cause suffering like so many other eschatological visions have in the past. We ought to remain humble about implementing our visions.

Summary – Cybernetic totalism is philosophically and technologically problematic.

10. Gregory Paul & Earl Cox: Going Beyond Humanity

Gregory Scott Paul (1954 -) is a freelance researcher, author and illustrator who works in paleontology, sociology and theology. Earl D. Cox is the founder of Metus Systems Group and an independent researcher. Their 1996 book, Beyond Humanity: CyberEvolution and Future Minds is an assault on the mindset of those who oppose their view of scientific progress.

Like many of our previous authors, Paul and Cox argue that the universe, as well as all life and mind within it, have evolved over time from the bottom up. However, genes now have little to do with our evolution—science and technology move the accelerating rate of evolution. In the course of that evolution a general pattern emerges—more change in less time. While it took nature a long time to produce a bio-brain, technology will produce a cyber-brain much faster.

Despite its promises people are ambivalent about science and technology (SciTech). They believe it will improve their lives, yet it has contributed to the death of millions. Its success has, in some sense, backfired. To be completely accepted SciTech must solve the problems of suffering and death which inevitably leads to questions about human nature. When taking a good look at human nature, the authors conclude that there is good news—we have brains that produce self-aware, conscious thought which is itself connected with wonderful auditory and visual systems. However, our bodies need sleep, demand exercise, lust for fatty foods, and have limited mobility and strength.

The bad news continues if we consider the limited memories and storage capacity of our brain. We upload information slowly; often cannot control our underdeveloped emotions; are easily conditioned by all sorts of irrationalities as children; have difficulty unlearning old falsehoods as adults; don't know how our brains work; often cannot change unwanted behavioral patterns; and brain chemicals control our moods—suggesting that we are much less free than we admit. Moreover, when individual minds join they are particularly destructive, often killing each other at astonishing rates. We are also vulnerable to: brainwashing, pain, sun, insects, viruses, trauma, broken bones, disease, infection, organ failure, paralysis, miniscule DNA glitches, cancer, depression, and psychosis. We degrade and suffer pain as we age, and we die without a backup system since evolution perpetuates our DNA not our minds. On the whole, this is not a pretty picture.

Disease and aging can be thought of as a war which matches our brains and computers versus the RNA and DNA computers of microbes and diseased cells. What is the best way to win this war? Regeneration from our DNA would only regenerate the body—the mind would still have died—so it is not a wholly promising approach. The way around this limitation is to have a nanocomputer within your brain that receives downloads from your conscious mind. If the mind storage unit receives continuous downloads you can always be brought back after death—you would be immortal. But why stop there? Why not just make an indestructible cyber-body and cyber-brain? Why not become immortal cyber-beings?

This all leads to questions about us becoming gods. The authors argue that the existence of gods is a science and engineering project—we can create minds as powerful as those of our imaginary gods with sufficient technology. Of course supernaturalism opposes this project, but SciTech will win the struggle, just as it has historically dismantled other supernatural superstitions one by one. Science will defeat supernaturalism by explaining it, by providing in reality what religions supply only in the imagination. When science conquers death and suffering, religion will die; religions fundamental reason for being—comforting our fear of death—will become irrelevant. As for the custodians of religion, the theologians, the authors issue a stern warning:

> Theologians are like a group of Homo erectus huddling around a fire, arguing over who should mate with whom, and which clan should live in the green valley, while paying no mind to the mind-boggling implications of the first Homo sapiens ... Theologians of the world ... the affairs you devote so much attention to are in danger of having as much meaning as the sacrifices offered to Athena ... science and technology may be about to deliver ... minds [that] will no longer be weak and vulnerable to suffering, and they will never die out. The gods will soon be dead, but they will be replaced with real minds that will assume the power of gods, gods that may take over the universe and even make new universes. It will be the final and greatest triumph of science and technology over superstition.[22]

Summary – We should proceed beyond humanity, overcoming the religious impulses which are the last vestige of superstition.

11. Bill Joy: We Should Relinquish These Technologies

Bill Joy (1954 -) is an American computer scientist who co-founded Sun Microsystems in 1982, and served as chief scientist at the company until 2003. His now famous Wired magazine essay, "Why the future doesn't need us," (2000) sets forth his deep concerns over the development of modern technologies.[23]

Joy traces his concern to a discussion he had with Ray Kurzweil at a conference in 1998. Taken aback by Kurzweil's predictions, he read an early draft of *The Age of Spiritual Machines*, and found it deeply disturbed. Subsequently he encountered arguments by the Unabomber Ted Kaczynski's. Kaczynski argued that if machines do all the work, as they inevitably will, then we can: a) let the machines make all the decisions; or b) maintain human control over the machines.

If we choose "a" then we are at the mercy of our machines. It is not that we would give them control or that they would take control, rather, we might become so dependent on them that we would have to accept their commands. Needless to say, Joy doesn't like this scenario. If we choose "b" then control would be in the hands of an elite, and the masses would be unnecessary. In that case the tiny elite: 1) would exterminate the masses; 2) reduce their birthrate so they slowly became extinct; or 3) become benevolent shepherds to the masses. The first two scenarios entail our extinction, but even the third option is no good. In this last scenario the elite would see to it that all physical and psychological needs of the masses are met, while at the same time engineering the masses to sublimate their drive for power. In this case the masses might be happy, but they would not be free.

Joy finds these arguments convincing and deeply troubling. About this time Joy read Moravec's book where he found more of the same kind of predictions. He found himself especially concerned by Moravec's claim that technological superiors always defeat the inferiors, as well as his contention that humans will become extinct as they merge with the robots. Disturbed, Joy consulted other computer scientists who basically agreed with these technological predictions but were themselves unconcerned. Joy was stirred to action.

Joy's concerns focuses on the transforming technologies of the 21st century—genetics, nanotechnology, and robotics (GNR). What is particularly problematic about them is that they have the potential to self-replicate. This makes them inherently more dangerous than 20th century technologies—nuclear, biological, and chemical weapons—which were expensive to build and require rare raw materials. By contrast, 21st century technologies allow for small groups or individuals to bring about massive destruction. Joy accepts that we will soon achieve the computing power to implement some of the dreams of Kurzweil and Moravec, worrying nevertheless that we overestimate our design abilities. Such hubris may lead to disaster.

Robotics is primarily motivated by the desire to be immortal—by downloading ourselves into them. (The terms uploading and downloading are used interchangeably.) But Joy doesn't believe that we will be human after the download or that the robots would be our children. As for genetic engineering, it will create new crops, plants, and eventually new species including many variations of human species, but Joy fears that we do not know enough to conduct such experiments. And nanotechnology confronts the so-called "gray goo" problem—self-replicating nanobots out of control. In short, we may be on the verge of killing ourselves! Is it not arrogant, he wonders, to design a robot replacement species when we so often make design mistakes?

Joy concludes that we ought to relinquish these technologies before it's too late. Yes, GNR may bring happiness and immortality, but should we risk the survival or the species for such goals? Joy thinks not.

Summary – Genetics, nanotechnology, and robotics are too dangerous to pursue. We should relinquish them.

12. A Critique of Joy's Pessimistic Futurism

Elsewhere we have offered a systematic critique of Joy's pessimistic futurism, identifying no less than a dozen separate arguments in Joy's article and critiquing each of them in turn.[24] In briefest form, here are Joy's arguments and our responses.

1. Technology has unintended consequences. Reply – So does every action, thus we ought to be careful.
2. Robots and other 21st century technology will kill us. Reply – It may be worse to not develop them.
3. Mad scientists will kill us with technology. Reply – Scientists are no more mad than anyone else.
4. Robots will self-replicate, become uncontrollable, and subdue us. Reply – Human self-replication can do the same thing.

5. Easy access to GNR makes our extinction more likely. Reply – Our extinction is inevitable without advanced technology.
6. We overestimate our design abilities. Reply – Sometimes we underestimate them, or we are too cautious.
7. Our humanity will be lost after uploading. Reply – This is partly true, but not necessarily bad.
8. Other technologies compound the problem. Reply – More knowledge is often a good thing.
9. We can now destroy ourselves. Reply – The species has always been in danger of extinction.
10. Science is arrogant. Reply - Science is humbler than most human pursuits.
11. We should seek self-knowledge, not artificial intelligence. Reply - Increasing knowledge generally aids self-understanding.
12. Relinquish these technologies. Reply - This is unrealistic, doesn't address threats from current technology, and forgoes future benefits.

Joy's worries blind him to the possible fruits of our knowledge; his pessimism won't allow him to see our knowledge and its applications as our possible salvation. Instead he appeals to the ethics of the Dalia Lama to save us, as if another religious ethics will offer an escape from our nature. I know of no good evidence that the prescriptions of religious ethics have, on the whole, increased the morality of the human race. Why not then use our knowledge to gain mastery over ourselves? If we do that, mastery of our technology will mostly take care of itself. Joy's concerns are legitimate, but his solutions unrealistic. His plea for relinquishment condemns human beings to an existence that cannot improve. If that's the case, what is the point of life?

We say forego Joy's pessimism; reject all barriers and limitations to our intelligence, health, and longevity. Be mindful of our past accomplishments, appreciative of all that we are, but be driven passionately and creatively forward by a hope in what we may become. Therein lays the hope of humankind and their descendents. There is no way ahead that is not without danger; let us then be both cautious and bold, but let us not stand still. In the words of Walt Whitman:

> This day before dawn I ascended a hill,
> and look'd at the crowded heaven,
> And I said to my Spirit,
> When we become the enfolders of those orbs,
> and the pleasure and knowledge
> of everything in them,
> shall we be fill'd and satisfied then?
> And my Spirit said:
> No, we but level that lift,
> to pass and continue beyond.[25]

Summary – We should not fear radical change.

13. Conclusion: Death Should Be Optional

We have established that there are serious thinkers—Kurzweil, Moravec, Kaku, Brain, and others—who foresee that technology may enable humans to overcome death. Searle and Lanier argue that it is exceedingly unlikely that robots could be conscious, thus we will not become immortal by uploading ourselves into them. Rubin and Joy believe that technologies for immorality will probably be developed, but find the prospect undesirable primarily because it signals the end of the human race as we know it.

As non-scientists we are not qualified to evaluate scientific claims about what science can and cannot do, but *we are sure that the future will be radically different from the past.* Understanding the evolution of technology makes this conclusion unavoidable. In the future the products of SciTech will increasingly allow us to vault barriers once thought insurmountable, as long as we accept the caveat that humans don't destroy themselves, and that science continues to progress. A realistic prospect that death will be eliminated in the future is something humans have never had before. All of this leads to a question that has been with us throughout the chapter: if you could choose immortality, should you? Alternatively, if our society could choose immortality, should they?

We believe the individual question has a straightforward answer—we should respect the right of autonomous individuals to choose for themselves. If an effective pill that stops or reverses aging becomes available at your local pharmacy, then you should be free to use it. *My guess is that such a pill would be wildly popular and only the equivalent of today's Amish would reject it.* (Just look at what people spend on vitamins and other elixirs on the basis of little or no evidence of their efficacy.) Or if, as you approach death, you are offered the opportunity to have your consciousness transferred to your younger cloned body, a genetically engineered body, a robotic body, or into a virtual reality, you should be free to do so. Again, *we believe that nearly everyone will use such technologies once they are demonstrated effective*, despite the critic's objections. But if individuals prefer to die in the hope that the gods will revive them in paradise, thereby granting them reprieve from everlasting torment, then we ought to respect that too. Individuals should be able to end their lives whenever they want, in good health, in bad health, after death has become optional for them, or whenever.

The argument about whether a society should fund and promote such research is more complex. Societies currently invest vast sums on entertainment as opposed to scientific research; although the case is strong that the latter is a better societal investment. Ultimately the arguments for and against immortality must speak for themselves, but we reiterate the caveat that once science and technology have overcome death the point will be moot. By then almost everyone will choose more life. If people do that now, at great cost and often gaining only precious additional months of bad health, imagine how quickly they will choose life over death when the techniques are proven to lead to long, healthy lives. As for the opponents, they will get used to new technologies just like they did to previous ones.

Nonetheless the virtual inevitability of advanced technologies does not equate to their being desirable and there are, as we have seen, many thinkers who have campaigned actively and vehemently against utilizing such options. Joy and Rubin exemplify this approach, with the former calling for relinquishment of the most important new technologies and the latter labeling some technology advocates—extinctionists. In contrast, we previously called the defenders of death—deathists. They advocate maintaining the status quo, with its daily dose of 150 thousand deaths worldwide. Prominent among such thinkers are Leon Kass, who chaired George W. Bush's Council on Bioethics from 2001-2005, Francis Fukuyama, a Senior Fellow at the Center on Democracy, Development and the Rule of Law at Stanford, and Bill McKibbon, the Schumann Distinguished Scholar at Middlebury College.

Kass opposes euthanasia, human cloning, and embryonic stem cell research and was an early opponent of in vitro fertilization, which he thought would obscure truths about human life and society. (IVF had none of the dire consequences that Kass predicted; in fact, the technology goes mostly unnoticed now.) One of Kass' main concerns is with the enhancement capability of biotechnology, which he fears will become a substitute for traditional human virtues in the quest to perfect the species. His concerns about modifying our biological inheritance extend to his worries about life extension. He values the natural cycle of life and views death as a desirable end—mortality, he says, is a blessing in disguise.[26] Kass is the quintessential deathist.

Fukuyama argues that biotechnology will alter human nature beyond recognition and have terrible consequences. One would be the undermining of liberal democracy due to radical inequality. But at an even more fundamental level:

> Nobody knows what technological possibilities will emerge for human self-modification. But we can already see the stirrings of Promethean desires in how we prescribe drugs to alter the behavior and personalities of our children. The environmental movement has taught us humility and respect for the integrity of nonhuman nature. We need a similar humility concerning our human nature. If we do not develop it soon, we may unwittingly invite the transhumanists to deface humanity with their genetic bulldozers and psychotropic shopping malls.[27]

McKibbon admits the allure of technological utopia, knowing that it will be hard to resist when presented, but he fears that the richness of human life would be sacrificed in a post-human world. Even if we were godlike, spending our time meditating on the meaning of the cosmos or reflecting on our own consciousness like Aristotle's god, McKibbon says he would not trade his life for such an existence. He wouldn't want to be godlike he says, preferring instead to smell the fragrant leaves, feel the cool breeze, and see the fall colors. Yes there is pain, suffering, cruelty, and death in the world, but this world is enough. "To call this world enough is not to call it perfect or fair or complete or easy. But enough, just enough. And us in it."[28]

There is a lot to say against all these views, but one wonders why these thinkers see human nature as sacrosanct. Is our nature really so sacred that we should be apologists for it? Is it not arrogant to think so highly of ourselves? This is the same human nature that produced what Hegel famously lampooned as "the slaughter-bench at which the happiness of peoples, the wisdom of States, and the virtue of individuals have been victimized." Surely we can do a better than natural selection.

Still, we must concede something to these warnings. The same technologies that may make us immortal are also the ones that bring robotic police, soldiers, and unmanned planes. There is no way to assure that we will not suffer a nightmarish future no matter how we proceed. With greater knowledge comes greater power; with greater power comes the possibility of making life better or worse. The future with all its promises and perils will come regardless—all we can do is do our best.

The defense of immortality against such attacks has been undertaken most thoroughly by the recent intellectual and cultural movement known as transhumanism. *The philosophy of transhumanism affirms the possibility and desirability of using technology to eliminate aging and overcome all other human limitations.* Adopting the evolutionary perspective mentioned earlier, transhumanists maintain that humans are in a relatively early phase of their development. They agree with humanism—that human beings matter and that reason, freedom, and tolerance make the world better—but emphasizes that we can become more than human by changing ourselves. This opens up the possibility of employing high-tech methods to transform the species and direct our own evolution, as opposed to relying on biological evolution or low-tech methods like education and training.

If science and technology develop sufficiently, this would lead to a stage where humans would no longer be recognized as human, but better described as post-human. But why would people want to transcend human nature? Because:

> they yearn to reach intellectual heights as far above any current
> human genius as humans are above other primates; to be
> resistant to disease and impervious to aging; to have unlimited
> youth and vigor; to exercise control over their own desires,
> moods, and mental states; to be able to avoid feeling tired,
> hateful, or irritated about petty things; to have an increased
> capacity for pleasure, love, artistic appreciation, and serenity;
> to experience novel states of consciousness that current human
> brains cannot access. It seems likely that the simple fact of
> living an indefinitely long, healthy, active life would take
> anyone to posthumanity if they went on accumulating
> memories, skills, and intelligence.[29]

And why would one want these experiences to last forever?
Transhumanists answer that they would like to do, think, feel,
experience, mature, discover, create, enjoy, and love beyond what
one can do in seventy or eighty years. All of us would benefit from
the wisdom and love that come with time.

> The conduct of life and the wisdom of the heart are based upon
> time; in the last quartets of Beethoven, the last words and
> works of 'old men' like Sophocles and Russell and Shaw, we
> see glimpses of a maturity and substance, an experience and
> understanding, a grace and a humanity, that isn't present in
> children or in teenagers. They attained it because they lived
> long; because they had time to experience and develop and
> reflect; time that we might all have. Imagine such individuals –
> a Benjamin Franklin, a Lincoln, a Newton, a Shakespeare, a
> Goethe, an Einstein [and a Gandhi] – enriching our world not
> for a few decades but for centuries. Imagine a world made of
> such individuals. It would truly be what Arthur C. Clarke
> called   'Childhood's End' – the beginning of the adulthood
> of humanity.[30]

As for the charge that creating infinitely long life spans tamper
with nature, transhumanists respond that something is not good or
bad because it's natural. Some natural things are bad, and some are
good; some artificial things are bad, and some are good. (Assuming

we can even make an intelligible distinction between the natural and the unnatural.) As for the charge that long lives undermine humanity, the transhumanist replies that the key is to be humane, not human. Merely being human does not guarantee you are humane. As for the claim that death is natural, again, that does not make it good. Moreover, it was natural to die before the age of thirty for most of human history, so we live unnaturally long lives now by comparison. And even if death is natural; so too is the desire for immortality. It is easy to see that people had to accept death when there was nothing they could do about it, but now such deathist attitudes impede progress in eradicating death. Again, transhumanism maintains that death should be optional.

Additionally there are important reasons to be suspicious about the anti-immortality arguments—many are made by those who profit from death. For example, if you are a church selling immortality your business model is threatened by a competitor's offering the real thing. Persons no longer need to join your institution if your promise of immortality is *actually* delivered elsewhere for a comparable cost. Those who make anti-technology arguments may thus be blinded by their short term self-interest. And, as we all know, most people hesitate to believe anything that is inconsistent with how they make money. Just look at the historical opposition to the rise of modern science and the accompanying *real* miracles it brought. Or to tobacco companies opposition to the evidence linking smoking with cancer, or to the oil companies opposition to the evidence linking burning fossil fuels with global climate change.

A closely connected reason to be suspicious of the deathists is that death is so interwoven into their world-view, eliminating it would essentially destabilize that world-view, thereby undercutting their psychological stability. If one has invested a lifetime in a world-view in which dying and an afterlife are an integral part, a challenge to that world-view will almost always be rejected. The great American philosopher Charles Sanders Pierce captured this point perfectly:

> Doubt is an uneasy and dissatisfied state from which we struggle to free ourselves and pass into the state of belief; while the latter is a calm and satisfactory state which we do not wish to avoid, or to change to a belief in anything else. On the

contrary, we cling tenaciously, not merely to believing, but to believing just what we do believe.[31]

The defeat of death completely obliterates most world-views that have supported humans for millennia; no wonder it undermines psychological stability and arouses fierce opposition. Thus monetary and psychological reasons help to explain much opposition to life-extending therapies. Still, people do change their minds. *We now no longer accept dying at age thirty and think it a great tragedy when it happens; I argue that our descendents will feel similarly about our dying at ninety.* Ninety years may be a relatively long lifespan compared with those of our ancestors, but it may be exceedingly brief when compared to those of our descendents. Our mind children may shed the robotic equivalent of tears at our short and painful lifespans, as we do for the short, difficult lives of our forbearers.

In the end death eradicates the possibility of complete meaning; surely that is the best reason to desire immortality for all conscious beings. For those who do not want immortality, they should be free to die; for those of us that long to live forever, we should free to do so. I am convinced. I want more freedom. I don't want to die. I want death to be optional.

Summary – There are good reasons to believe that science can make death optional, good reasons to believe that death should be optional, and good reasons to think that most people will exercise that option when it becomes available.

CHAPTER 9 – THE EVOLUTION OF A FULLY MEANINGFUL COSMOS

All the past is but the beginning of a beginning; all that the human mind has accomplished is but the dream before the awakening.
~ H.G. Wells

Man is a rope stretched between the animal and the Superman -- a rope over an abyss. A dangerous crossing, a dangerous wayfaring, a dangerous looking-back, a dangerous trembling and halting. What is great in man is that he is a bridge and not a goal.
~ Frederick Nietzsche

Mankind is still embryonic ... man is the bud from which something more complicated and more centered than man himself should emerge.
~ Pierre Teilhard de Chardin

But at the same time, in reality, what a difference there is between the world today, and what it used to be! And with the passage of more time, some two or three hundred years, say, people will look back at our own times with horror, or with sneering laughter, because all of our present day life will appear so clumsy, and burdensome, extraordinarily inept and strange. Yes, certainly, what a life it will be then, what a life!
~ Anton Chekhov

There is a grandeur in this view of life, with its several powers, having been originally breathed into a few forms or into one; and that, whilst this planet has gone cycling on according to the fixed law of gravity, from so simple a beginning endless forms most beautiful and most wonderful have been, and are being, evolved.
~ Charles Darwin

1. Does Evolution Imply That Life is Meaningful?

We argued at the end of Chapter 7 that it is helpful to be optimistic about the meaning of life in the face of death—thus there is a *pragmatic* justification for believing that life has meaning. At the beginning of Chapter 8 we argued there are good reasons to believe that death can be defeated—thus there is a *scientific* justification for believing that we can erase an essential impediment to a meaningful life. At the end of Chapter 8 we argued that it is desirable to defeat death—thus there is a *moral* justification for defeating death inasmuch as a completely meaningful life is otherwise impossible. *In the conquering of death lies our most immediate hope of making life more meaningful.*

Still, none of this guarantees that our life or cosmic life is meaningful. Why? For one thing, a positive attitude says nothing about the reality of our situation. For another, we cannot know if the technology to defeat death will ever come to fruition or, if it does, that it will do so in our lifetime. Not knowing if the technology will ever come to fruition, or be developed in our lifetimes, our best response is optimism. But even if technology does defeats death in our lifetime, or revives us after death, a meaningful life is still not assured because a long life is no guarantee of a meaningful one. In other words, immortality is only a necessary condition for full meaning, not a sufficient one; *we need quality as well as quantity for fully meaningful lives.*

But if immortality is not enough for full meaning, what is? It is audacious to attempt to answer this question, since we probably do not possess the intellectual wherewithal to specify all the necessary and sufficient conditions of full meaning—assuming the question even makes sense. Fortunately the inability to capture the essence of meaning need not impede our search, an insight noted also by Thaddeus Metz:

> Fortunately the field does not need an extremely precise analysis of the concept of life's meaning ... in order to make progress on the substantive question of what life's meaning is. Knowing that meaningfulness analytically concerns a variable and gradient final good in a person's life that is conceptually distinct from happiness, rightness, and worthwhileness provides a certain amount of common ground.[1]

So while we cannot apprehend meaning with precise conceptual clarity, we can assume that it is some good in addition to, enmeshed in, intertwined with, or emergent from being, truth, joy, beauty, and all the other good things. Meaning is a variable and gradient good that is desirable, something we want desperately. Therefore we will not pursue further abstruse questions about the essence or logical possibility of complete meaning.

Instead, in this penultimate chapter, *we ask if the idea of evolution supports the claim that life is meaningful, or is becoming meaningful, or is becoming increasingly meaningful.* Does evolution add to the case for meaning? Is there anything about evolution in general—as opposed to technological evolution specifically—which sheds light on meaning? Is there anything about evolution as a whole—cosmic, biological, and cultural—which implies that life is meaningful, or that meaning emerges, or that, given enough time, complete meaning will be attained, actualized, or approached as a limit? Does an a posteriori analysis of past evolution allow us to draw positive conclusions about the meaning of life?

Perhaps there is a *progressive* directionality to evolution, perhaps the meaningful eschatology of the universe will gradually unfold as we evolve, and perhaps we can articulate a cosmic vision to describe this unfolding—or perhaps not. Essentially, what we want to know is: *are there any other good reasons to believe that life meaningful besides the practical effects of optimism and the possibility of technological immortality?* It is to such concerns that we now turn.

2. A Recap of Cosmic and Biological Evolution

Our universe is 13.7 billion years old, our solar system is 8 billion years old, and the earth is 4.5 billion years old. A timeline on earth from that point on reads like this (and what a testimony to scientific achievement this list is):

- billion years of simple cells (prokaryotes),
- 3 billion years of photosynthesis,
- 2 billion years of complex cells (eukaryotes),
- 1 billion years of multi-cellular life,
- 600 million years of simple animals,
- 550 million years of complex animals,

- 500 million years of fish and proto-amphibians,
- 475 million years of land plants,
- 400 million years of insects and seeds,
- 360 million years of amphibians,
- 300 million years of reptiles,
- 200 million years of mammals,
- 150 million years of birds,
- 130 million years of flowers,
- 65 million years since the dinosaurs died out
- 40 million years of butterflies and moths
- 20 million years of giraffes
- 15 million years of hominids
- 13 million years since orangutan-hominid split
- 10 million years since gorilla-hominid split
- 6 million years since chimpanzee-hominid split
- 5 million years of Australopithecines
- million years of *Ardipithecus*
- million years of *Australopithecus afarensis*
- 2.5 million years of Homo habilis
- 1.8 million years of Homo erectus
- 1.2 millions years of Homo antecessor
- 600 thousand years of *Homo heidelbergensis*
- 350 thousand years of Neanderthals
- 200 thousand years of Anatomically modern humans
- 160 thousand years of Homo sapiens
- 50 thousand years since migration to South Asia
- 40 thousand years since migration to Australia and Europe
- 15-40 thousand years since migration to Americas
- 12 thousand years since evolution of light skin in Europeans

Is something happening here? Is there anything we can infer from all this?

3. Has There Been Biological Progress?

We have already seen thinkers like Kurzweil and Moravec defend the idea that cosmic evolution is progressive. But what of biological progress? The debate between those who defend evolutionary progress and those who deny it has been ongoing throughout the history of biology. On the one hand, more recent biological forms seem more advanced, on the other hand no one agrees on precisely what progress is.

Darwin's view of the matter is summarized nicely by Timothy Shanahan: "while he rejected any notion of evolutionary progress, as determined by a necessary law of progression, he nonetheless accepted evolutionary progress as a contingent consequence of natural selection operating within specified environments."[2] This fits well with Darwin's own words:

> There has been much discussion whether recent forms are more highly developed than ancient . . . But in one particular sense the more recent forms must, on my theory, be higher than the more ancient; for each new species is formed by having had some advantage in the struggle for life over other and preceding forms I do not doubt that this process of improvement has affected in a marked and sensible manner the organization of the more recent and victorious forms of life, in comparison with the ancient and beaten forms; but I can see no way of testing this sort of progress.[3]

The most vociferous critic of biological progress was Harvard's Stephen Jay Gould (1941 – 2002) who thought progress an annoying and non-testable idea that had to be replaced if biological history were to be understood. What we call evolutionary progress is really just a random moving away from something, not an orienting toward anything. Starting from simple beginnings, organisms become more complex but not necessarily better. In Gould's image, if a drunk man staggers from a wall that forces him to move toward a gutter, he will end up in the gutter. Evolution acts like that wall pushing individuals toward behaviors that are mostly random but statistically predictable. Nothing about it implies progress.

The biologist Richard Dawkins is more sanguine regarding progress, arguing that if we define progress as adaptive fit between organism and environment then evolution is clearly progressive. To see this consider the predator/prey arms race, where positive feedback loops drive evolutionary progress. Dawkins believes in life's ability to evolve further, in the "evolution of evolvability." He believes in progressive evolution.

Darwin seemingly reconciled these two views.

> ... as the forms became complicated, they opened *fresh* means
> of adding to their complexity ... but yet there is no *necessary*
> tendency in the simple animals to become complicated
> although all perhaps will have done so from the new relations
> caused by the advancing complexity of others ... if we begin
> with the simpler forms & suppose them to have changed, their
> very changes tend to give rise to others.[4]

Simple forms become increasingly complex, thus stimulating
the complexity of other forms. This did not happen by necessity
and no law need be invoked to drive the process, nonetheless
competition between organisms will likely result in progressively
complex forms.

There is probably no greater authority on the idea of
evolutionary progress than Michael Ruse whose book, *Monad to
Man: The Concept of Progress in Evolutionary Biology*, is the most
comprehensive work on the subject. Ruse observes that museums,
charts, displays, and books all depict evolution as progressive, and
he thinks that the concept of progress will continue to play a major
role in evolutionary biology for the following reasons. First, as
products of evolution, we are bound to measure it from our own
perspective, thus naturally valuing the intelligence that asks
philosophical questions. Second, whatever epistemological
relativists might think, nearly all practicing scientists strongly
believe their theories and models get closer to the truth as science
proceeds. From there scientists typically transfer that belief in
scientific progress to a belief in organic progress. Finally, Ruse
maintains that the kinds of scientists drawn to evolution are those
particularly receptive to progressive ideas. Evolution and the idea
of progress are intertwined and nearly inseparable.

4. Will Durant: A Historian's View of Cultural Progress

Will Durant (1885-1981) was a prolific writer, historian, and
philosopher best known for his eleven volume, The Story of
Civilization, and his 1926 book, The Story of Philosophy, one of
the best-selling philosophy books of all time. He is generally
regarded as a gifted prose stylist, was a winner of the Pulitzer Prize
for General Non-Fiction and a Presidential Medal of Freedom, and

was one of the most beloved public intellectuals of the twentieth-century.

In a 1941 magazine essay entitled "Ten Steps Up From the Jungle," Durant makes a historian's case for cultural progress. He begins by retelling the story of Nicolas de Condorcet, the young French aristocrat, mathematician, and Enlightenment philosopher who penned one of the greatest tributes to progress ever written while hiding from the guillotine, the Historical Record of Progress of the Human Race. Given expanding scientific knowledge and universal education, Condorcet believed that there was no limit to human progress. Of him Durant exclaims:

> I have never ceased to marvel that a man so placed—driven to the very last stand of hope, with all his personal sacrifices of aristocratic privilege and fortune gone for nothing, with that great revolution upon which the youth of all Europe had pinned its hopes for a better world issuing in indiscriminate suspicion and terror—should, instead of writing an epic of despondency and gloom, have written a paean to progress. Never before had man so believed in mankind, and perhaps never again since.[5]

Of course many legitimately question whether progress is real, whether our knowledge and technological achievements are good, for though knowledge is power, it is not justice or wisdom or beauty or kindness or hope. Civilizations have crumbled to dust and our technology may destroy us—thus pessimism may be warranted. So is progress real? Despite misgivings, Durant answers in the affirmative, for though history is full of war, it is also full of genius, the true source of the advance of civilization. The achievement of genius, preserved and transmitted as cultural heritage, transcends the fleetingness of states and empires, leaving us a legacy for which we are richer. Progress is real.

To specify this progress, Durant focused on ten salient progressive steps that together reveal cultural progress as self-evident. They are: 1) speech; 2) conquering animals; 3) conquering fire and light; 4) agriculture; 5) social organization; 6) morality; 7) developing the aesthetic sense; 8) science; 9) communication; and 10) education to transmit our cultural heritage.

Seen from a distance these steps show progress to be real and optimism justified. In the end this upward trajectory left Durant as optimistic about the future as Condorcet and Voltaire.

> Do I have doubts about the future? Yes. Certainly, we shall pass through misery and terror. But I envy our children. I feel toward them as Voltaire felt when he came to Paris in 1778, aged 83, to die. He looked at the young men in Paris; he could see in their eyes the coming revolution. He knew they would suffer. That great men had died so many deaths to live so many lives—how gladly he would have died one more death to live one more life for those young men in Paris, to go through with them their revolution and their terror, their suffering and their creation. So he said to them what I should say to you: "The young are fortunate, for they will see great things. For us older ones, parents and teachers, it only remains to make straight their way.[6]

Summary – There has been cultural progress.

5. Jean Piaget: Knowledge Evolves in a Progressive Direction

Jean Piaget (1896-1980) was a Swiss biologist, psychologist, and philosopher known most prominently for his studies of the cognitive development of children. He was a voluminous writer in multiple fields whose publishing career began at age ten and continued unabated for about seventy years. He is one of the most important and cited intellectuals of the twentieth-century.

The desire to find a bridge between biology and knowledge was Piaget's lifelong goal, and evolution provided that bridge, since both life and mind evolve.[7] What Piaget discovered after decades of empirical study was that interactions between biological organisms and their physical environment were strikingly parallel to those found in the relation between minds and reality—in both domains evolution proceeds similarly.

The key concepts in Piaget's thought were: organization, adaptation, assimilation, accommodation, and equilibration. An animal is an organization, a complex, physical structure. If a biological organism is in a state of disequilibrium—for example it's hungry—it is motivated to adapt to its environment—search for food. This process of adaptation comes about by assimilating from the environment—eating—and then accommodating to what's been assimilation—undergoing the digestive process. The end result of the adaptive process is that the organism returns to a state of biological equilibrium—its hunger satisfied.

Similarly, humans exist as organisms in cognitive environments. If an organism is in a state of cognitive disequilibrium—say it's unsure of a truth claim—it is motivated to adapt to its cognitive environment—say by signing up for a class about the topic. This process of adaptation consists of both the process of assimilating new knowledge—attending a lecture—as well as accommodating to what's been assimilated—by reconciling the new information with previous cognitive structures. The end result of the adaptive process is that the organism achieves a higher level of cognitive equilibrium.

Together organization and adaptation constitute what Piaget calls the process of equilibration—essentially a biological drive to produce optimal states of equilibrium between organisms and their physical and cognitive environments. The result in biological evolution is organisms more adapted to or equilibrated with their physical environments, and in cognitive evolution organisms more adapted to or equilibrated with their cognitive environment.

The empirical evidence to support his view comes from multiple sources. For instance, the cognitive development of a child—the evolution of individual mind—and the development of better scientific theories—the evolution of the group mind—both provide overwhelming evidence for the progressive evolution of knowledge toward better theories about the world, contra Kuhn. The equilibration process drives both individuals and groups to higher levels of equilibrium between mind and reality. In other words thought gradually adapts to reality. While Piaget did not discuss whether the evolution of cognitive structures would construct or discover meaning, we might infer that meaning, if real, will be approached by the increasing power of mind—mind that is the product of the process of equilibration that in turn moves mind closer and closer to truth.

Summary – Knowledge evolves in a progressive direction characterized by a better fit between mind and the real.

6. Robert Wright: Game Theory, Evolution, and Meaning

Robert Wright (1957 -) is a journalist, and prize-winning author of books about evolutionary psychology, science, religion, and game theory. He is a graduate of Princeton University, where he has taught courses on the evolution of religion.

In *Non-Zero: The Logic of Human Destiny* (2000), Wright argues that biological and cultural evolution are shaped and directed primarily by non-zero-sumness—a concept in game theory that describes situations where both parties involved in an interaction can gain something. (As opposed to zero-sum games where one party's gain is the other party's loss, that is, the sum is zero.) As a result of the interactions between individuals in non-zero sum situations, increasingly complex information-processing individuals who cooperate more readily with each other emerge, implying that we are here because of a process that made the evolution of intelligent beings likely. As the complexity of individuals and societies increases, their ability to reap the rewards of cooperation increases, thus perpetuating further cooperation and developmental complexity.

The majority of Wright's book summarizes the biological and cultural development which follows almost by necessity from non-zero sum interactions. However, at the end of his book, Wright intimates that we may be on the threshold of developing a global consciousness along the lines suggested by Pierre Teilhard de Chardin, a thinker we will discuss later. This leads him to wonder if there is any spiritual or moral directionality in evolution, and ultimately to the question of whether such progress is connected with the meaning of life. The connection, as Wright sees it, resides in the fact that consciousness imparts meaning.

> A strictly empirical analysis of both organic and cultural evolution … reveals a world with direction—a direction suggestive of purpose … Life on earth was, from the beginning, a machine for generating meaning and then deepening it, a machine that created the potential for good and began to fulfill it.[8]

Summary – An analysis of biological and cultural evolution suggest a purposeful direction toward more meaning and goodness.

7. Steven Pinker: A Critique of Wright's Progressivism

Steven Pinker (1954 -) is an experimental psychologist, cognitive scientist, linguist, popular science author, and the Johnstone Family Professor in the Department of Psychology at Harvard University, where he earned his PhD in 1979. He regularly appears on lists of today's most influential scientists, thinkers, and public intellectuals.

Pinker agrees with Wright that biological organisms and cultures get more complex over time and that there has been cultural and moral progress. Yet he is not convinced "that the cosmos has, in some sense, the "goal," "end," "purpose," or "destiny" of producing complex life, intelligent species, societies, and global cooperation ... natural selection is a feedback process with a kind of "goal," and so is human striving. But do the two have the *same* goal, and is that goal an increase of complexity in the service of cooperation?"[9] Pinker argues that the answer to both parts of this question is no. But why?

First, the goal of natural selection is to enhance reproduction; increasing complexity and cooperation are sub-goals in the service of this primary goal, as are increased size, speed, energy efficiency, parental care, weapons, etc. All may have increased over time, but they are not the goal or destiny of evolution. Second, human intelligence was no more destined to be than elephant trunks or any other biological adaptation. Brains evolve only when their benefits exceed their costs, an occurrence quite rare in living things since most things never develop brains. Third, humans don't seek cooperation and societal complexity; they seek pleasure, friendship, knowledge and the like. Complexity may help us be happy, and it may help organisms reproduce, but that doesn't mean they were evolution's goal. Finally, Pinker argues that cooperation and moral progress will not increase toward a limit, but cease when the benefits of cooperation are balanced by its costs. Organisms and societies have become more complex, intelligent, and cooperative over time, but that doesn't mean they were destined to become so. There may be some progress, but it is not inevitable, it is not built into the nature of things.

Summary - Biological and cultural evolution do not have a destiny.

8. Daniel Dennett: Evolution as the Universal Acid

In his book, *Darwin's Dangerous Idea: Evolution and the Meanings of Life*, Dennett describes evolution as a universal acid that eats through everything it touches; everything from the cell to consciousness to the cosmos is best explained from an evolutionary perspective, as is metaphysics, epistemology, ethics, religion, and the meaning of life. To better understand this, Dennett considers the "great cosmic pyramid. Traditionally this pyramid explains design from the top down—from god down through mind, design, order, chaos, and nothingness. In this interpretation, god acts as the ultimate "skyhook," a miraculous source of design that does not build on lower, simpler layers. By contrast, evolution reverses the direction of the pyramid explaining design from the bottom up, by what Dennett calls "cranes." Here physical matter and the algorithmic process of evolution explain the evolution of more complex structures from simpler ones, and they do so without miraculous intervention.

Now applied to meaning, evolution implies that no godlike skyhook is needed to derive meaning; instead, meaning must be created from the ground up, as the subjectivists argued in Chapter 5. While subjectivists have a hard time explaining how you create meaning, evolution does not. If we abandon the idea that god or mind comes first, we see that meaning evolves from the bottom up as order, design and mind are created. At one time there was no life, no mind, and no meaning, but slowly, imperceptibly they emerged. Meaning does not then descend from on high; it percolates up from below as mind develops. The meaning that mind now experiences is not full-fledged meaning, but it is moving in that direction as mind develops. From a mind that itself was built by cranes, composed of molecules, atoms, and neurons in ever more complex arrangements, meaning evolves.

The mental states that give rise to meaning are themselves grounded ultimately in biology. Darwin showed us that everything of importance, including our minds, evolved from below, slowly, by happenstance, and all connected in a tree of life. The tree of life created by evolution is no god to be prayed to, but it inspires awe nonetheless. It is something sacred.

Summary – Meaning is not complete, but it is evolving along with the minds with which it co-exists.

9. Michael Shermer: Meaning Is Built Into Us

Michael Shermer (1954 -) is an American science writer, historian of science, founder of The Skeptics Society, and Editor in Chief of its magazine *Skeptic*, which is largely devoted to investigating pseudoscientific and supernatural claims. He is also the author of numerous well-received popular books. He received his PhD in the history of science in 1991 from the Claremont Graduate University.

In his commencement speech at Whittier College in May of 2008 titled, "The Meaning of Life, The Universe, and Everything," Shermer makes his case for the relationship between evolution and meaning. He asserts that while the question of the existence of an afterlife is an open one, we should live as if this life is the only one, treating others and each moment as the most important thing. In this way our lives become meaningful by valuing things in the here and now, as opposed to treating this life as a prelude to another one. The values and purposes and meanings we create are provisional of course, since we have no access to ultimate truth. In this way they are analogous to the provisional truths of science—facts confirmed to such a degree we give them our provisional assent. The self-correcting nature of science determines provisional scientific truths, while life itself shows the way to provisional purpose.

The most basic purpose of life is survival and reproduction, and we are the product of those billions of years of evolution. We might conclude that there was a cosmic destiny or divine providence that led to us, but in fact the existence of life was contingent on a billion circumstances. If an asteroid like the one that destroyed the dinosaurs had hit the earth a million years ago, if a few Homo sapiens had not migrated from Africa a hundred thousand years ago, if Neanderthals had killed our ancestors thirty thousand years ago, if any of these or countless other perturbations had occurred, we would have vanished. We are contingent.

But from our humble beginnings, a sense of purpose and the desire to achieve goals has evolved. We love, work, play, become involved, and transcend, finding transcendent meaning in the world revealed by science and the awe it inspires. Shermer experiences awe by looking at the Andromeda galaxy through his backyard telescope, by contemplating that the light of that galaxy took three million years to reach his retina, and by the fact that this galaxy was unknown until recently. The vastness of deep space and time are themselves more than enough to generate awe, and what generates awe is a source of meaning. Evolution has produced creatures with meaning built into them, and with the ability to experience it, if they choose to do so.

Summary – Evolution has built meaning and purpose into us.

10. Steve Stewart-Williams: Darwin and the Meaning of Life

Steve Stewart-Williams is a lecturer in evolutionary psychology at Swansea University in Wales. He received his PhD from Massey University in New Zealand in psychology and philosophy and was a post-doctoral fellow at McMaster University in Canada. His book, *Darwin, God and the Meaning of Life: How Evolutionary Theory Undermines Everything You Thought You Knew* (2010), applies evolutionary insights directly to questions of ethics, religion, and meaning.

Like the previous authors we have discussed in this chapter, Stewart-Williams thinks evolution bears significantly on the issue of the meaning of life. Humans have a perennial interest in the question of life's meaning, advancing religious and secular answers to the question but, as we have seen and as Stewart-Williams notes, there are difficulties with all the proposed solutions even before we take evolutionary theory into account. Let us look then more closely at the implications of evolution for meaning.

Why are we here? We are here because we evolved, but the purpose of our existence is not to survive, reproduce, or propagate genes; the fact that we evolved to do these things does not tell us what our purpose is now. So in this sense evolution is not relevant to questions of meaning. Nonetheless evolutionary theory is relevant to questions of meaning in another way. To see how we must understand that evolutionary theory offers historical explanations, not teleological ones. Teleological explanations explain apparent design, like the giraffe's long neck, in terms of purposes—they have long necks to feed on tall trees. (Aristotle's explanation of water running downhill to reach its natural resting place is another example of a teleological explanation.) Biology tells us instead that giraffes have long necks because *in the past* long necks helped them survive, reproduce, and thereby pass along their genes. In modern biology, all adaptations have historical rather than teleological explanations.

The important point is that explanations for why we are here—to get to heaven, be happy, help others, reproduce—are all teleological explanations. In evolutionary theory these are the wrong kinds of answers because again, in biology, there are no teleological answers only historical ones. From evolutionary theory it follows that we are here because we evolved, we are not here for a purpose. Notice that this does not preclude us choosing goals and purposes for ourselves from which we derive emotional or psychological meaning. "However, if we're interested in the question of whether life is *ultimately* meaningful, as opposed to whether it's potentially emotionally meaningful, well, after Darwin, there is no reason to suppose that it is."[10]

Yet Stewart-Williams does not find this conclusion gloomy. Just because life has no ultimate purpose, it does not follow that life is not worth living—life can still be good although it is ultimately meaningless. (Many subjectivists made the same point.) Like the existentialists we might even find this idea liberating, inasmuch as this state of affairs allows us the freedom to give life meaning, rather than having it imposed on us externally. For many subjective meaning may not be enough, but for Stewart-Williams we can appreciate beauty, kindness, and the other good things in life even if they don't have an ultimate purpose.

Surprisingly, we should not draw from all this the conclusion that we have purposes but the universe does not. *The minds from which purposes emerge are a part of the universe, and this means that if you have purposes then part of the universe does too.* The universe does not have a single purpose, but the many purposes of the beings that are part of it:

... it is false to say that the universe is purposeless. It was purposeless before the first life forms with purposes and drives evolved, and it will be devoid of purpose once more when the last life form takes its final gasp of breath. However, as long as we're here to contemplate such matters, to struggle and strive, the universe is not without purpose.[11]

Finally, the fact our minds are part of the universe has an interesting implication—the universe is partly conscious. When we contemplate the universe, part the universe is conscious; when we know something of the universe, part of the universe is self-conscious. From an evolutionary perspective this means that after eons of unconsciousness, the universe is gradually becoming self-aware. As for the destiny of consciousness Stewart-Williams is not optimistic. Given the shadow cast over us by universal death he expects the universe will lapse back into unconsciousness. As we will see, some of the thinkers that follow will offer more positive cosmic visions.

Summary – Evolution reveals that the universe has no objective purpose. However, we are part of the universe and we have purposes, so the universe has as many purposes as we give it. This means that the universe is partly conscious.

11. John Stewart: The Meaning of Life in an Evolving Cosmos

John Stewart is a member of the Evolution, Complexity and Cognition Research Group at The Free University of Brussels, and the author of: *Evolution's Arrow: the direction of evolution and the future of humanity*. In his essay "The Meaning of Life In A Developing Universe," he argues that evolution and meaning should be understood together.

Evolution has produced an organism that has begun to model and understand cosmic evolution, as well as the possible future evolution of life. The models reveal that there is a trajectory to evolution, specifically the increasing scales over which living processes evolve into organized cooperatives. For example, molecular processes were organized into cells; cells into organisms; and human organisms into families, bands, tribes, cities, and nations. Evolution favors cooperation because of the advantages bestowed upon organized cooperatives; in turn larger cooperatives have a greater ability to adapt to changing circumstances. Uninterrupted, this should lead to global and interstellar cooperatives, with a concomitant increase in intelligence that would eventually lead to a nearly omnipotent command of matter and energy.

While the trajectory of evolution has moved largely of its own accord, at some point it will probably continue only if we direct or steer it—an act Stewart calls intentional evolution. Intelligent beings such as ourselves must be committed to intentionally directing evolution, driving the development of life and intelligence even though our ultimate destination is unknown. This transition, from passive recipient to active participator must be taken in order to further evolve. "If humanity goes on to complete this great evolutionary transition, we will have embraced a role that provides meaning and purpose for our existence."[12]

Summary – The meaning of life is to direct evolution to new heights.

12. Pierre Teilhard de Chardin: Universal Progressive Evolution

Pierre Teilhard de Chardin (1881 – 1955), a Jesuit priest trained as a paleontologist and geologist, was one of the most prominent thinkers to attempt to reconcile evolutionary theory, religion, and the meaning of life. In his magnum opus, *The Phenomenon of Man*, he sets forth a sweeping account of cosmic unfolding.

While Teilhard's philosophy is notoriously complex, his key notion is that cosmic evolution is directional or teleological. Evolution brings about an increasing complexity of consciousness, leading from an unconscious geosphere, to a semi-conscious biosphere, and eventually to conscious sphere of mind. The arrival of human beings on the cosmic scene is particularly important, signaling that evolution is becoming conscious of itself. As the process continues the human ability to accumulate and transmit ideas increases, along with the depth and complexity of those ideas. This will lead to the emergence of what Teilhard calls the "noosphere," a thinking layer containing the collective consciousness of humanity which will envelope the earth. (Some contemporary commentators view the World Wide Web as a partial fulfillment of Teilhard's prophecy.)

Not only does evolution explain how mind arose from matter, it is also the key to all metaphysical understanding, if such understanding is to be based on a firm foundation.

> Is evolution a theory, a system or a hypothesis? It is much more: it is a general condition to which all theories, all hypotheses, all systems must bow and which they must satisfy henceforth if they are to be thinkable and true. Evolution is a light illuminating all facts, a curve that all lines must follow.[13]

Teilhard recognized this new, evolutionary worldview, with its oceans of space and time, as a source of disquiet for minds previously comforted by childlike myths. Anxiety begins when we reflect, and reflection on the nature of the universe clearly discomforts.

> Which of us has ever in his life really had the courage to look squarely at and try to 'live' [in] a universe formed of galaxies whose distance apart runs into hundreds of thousands of light years? Which of us, having tried, has not emerged from the ordeal shaken in one or other of his beliefs? And who, even when trying to shut his eyes as best he can to what the astronomers implacably put before us, has not had a confused sensation of gigantic shadow passing over the serenity of his joy?[14]

The cause of our psychic troubles derives mostly from this evolutionary worldview."What disconcerts the modern world at its very roots is not being sure, and not seeing how it ever could be sure, that there is an outcome—a suitable outcome—to that evolution."[15] But alas the source of our discomfort is also the fount of our salvation. For if the future is open to our further development, then we have the chance to fulfill ourselves, "to progress until we arrive ... at the utmost limits of ourselves."[16]

The increasing power and influence of the noosphere or world of mind will culminate in the Omega Point—a supreme consciousness or God. At that point all consciousness will converge, although Teilhard argues that individual consciousness will somehow still be preserved. While the Omega point is extraordinarily difficult to describe, it must be a union of love if it is to be a sublimely suitable outcome of evolution. Here Teilhard waxes poetic:

> Love alone is capable of uniting living beings in such a way as to complete and fulfill them, for it alone takes them and joins them by what is deepest in themselves. This is a fact of daily experience. At what moment do lovers come into the most complete possession of themselves if not when they say they are lost in each other? In truth, does not love every instant achieve all around us, in the couple or the team, the magic feat, the feat reputed to be contradictory, of personalizing by totalizing? And if that is what it can achieve daily on a small scale, why should it not repeat this one day on world-wide dimensions?[17]

In Teilhard's vision, all reality evolves toward higher forms of being and consciousness, which are at the same time more intense and satisfying forms of love. Thus spirit or mind, not matter or energy, ground the unity of the universe; they are the inner driving force propelling evolution forward. Teilhard found meaning and purpose in this sweeping epic of cosmic evolution in which the endpoint of all evolution will be the highest good.

Summary – Cosmic evolution leads to the fully meaningful Omega Point.

13. Jacques Monod: Banishing Cosmic Meaning

Jacques Monod (1910 – 1976) was a French biologist who was awarded a Nobel Prize in Physiology or Medicine in 1965 for his discoveries in molecular biology. His classic book Chance and Necessity: An Essay on the Natural Philosophy of Modern Biology (1971) is an antipode to Teilhard's The Phenomena of Man, as well as other versions of progressivism.

Monod presumes that our early ancestors did not feel themselves strangers in the world amongst plants that grew and died, and animals that ate, fought, and protected their young. In short they saw things like themselves whose purpose was to survive and produce progeny. They also saw rivers, mountains, oceans, lighting, rain, and stars in the sky, assuming no doubt that these objects had purposes too. If humans have purposes, nature must too—and with that single thought animism was born, nature and humans were connected.

However, modern science largely severed this connection, whereas Teilhard tried to revive it, placing him squarely in company of other thinkers who tried to restore the connection between human and nature's purposes. Hegel's grand system, Spencer's evolutionism, and Marx and Engels' dialectical materialism all insert meaning and purpose into purposeless evolution, but at the cost of abandoning objectivity, for chance is the source of innovation in biology. In Monod's famous words:

> Pure chance, absolutely free but blind, at the very root of the stupendous edifice of evolution: this central concept of modern biology is no longer one among other possible or even conceivable hypothesis. It is today the sole hypothesis, the only one that squares with observed and tested fact. And nothing warrants the supposition—or the hope—that on this score our position is likely ever to be revised.[18]

For Monod chance destroys both teleology and anthropocentrism. Errors in the replication of the genetic messages—genetic mutations—are essentially random; the mutations of DNA that moves evolution are random. The process is explicitly non-teleological—they are not goal seeking processes initiated and controlled by rational entities. (Still, Monod does invoke the softer term teleonomy—goal-oriented structures and functions that derive from evolutionary history without guiding foresight.) As for anthropocentrism, we were not destined to be, we are accidents. "The universe was not pregnant with life nor the biosphere with man. Our number came up in the Monte Carlo game. Is it any wonder if, like the person who has just made a million at the casino, we feel strange and a little unreal?"[19] We are neither the goal nor the center of creation.

So we seem lost; but it was not always so. For eons of time humans survived in groups with the cohesive social structures necessary for survive, leading to the acceptance of tribal laws and the mythological explanations that gave them sovereignty. From such people

…we have probably inherited our need for an explanation, the profound disquiet which goads us to search out the meaning of existence. That same disquiet has created all the myths, all the religions, all the philosophies, and science itself. That this imperious need develops spontaneously, that it is inborn, inscribed somewhere in the genetic code, strikes me as beyond doubt.[20]

Human social institutions have both a cultural and biological basis, with religious phenomena invariably at the base of social structures to assuage human anxiety with narratives, stories, and histories of past events. Given our innate need for explanation, the absence of one begets existential angst, alleviated only by assigning humans a proper place in a soothing story of a meaningful cosmos. But just a few hundred years ago science offered a new model of objective knowledge as the sole source of truth.

It wrote an end to the ancient covenant between man and nature, leaving nothing in place of the precious bond but an anxious quest in a frozen universe of solitude. With nothing to recommend it but a certain puritan arrogance, how could such an idea win acceptance? It did not; it still has not. It has however commanded recognition; but that is because, solely because, of its prodigious power of performance.[21]

Science undermines the ancient stories as well as the values that were derived from them, leaving us with an ethic of knowledge. Unlike animistic ethics, which claim knowledge of innate, natural, or religious law, an ethics of knowledge is self-imposed. An ethic of knowledge created the modern world—through its technological applications—and it is the only thing that can save the world. Our knowledge has banished cosmic meaning, yet it might also be our redemption. As Monod concludes: "The ancient covenant is in pieces; man knows at last that he is alone in the universe's unfeeling immensity, out of which he emerged only by chance. His destiny is nowhere spelled out, nor is his duty. The kingdom above or the darkness below: it is for him to choose."[22]

Summary – There is no meaning to be found in the cosmos—we are alone, and only we can decide where we want to go.

14. Julian Huxley: Guiding Evolution Gives Meaning to Life

Sir Julian Huxley (1887–1975) was an English evolutionary biologist, humanist and internationalist. He was a leading figure in the mid-twentieth century evolutionary synthesis which united Darwinian natural selection and Mendelian genetics—one of the great scientific achievements of all time. Huxley hailed from one of the most famous intellectual families in English history. His brother was the celebrated writer Aldous Huxley; his half-brother a fellow biologist and Nobel laureate, Andrew Huxley; his father was the writer and editor Leonard Huxley; his paternal grandfather was the acclaimed writer and intellectual Thomas Henry Huxley, a friend and supporter of Charles Darwin; his maternal grandfather was the academic Tom Arnold; and his great-uncle the famous poet Matthew Arnold.

In his 1939 essay, "The Creed of a Scientific Humanist," Huxley argues that much of our unhappiness derives from our asking unanswerable or ill-conceived questions, something philosophy, religion, and science often discover after much wasted effort. For example, asking what form of magic kills people is the wrong kind of question because nothing magical kills people. Similarly, asking who rules the universe is the wrong kind of question—all the scientific evidence points to it ruling itself, and besides, even if there were godlike rulers we could not know them. Gods have been created by humans from various elements of their experience; they are probably anthropomorphic idealizations without any basis in reality. As for the question of an immortal afterlife, it is irresolvable, and we waste time considering it. Real salvation is to be found in the possible harmony between ourselves and the external world. Huxley is not deterred by those who say repudiating god and immortality leaves life meaningless, pointing to Buddhists, agnostics, and Stoics as exemplars of individuals who have led noble and devoted lives without such beliefs.

According to Huxley science provides the best means of realizing meaning in the modern world. It explains forces that were once dark and mysterious; it provides insights into our psychology; it improves both us and our world; and it reveals the vast history and future of the cosmos as well as the immensity of space and time. From the scientific perspective we have reason to hope that the future will be better than the past, that we can expedite biological evolution by our knowledge. Most importantly, "In man evolution could become conscious."[23] While we have taken only the first brief steps toward such consciousness, we should continue onward, as all of human history represents but the infancy of human potential. The most important faith we should have is in life and its potentially unlimited progress. Evolutionary biology thus has gives us a new view of human destiny, with us as the protagonists of evolution, agents of a process who can impose their principles to guide evolution in realizing new possibilities. This is the purpose of our lives.

> Man is that part of reality in which and through which the cosmic process has become conscious and has begun to comprehend itself. His supreme task is to increase that conscious comprehension and to apply it as fully as possible to guide the course of events. In other words, his role is to discover his destiny as an agent of the evolutionary process, in order to fulfill it more adequately.[24]

Almost twenty years later in his 1957 book *New Bottles for New Wine*, Huxley presented a more complete account of cosmic evolution akin to Teilhard's, but without the religious overtones. He began with the now familiar idea that the universe becomes conscious of itself in human beings, given their awareness of the past history and possible future of that universe. Evolution is the history of the realization of new possibilities—the flight of birds; the social interaction of insects; the emergence of mind, intelligence, and language; as well as self-conscious awareness of purpose. It is our duty to realize as many of these potentialities as possible or, as Huxley dramatically and insightfully puts it:

> It is as if man had been suddenly appointed managing director of the biggest business of all, the business of evolution— appointed without being asked if he wanted it, and without proper warning and preparation. What is more, he can't refuse the job. Whether he wants to or not, whether he is conscious of what he is doing or not, he *is* in point of fact determining the future direction of evolution on this earth. That is his inescapable destiny, and the sooner he realizes it and starts believing in it, the better for all concerned.[25]

The process of evolution began with inorganic/cosmic evolution, followed successively by organic/biological evolution, and now psychosocial/cultural evolution. As we have seen cosmic evolution proceeded excruciatingly slow, but pockets of increasingly complex matter gradually coalesce. Living matter arose which imperfectly copied itself, and from this material natural selection initiates a faster process of change, eventually producing the staggering complexity of animals. (A rabbit or a dog is an amazingly complex organization of matter.) In our species mind arose, possessing the power of language and conceptual thought, with the capability of transmitting behaviors, ideas, and values from one mind to another. We now spearhead the evolutionary process. We are its trustees.

Huxley saw his vision of evolution replacing traditional religious views of human destiny. While historically the function of religion has been to cope with human ignorance and fear, and to maintain social and spiritual stability, new belief systems must utilize our knowledge to guide and advance our development. Huxley suggests his new belief system is a type of religion.

> The religion indicated by our new view of our position in the cosmos must be once centered on the idea of fulfillment. Man's most sacred duty, and at the same time his most glorious opportunity, is to promote the maximum fulfillment of the evolutionary process on this earth; and this includes the fullest realization of his own inherent possibilities.[26]

Huxley's evolutionary humanism prescribes both our present fulfillment and the progressive realization of our potentialities. This leads to his exaltation of the scientific spirit. We find fulfillment in our duty to understand, accumulate, and organized knowledge. "Thus scientific research in all fields is essential, and its encouragement is one of the most important tasks of civilization."[27] Moreover, science has discovered that truth is provisional, with science progressing toward that truth. The provisional nature of science invokes humility, yet at the same time takes pride in the extraction of knowledge from the ignorance that long engulfed us—science is progressive although incomplete. Most importantly, evolutionary humanism gave meaning to Huxley's life.

[Evolutionary humanism] has enabled me to see this strange universe into which we are born as a proper object both of awe and wondering love and of intellectual curiosity. More, it has made me realize that both my wonder and curiosity can be of significance and value in that universe. It has enabled me to relate my experiences of the world's delights and satisfactions, and those of its horrors and its miseries to the idea of fulfillment, positive or negative. In the concept of increased realization of possibilities, it provides a common measuring rod for all kinds of directional processes, from the development of personal ethics to large-scale evolution, and gives solid ground for maintaining an affirmative attitude and faith, as against that insidious enemy … the spirit of negation and despair. It affirms the positive significance of effort and creative activity and enjoyment. In some ways most important of all, it has brought back intellectual speculation and spiritual aspiration out of the abstract and isolated spheres they once seemed to me to inhabit, to a meaningful place in concrete reality; and so has restored my sense of unity with nature.[28]

Summary – Guiding the evolutionary progress gives meaning to our lives.

15. E. O. Wilson: Evolution as Religion

Edward O. Wilson (1929 -) is a biologist, theorist, naturalist, and two-time Pulitzer Prize winning author for general non-fiction. He is the father of sociobiology and as of 2007 was the Pellegrino University Research Professor in Entomology in the Department of Organismic and Evolutionary Biology at Harvard University. He is also a Fellow of the Committee for Skeptical Inquiry, a Humanist Laureate of the International Academy of Humanism, and one of the world's most famous living scientists.

In his Pulitzer Prize winning book *On Human Nature* (1978), Wilson extended sociobiology, the study of the biological basis of human social behavior, into the realms of human sexuality, aggression, morality, and religion. Deploying sociobiology to dissect religious myths and practices, led him to affirm: "The predisposition to religious belief is the most complex and powerful force in the human mind and in all probability an ineradicable part of human nature."[29] Religion is a universal of social behavior, recognizable in every society in history and prehistory, and skeptical dreams that religion will vanish are futile. Scientific humanists, consisting mostly of scholars and scientists, organize into small groups which try to discredit superstition and fundamentalism but:

> Their crisply logical salvos, endorsed by whole arrogances of Nobel Laureates, pass like steel-jacketed bullets through fog. The humanists are vastly outnumbered by true believers ... Men, it appears, would rather believe than know. They would rather have the void as purpose ... than be void of purpose.[30]

Other scholars have tried to compartmentalize science and religion—one reads the book of nature, the other the book of scripture. However, with the advance of science, the gods are now to be found below sub-atomic particles or beyond the farthest stars. This situation has led to process theology where the gods emerge alongside molecules, organisms and mind, but, as Wilson points out, this is a long way from ancient religion. Elementary religion sought the supernatural for mundane rewards like long life, land, food, avoiding disasters and conquering enemies; whereas advanced religions make more grandiose promises. This is what we would expect after a Darwinian competition between more advanced religions, with competition between sects for adherents who promotes the religion's survival. This leads to the notorious hostility between religions where, "The conqueror's religion becomes a sword, that of the conquered a shield."[31]

The clash between science and religion will continue as science dismantles the ancient myths that gave religion its power. Religion can always maintain that gods are the source of the universe or defend esoteric arguments, but Wilson doubts the strategy will ultimately succeed, due to the power of science.

> It [science] presents the human mind with an alternative mythology that until now has always, point for point in zones of conflict, defeated traditional religion ... the final decisive edge enjoyed by scientific naturalism will come from its capacity to explain traditional religion, its chief competitor, as a wholly material phenomenon. Theology is not likely to survive as an independent intellectual discipline.[32]

Still, *religion* will endure because it possesses a primal power that science lacks. Science may explain religion, but it has no apparent place for the immortality and objective meaning that people crave and religion claims to provide. To fully address this situation, humanity needs a way to divert the power and appeal of religion belief into the service of scientific rationality.

However, this new naturalism leads to a series of dilemmas. The first is that our species has no "purpose beyond the imperatives created by its genetic history."[33] In other words, we have no pre-arranged destiny. This suggests the difficulty human society will have in organizing its energy toward goals without new myths and new moralities. This leads to a second dilemma "which is the choice that must be made among the ethical premises inherent in man's biological nature"[34] Ethical tendencies are hard-wired, so how do we choose between them? A possible resolution to the dilemmas combines the powerful appeal of religion and mythology with scientific knowledge. One reason to do this is that science provides a firmer base for our mythological desires because of:

> Its repeated triumphs in explaining and controlling the physical world; its self-correcting nature open to all competent to devise and conduct tests; its readiness to examine all subjects sacred and profane; and now the possibility of explaining traditional religion by the mechanistic models of evolutionary biology.[35]

When the latter has been achieved religion will be explained as a product of evolution, and its power as an external source of morality will wane. This will leave us with the evolutionary epic which claims, among other things, that life and mind, the world and universe, are all obedient to the same physical laws. "What I am suggesting ... is that the evolutionary epic is probably the best myth we will ever have."[36] (Myth as in grand narrative.) None of this implies that religion will be fully eradicated, for rationality and progressive evolutionism hold little affection for most, and the tendency for religious belief is hard-wired into the brain by evolution. Still, the pull of knowledge is strong—technologically skilled people and societies have tremendous advantages and they tend to win out in the struggle for existence.

Our burgeoning knowledge of human nature will lead in time to a third dilemma: should we change our nature? Wilson leaves the question open, counseling us to remain hopeful.

> The true Promethean spirit of science means to liberate man by giving him knowledge and some measure of dominion over the physical environment. But at another level, and in a new age, it also constructs the mythology of scientific materialism, guided by the corrective devices of the scientific method, addressed with precise and deliberately affective appeal to the deepest needs of human nature, and kept strong by the blind hopes that the journey on which we are now embarked will be farther and better than the one just completed.[37]

Summary – Evolution can be the basis of a new and better religious mythology. It can provide both hope and meaning.

16. A Summary

Cosmic evolution evokes the idea of *evolutionary progress*, as we saw earlier in thinkers like Kurzweil and Moravec, while progressivism imbues the work of most biologists, a trend Ruse thinks will continue. When we turn to culture, a compelling argument can be made for the reality of progressive evolution. (A case bolstered in the epistemic realm by the theory of memetics.) Durant argues for cultural progress, a conclusion that follows straightforwardly from elements of human history, while Piaget makes the case for cognitive progress, based on his studies of cognitive development in children and his analysis of the history of science. Wright believes in a generally progressive evolution based on the structure of non-zero sum interactions, whereas Pinker counters that complexity and cooperation are sub-goals of evolution, not its natural destiny. While the overall strength of the arguments for evolutionary progress is unclear, we cannot gainsay that such arguments have philosophical merit. Clearly there have been some progressive trends in evolution, which intimates that life as a whole may become increasingly meaningful.

As we have seen a number of thinkers argue for the *relevance of evolution to meaning*. Dennett extends the heuristic reach of evolution, showing how it acts as a universal solvent that eats through philosophical problems, while Shermer says that we create provisional meanings in our lives, even though our existence depends on a billion evolutionary happenstances. Stewart-Williams argues that the universe does have purposes, since we have purposes and we are part of the universe, while John Stewart claims that the universe will be increasingly meaningful if we direct the process. Still, other philosophers have argued that evolution is irrelevant to meaning; for example, Wittgenstein notoriously maintained that "Darwin's theory has no more to do with philosophy than any other hypothesis in natural science."[38] Yet this claim was made in a philosophical milieu where the scope of philosophical inquiry was narrow, whereas today the impact of scientific theories on philosophy is enormous. Today most thinkers would say that the emergence of conscious purposes and meanings in cosmic evolution is relevant to concerns about meaning.

Turning to grand *cosmic visions*, Teilhard articulates a universal vision of the evolutionary process, with that universe moving toward a fully meaningful end point, although Monod questions Teilhard's optimism, noting that biology reveals no meaning. Huxley conveys a vision—similar to Teilhard's but without the religious connotations—in which we are encouraged to play the leading role in the cosmic drama by guiding evolution to realize its possibilities, thereby finding meaning for ourselves in the process. Wilson follows this line of thinking—the evolutionary epic is mythic and sweeping—and exhorts us to create a better future. Thus many thinkers believe that evolution is both progressive and relevant to meaning; in fact it is a key that unlocks the secret of meaning. For Teilhard, Huxley, and Wilson, *life is meaningful because it evolves, and we live meaningful lives precisely because we play a central role in this evolving meaning.*

17. Evolution As Metaphysics

Returning then to the query we posed at the beginning of the chapter, a study of cosmic evolution supports the claim that life has become increasingly meaningful, a claim buttressed primarily by the emergence of beings with conscious purposes and meanings. Where there once was no meaning or purpose—in a universe without mind—there now are meanings and purposes. These meanings have their origin in the matter which coalesced into stars and planets, and which in turn supported organisms that evolved bodies with brains and their attributes—behavior, consciousness, personal identity, freedom, value, and meaning. Meaning has emerged in the evolutionary process. It came into being when complexly organized brains, consisting of constitutive parts and the interactive relationships between those parts, intermingled with physical and then cultural environments. This relationship was reciprocal—brains effected biological and cognitive environments which in turn affected those brains. The result of this interaction between organisms and environments was a reality that became, among other things, infused with meaning.

But will meaning continue to emerge as evolution moves forward? Will progressive evolutionary trends persevere to complete or final meaning, or to approaching meaning as a limit? Will the momentum of cognitive development make such progress nearly inevitable? These are different questions—ones which we cannot answer confidently. We could construct an inductive argument, that the past will resemble the future in this regard, but such an argument is not convincing. For who knows what will happen in the future? The human species might bring about its own ruin tomorrow or go extinct due to some biological, geophysical, or astronomical phenomenon. We cannot bridge the gap between what has happened and what will happen. The future is unknown.

And this leads naturally to another question. Is the emergence of meaning a good thing? It is easy enough to say that conscious beings create meaning, but it is altogether different to say that this is a good thing. Before consciousness no one derived meaning from torturing others, but now they sometimes do. In this case a new kind of meaning came to be, but few would wish for this outcome. Although we can establish the emergence of meaning, we cannot establish that this is good.

Still, we fantasize that our scientific knowledge will improve both the quality and quantity of life. We will make ourselves immortal, build ourselves better brains, and transform our moral natures—making life better and more meaningful, perhaps fully meaningful. We will become pilots worthy of steering evolution to fantastic heights, toward creating a heaven on earth or in simulated realities of our design. If meaning and value continue to emerge we will find meaning by partaking in, and hastening along, that meaningful process. As the result of past meanings and as the conduit for the emergence of future ones, we could be the protagonists of a great epic that ascends higher, as Huxley and Teilhard had hoped.

In our imagination we exist as links in a golden chain leading onward and upward toward greater levels of being, consciousness, joy, beauty, goodness, and meaning—perhaps even to their apex. As part of such a glorious process we would find meaning instilled into our lives from previously created meaning, and we would reciprocate by emanating meaning back into a universe with which we are ultimately one. Evolutionary thought, extended beyond its normal bounds, is an extraordinarily speculative, quasi-religious metaphysics in which a naturalistic heaven appears on the horizon.

18. Conclusion: Sobriety and Skepticism

Yet, as we ascend these mountains of thought, we are brought back to earth. When we look to the past we see that evolution has produced meaning, but it has also produced pain, fear, genocide, extinction, war, loneliness, anguish, envy, slavery, despair, futility, torture, guilt, anxiety, depression, alienation, ignorance, torture, inequality, superstition, poverty, heartache, death, and meaninglessness. *Surely serious reflection on this misery is sobering.* Turning to the future, our optimism must be similarly restrained. Fantasies about where evolution is headed should be tempered, if for no other reason than that our increased powers can be used for evil as well as for our improvement. Our wishes may never be fulfilled.

But this is not all. It is not merely that we cannot know if our splendid speculations are true—which we cannot—it is that we have an overwhelmingly strong reason to reject our flights of fancy. And that is that *humans are notorious pattern-seekers, story-tellers, and meaning-makers who invariably weave narratives around these patterns and stories to give meaning to their lives.* It follows that the patterns of progress we glimpse likely exist only in our minds. There is no face of a man on Mars or of Jesus on grilled cheese sandwiches. Finding patterns of progress in evolution, we are probably victims of simple confirmation bias.

After all progress is hardly the whole story of evolution, as most species and cultures have gone extinct, a fate that may soon befall us. Furthermore, as this immense universe (or multiverse) is largely incomprehensible to us, with our three and a half pound brains, we should hesitate to substitute an evolutionary-like religion for our frustrated metaphysical longings. We should be more reticent about advancing cosmic visions, and less credulous about believing in them. Our humility should temper our grandiose metaphysical speculations. *In short, if reflection on a scientific theory supposedly reveals that our deepest wishes are true, our skeptical alarm bell should go off.* If our searching easily finds precisely what we are looking for, we are likely moved by our wishes, not the implications of our science. We need to be braver than that. Like E.O. Wilson we want to know, not just to believe. In our job as serious seekers of the truth, the credulous need not apply.

In the end cosmic and biological evolution—and later the emergence of intelligence, science, and technology—leave us awestruck. The arrival of intelligence and the meaning it creates is important, an idea echoed by the physicist Paul Davies: "the existence of mind in some organism on some planet in the universe is surely a fact of fundamental significance. Through conscious beings the universe has generated self-awareness. This can be no trivial detail, no minor byproduct of mindless, purposeless forces. We are truly meant to be here."[39] Similar ideas reverberate in the work of the Cambridge evolutionary palaeobiologist and evangelical Christian, Simon Conway Morris. Morris argues that if intelligence had not developed in humans, it would have done so in another species—in other words, the emergence of intelligence on our planet was inevitable.[40]

We agree with both Davies and Morris that mind and its attendant phenomena are important, but it does not follow that we are therefore meant to be here or that intelligence was inevitable. It is only because we value our life and intelligence that we succumb to such anthropocentrism. Homo sapiens might easily have never been, as countless events could have led to their downfall. This fact alone should give us pause when we imbue our existence with undue significance. We were not inevitable, we were not meant to be here—we are serendipitous. The trillions and trillions of evolutionary machinations that led to us might easily have led to different results—and ones that didn't include us. As for the inevitability of intelligence, are we really to suppose that dinosaurs, had they not been felled by an asteroid, were on their way to human-like intelligence? Of course not, and such a view strains credulity. Dinosaurs were around for millions of years without developing greater intelligence. We want to believe evolution had us and our minds as it goal or central concern—but it did not—and we were not meant to be. We should forgo our penchant for detecting patters and accept our radical contingency. Like the dinosaurs, we too could be felled by an asteroid.[41]

Thus we cannot confidently answer all of the questions we posed at the beginning of this chapter in the affirmative. We can say that there has been some progress in evolution and that meaning has emerged in the process, but we cannot say these trends will continue, or that they were good. And we certainly must guard against speculative metaphysical fantasies, inasmuch as there are good reasons to think we are not special, however pleasant it may be to think otherwise. We do not know that a meaningful eschatology will gradually unfold as we evolve, much less that we could articulate a cosmic vision to describe it. *We don't even know if the reality of any grand cosmic vision is possible.* We are moving, but we might be moving toward our own extinction, toward universal death, or toward eternal hell. And none of those offer much comfort.

We long to dream but always our skepticism awakens us from our Pollyannaish imaginings. The evolution of the cosmos, our species, and our intelligence gives us some grounds for believing that life might become more meaningful, but not enough to satisfy our longings. For we want to *really* believe that tomorrow will be better than yesterday. We want to believe with Kurzweil and Moravec, with Teilhard and Huxley, that a glorious future awaits but, detached from our romanticism, we know that the Monod may be right—there may be no salvation, there may be nothing over the rainbow, there may be no comfort to be found for our harassed souls. Confronted with such meager prospects and the anguish that accompanies them, we are lost, and the most we can do, once again, is hope. That doesn't give us what we want or need, but it does give us something we don't have to be ashamed of. There is nothing irrational about the kind of hope that is elicited by, and best expressed from, an evolutionary perspective. Julian Huxley, scientist and poet, best conveyed these hopes.

I turn the handle and the story starts:
Reel after reel is all astronomy,
Till life, enkindled in a niche of sky,
Leaps on the stage to play a million parts.

Life leaves the slime and through the oceans darts;
She conquers earth, and raises wings to fly; Then spirit
blooms, and learns how not to die,
Nesting beyond the grave in others' hearts.

I turn the handle; other men like me
Have made the film; and now I sit and look
In quiet, privileged like Divinity
To read the roaring world as in a book.
If this thy past, where shall thy future climb,
O Spirit, built of Elements and Time![42]

CHAPTER 10 – CONCLUSION

Zorba: Why do the young die?
Why does anybody die?
Basil: I don't know.
Zorba: What's the use of all your damn books?
If they don't tell you that,
what the hell do they tell you?
Basil: They tell me about the agony of men
who can't answer questions like yours.
Zorba: I spit on this agony.
~ Nikos Kazantzakis (from *Zorba the Greek*)

1. A Recap of Our Journey

We declared at the outset that life is problematic—there is something amiss in life. We have concentrated on the problem of meaning and on proposed religious, philosophical, and scientific solutions to our quandary. We have found religious answers to be generally unsatisfying as they depend on problematic philosophical assumptions; moreover, even if religious claims are true, they seem largely irrelevant to our concerns. Turning to philosophy, we could not initially accept agnosticism, since we were forced by constraints of consistency to be skeptical of our own skepticism. Nihilism haunts us, and no amount of philosophizing is palliative in its wake. Yet we reject it too, for why accept such a depressing conclusion when we cannot be any more sure of its truth than of Pollyannaish religious assertions?

Subjectivism is a more promising philosophical response—we can create limited meaning without accepting religious, agnostic, or nihilistic provisos. The main problem is the meaning created doesn't seem to be enough; we want more than just subjective meaning. This led us to consider objective values and meanings external to us. In the meeting of subjective desires and objectively good things, we may have found the most meaning we can in this life; given our current state of intellectual and moral development and the present reality of the human condition. In the present we derive the limited meaning life offers by attraction to, and engagement in, the really good things of life.

Nevertheless, our musings fall short—because we die. How can anything matter, even subjective immersion in objectively good things, if all leads to nothingness? True, things may have mattered while they were happening, but the present is too fleeting for this to be enough. If reality ends in nothingness, all was for naught. Yet we have a reprieve; *science may grant us immortality, ultimately giving us the power to decide the fate of both ourselves and the universe.* In that case life could be made completely meaningful. Unfortunately we do not know if our science will succeed in this regard, or that it will defeat death soon enough for us, or even that immortality will provide the meaning we desire. We have no guarantees. Such considerations led us to ask if evolution unfolds progressively, toward greater meaning, according to a trajectory that leads to higher levels of being, consciousness, goodness, and meaning. (If true, this would bolster the case for meaning immensely.) These are attractive ideas and ones the credulous readily accept. But we cannot. We must be intellectually honest, proportioning our assent to the evidence while rejecting dubious metaphysical speculation; no matter how emotionally appealing we find it.

Lacking a definitive solution to our problem, perhaps we need to supplement these intellectual findings with *something else* in order to better satisfy our desire for meaning. It is to such considerations that we turn.

2. Optimism and Hope; Wishes and Longings

Thus we turn to optimism and hope to enhance our limited intellectual replies. Perhaps an optimistic or hopeful disposition is the missing ingredient in our search for meaning. We have hinted throughout our treatise that part of the solution to our problem may come from optimism or hope. But what is optimism, and what is hope? The American Heritage Dictionary of the English Language defines optimism as: "A tendency to expect the best possible outcome or dwell on the most hopeful aspects of a situation." In neither of these senses are we optimists. We do not *expect* our most fervent wishes to come true, nor do we *dwell* on the most hopeful possibilities. Might hope be the proper supplement instead? The same source defines hope as: "To wish for something with expectation of its fulfillment. To look forward to with confidence or expectation." In neither of these senses do we have hope. We have wishes and longings, but we do not *expect* them to be fulfilled. To expect is to look forward to a probable occurrence, but we don't claim that the objects of our hopes will be actualized. Optimism or hope may be useful, but we will not subscribe to them—and they don't answer our *questions*. Having neither optimism nor hope to what else may we appeal?

We could appeal to our wishes and longings. We wish that life made sense; we long for life to be worth the trouble. But to wish that life is meaningful does *not* imply that we believe, have faith in, anticipate, expect, or hope that life is meaningful. Instead we just wish, want, desire, or long for meaning. Wishes and longings are less amenable to criticism than optimism or hope because the former don't imply expectations. Our wishes and longings exist exclusively in the realm of emotions, and are thereby immune from most intellectual criticism. After all there is nothing irrational about flipping a coin and wishing for a certain outcome, anymore than it is irrational to wish we win a lottery! We may know the chances of winning are remote, but as long as it's possible to win, there is nothing wrong with wanting a certain outcome. It's stupid to think that we'll win a typical lottery, or to plan our life as if we'll win, but surely it is permissible to *want* to win. Similarly one can maintain intellectual integrity yet wish that life has meaning. So it seems we can live *as if* live has meaning even though we don't know that for sure.

So our wishes and longings are relatively immune from intellectual critique, inasmuch as they exist in the affective domain. I wish for meaning and that's all; there is nothing incoherent about wanting. The problem with wishes and wants is that they don't answer *questions* about the meaning of life. They may satisfy our emotions and be pragmatically useful, but they leave the intellect starved. Their cognitive content has been so watered down that their hardly worth the trouble. Vague wishes don't provide much comfort anyway, and even if they did we want some reasonable assurance that our wishes could come true. But we have no such assurances. Emotions satisfy emotionally, but our intellectual skepticism destabilizes them. In the end, wishes and longings help us no more than did optimism and hope. If we have no answers, wishing that we do does not help.

3. Alfred Lord Tennyson: The Struggles of Ulysses

Maybe the key is not in our answers, our hopes, or our wishes, but in our struggles. This is a salient theme in Homer's epic poem *The Odyssey*, which tells the story of Odysseus, the king of Ithaca, and his ten year journey home after the end of the ten year long Trojan War. Odysseus' tribulations on his homeward journey are legendary, as he battles giants, monsters, storms, and the sirens of beautiful women who call sailors to their death. After finally reaching home, reunited with his wife and his kingdom, Homer suggests that Odysseus desired to leave again, an idea picked up centuries later by Dante.

In the nineteenth century Alfred Lord Tennyson (1809 – 1892) expanded on this theme. Tennyson was the Poet Laureate of the United Kingdom during much of Queen Victoria's reign, and one of the most popular poets in the English language. His poem *Ulysses*, Odysseus' name in Latin, famously captured Ulysses' dissatisfaction with life in Ithaca after his return, and his subsequent desire to set sail again. Perhaps nothing in Western literature conveys the feeling of going forward and braving the struggle of life more movingly than this poem.

Tennyson begins by describing the boredom and restlessness Ulysses experiences after finally returning to rule his kingdom.

> It little profits that an idle king,
> By this still hearth, among these barren crags,
> Matched with an aged wife, I mete and dole
> Unequal laws unto a savage race,
> That hoard, and sleep, and feed, and know not me.

Contrast these sentiments with his excitement that his memories elicit.

> I cannot rest from travel: I will drink
> Life to the lees: all times I have enjoyed
> Greatly, have suffered greatly, both with those
> That loved me, and alone; on shore, and when
> Through scudding drifts the rainy Hyades
> Vexed the dim sea: I am become a name;
> For always roaming with a hungry heart
> Much have I seen and known; cities of men

And manners, climates, councils, governments,
Myself not least, but honoured of them all;
And drunk delight of battle with my peers;
Far on the ringing plains of windy Troy.

He's nostalgic about his past, but he also longs for new experiences. He describes his restlessness perfectly:

I am a part of all that I have met;
Yet all experience is an arch wherethrough
Gleams that untravelled world, whose margin fades
For ever and for ever when I move.
How dull it is to pause, to make an end,
To rust unburnished, not to shine in use!
As though to breathe were life.

Looking toward the sea with a restless heart, he again feels its pull.

There lies the port; the vessel puffs her sail:
There gloom the dark broad seas. My mariners,
Souls that have toiled, and wrought, and thought
with me—
That ever with a frolic welcome took
The thunder and the sunshine, and opposed
Free hearts, free foreheads—you and I are old;
Old age hath yet his honour and his toil;
Death closes all: but something ere the end,
Some work of noble note, may yet be done,
Not unbecoming men that strove with Gods.

Finally, he gathers his fellow sailors and pushes out of the harbor for new adventures. Tennyson describes the scene and the sentiment with some of the greatest lines in the English language.

The lights begin to twinkle from the rocks:
The long day wanes: the slow moon climbs: the deep
Moans round with many voices. Come, my friends,
'Tis not too late to seek a newer world.
Push off, and sitting well in order smite
The sounding furrows; for my purpose holds

To sail beyond the sunset, and the baths
Of all the western stars, until I die.
It may be that the gulfs will wash us down:
It may be we shall touch the Happy Isles,
And see the great Achilles, whom we knew
Though much is taken, much abides; and though
We are not now that strength which in old days
Moved earth and heaven; that which we are, we are;
One equal temper of heroic hearts,
Made weak by time and fate, but strong in will
To strive, to seek, to find, and not to yield.

Ulysses found joy and meaning, not in port, but in his journeys, in the dark troubled sea of life which tosses us as we wrestle against it. There we find the thrill and the meaning of our lives as we battle without hope of ever finding a home. For Ulysses, the struggle was the meaning.

4. Nikos Kazantzakis: A Rejection of Hope

The power of the story of Ulysses was picked up by the famous Greek novelist Nikos Kazantzakis (1883 – 1957), who wrote a 33,333 line sequel to Homer's poem. In it the bored Ulysses gathers his followers, builds a boat, and sails away on a final journey, eventually dying in the Antarctic. According to Kazantzakis, Ulysses does not find what he's seeking, but it doesn't matter. Through the search itself he is ennobled—and the meaning of his life was found in the search. In the end his Ulysses cry out "My soul, your voyages have been your native land."[1]

Perhaps no one thought deeper about longings, hope, and the meaning of life than Kazantzakis. In his early years he was particularly impressed with Nietzsche's Dionysian vision of humans shaping themselves into the superman, and with Bergson's idea of the *elan vital*. From Nietzsche he learned that by sheer force of will humans can be free as long as they proceed without fear or hope of reward. From Bergson, under whom he studied in Paris, he came to believe that a vital evolutionary life force molds matter, potentially creating higher forms of life. Putting these ideas together, Kazantzakis declared that we find the meaning of life by struggling against universal entropy, an idea he connected with god. For Kazantzakis the word god referred to "the anti-entropic life-force that organizes elemental matter into systems that can manifest ever more subtle and advanced forms of beings and consciousness."[2] The meaning of our lives is to find our place in the chain that links us with these undreamt of forms of life.

> We all ascend together, swept up by a mysterious and invisible urge. Where are we going? No one knows. Don't ask, mount higher! Perhaps we are going nowhere, perhaps there is no one to pay us the rewarding wages of our lives. So much the better! For thus may we conquer the last, the greatest of all temptations—that of Hope.[3]

The honest and brave struggle without hope or expectation that they will ever arrive, ever be anchored, ever be at home. Like Ulysses, the only home Kazantzakis found was in the search itself. The meaning of life is found in the search and the struggle.

In the prologue of his autobiography, *Report to Greco*, Kazantzakis claims that we need to go beyond both hope and despair. Both expectation of paradise and fear of hell prevent us from focusing on what is in front of us, our heart's true homeland … the search for meaning itself. We ought to be warriors who struggle bravely to create meaning without expecting anything in return. Unafraid of the abyss, we should face it bravely and run toward it. Ultimately we find joy by taking full responsibility for our lives— joyous in the face of tragedy. Life is essentially struggle, and if in the end it judges us we should bravely reply:

> General, the battle draws to a close and I make my report. This is where and how I fought. I fell wounded, lost heart, but did not desert. Though my teeth clattered from fear, I bound my forehead tightly with a red handkerchief to hide the blood, and ran to the assault."[4]

Surely that is as courageous a sentiment in response to the ordeal of human life as has been offered in world literature. It is a bold rejoinder to the awareness of the inevitable decline of our minds and bodies, as well as to the existential agonies that permeate life. It finds the meaning of life in our actions, our struggles, our battles, our roaming, our wandering, and our journeying. It appeals to nothing other than what we know and experience—and yet finds meaning and contentment there.

Just outside the city walls of Heraklion Crete one can visit Kazantzakis' gravesite, located there as the Orthodox Church denied his being buried in a Christian cemetery. On the black, jagged, cracked, unpolished Cretan marble you will find no name to designate who lies there, no dates of birth or death, only an epitaph in Greek carved in the stone. It translates: "I hope for nothing. I fear nothing. I am free."

5. Andre Maurois: Finding Meaning in Living

Picking up on the theme found in both Tennyson and Kazantzakis, the French author Andre Maurois (1885 -1967) wrote that the meaning of life is found nowhere else but in our living struggles, in the experience and activity of life. To illustrate he tells the story of a group of Englishmen who establish a colony on the moon, but do not hear anything from the Earth for many generations. Some of their descendents now doubt the story of a king who lives on the earthly orb they see in the night sky, others still believe. Then a philosopher among them utters:

> Why search for the meaning of life outside of life itself? The King of whom our legends speak—does he exist? I do not know, and it does not matter. I know that the mountains of the moon are beautiful when the crescent of the earth illuminates them. If the King remains, as always since my birth, invisible and silent, I shall doubt his reality; but I shall not doubt life, or the beauty of the moment, or the happiness of action. Sophists teach you today that life is only a brief moment in the trajectory of a star; they tell you that nothing is certain except defeat and death. As for me, I tell you that nothing exists except victory and life. What shall we know of death? Either the soul is immortal and we shall not die, or it perishes with the flesh and we shall not know that we are dead. Live, then, as if you were eternal, and do not believe that your life is changed merely because it seems proved that the Earth is [the Heavens are] empty. You do not live in the Earth [the Heavens], you live in yourself.[5]

Maurois also tells another story of a philosophical ant who

discovers that there is no Great Ant above all others; and that hers is one among millions of ant heaps which are just drops of mud in an endless universe. This philosophical ant counsels her sisters to stop working, to stop being slaves, as life is apparently pointless. To this a young ant replies "This is all very well sister, but we must build our tunnel."[6] We find meaning it seems, in what's in front of us.

Maurois' insights preview those of another Frenchman, Albert Camus. When a priest visits Meursault—the protagonist of Camus' novel *The Stranger*—before Meusault's impending execution and makes metaphysical promises, Meursault responds "none of his [a priest's] certainties were worth one strand of a woman's hair." Camus sees that abstract ideas bring about a distance from the world; they draw us away from the actual. But we must always come back to the commonplace for meaning, to what surrounds us, to what we previously called the ordinary extraordinary. No theory or abstract truths mitigate existential realities. He also put the point clearly in his essay *Summer in Algiers*. There amidst sea, sun, sand, and sex he mused: "Between this sky and these faces turned toward it, nothing on which to hang a mythology, a literature, an ethic, or a religion, but stones, flesh, stars, and those truths the hand can touch."[7]

6. Will Durant: Finding Meaning in Everything

Will Durant wondered if there is something suggestive about the cycle of a human life which sheds light on meaning, a theme explored in his 1929 book *The Mansions of Philosophy*. He grants that "life is in its basis a mystery, a river flowing from an unseen source; and in its development an infinite subtlety too complex for thought, much less for utterance."[8] Yet we seek answers nonetheless. Undeterred by the difficulty of his task, Durant suggests that reflection on the microcosm of a human life might yield insights about the meaning of all life and death. Thus he looks at a typical human life cycle for clues about cosmic meaning.

In children Durant saw curiosity, growth, urgency, playfulness, and discontent. In later youth the struggle continues as we learn to read, work, love, and learn of the world's evils. In middle age we are often consumed by work and family life, and for the first time we see the reality of death. Still, in family life people usually find great pleasure, and the best of all human conditions.

In old age the reality of death comes nearer. If we have lived well we might graciously leave the stage for better players to perform a better play. But what if life endlessly repeats its sufferings, with youth making the same mistakes as their elders, and all leading to death? Is this the final realization of old age? Such thoughts gnaw at our heart and poison aging.

So Durant wonders if we must die for life. If we are not individuals but cells in life's body, then we die so that life remains strong, death removing the rubbish as the new life created defeats death. This perpetuation of life gives life meaning. "If it is one test of philosophy to give life a meaning that shall frustrate death, wisdom will show that corruption comes only to the part, that life itself is deathless while we die."[9] So the individual dies, but life goes on endlessly forward. Durant paints the most moving and poignant image to describe the cycle of life and death that I know of in all of world literature.

> Here is an old man on the bed of death, harassed with helpless friends and wailing relatives. What a terrible sight it is - this thin frame with loosened and cracking flesh, this toothless mouth in a bloodless face, this tongue that cannot speak, these eyes that cannot see! To this pass youth has come, after all its hopes and trials; to this pass middle age, after all its torment and its toil. To this pass health and strength and joyous rivalry; this arm once struck great blows and fought for victory in virile games. To this pass knowledge, science, wisdom: for seventy years this man with pain and effort gathered knowledge; his brain became the storehouse of a varied experience, the center of a thousand subtleties of thought and deed; his heart through suffering learned gentleness as his mind learned understanding; seventy years he grew from an animal into a man capable of seeking truth and creating beauty. But death is upon him, poisoning him, choking him, congealing his blood, gripping his heart, bursting his brain, rattling in his throat. Death wins

> Outside on the green boughs birds twitter, and Chantecler sings his hymn to the sun. Light streams across the fields; buds open and stalks confidently lift their heads; the sap mounts in the trees. Here are children: what is it that makes them so joyous,

running madly over the dew-wet grass, laughing, calling, pursuing, eluding, panting for breath, inexhaustible? What energy, what spirit and happiness! What do they care about death? They will learn and grow and love and struggle and create, and lift life up one little notch, perhaps, before they die. And when they pass they will cheat death with children, with parental care that will make their offspring finer than themselves. There in the garden's twilight lovers pass, thinking themselves unseen; their quiet words mingle with the murmur of insects calling to their mates; the ancient hunger speaks through eager and through lowered eyes, and a noble madness courses through clasped hands and touching lips. Life wins.[10]

This is stirring prose, but we remain forlorn. Perhaps we should give up our ego attachment, and leave for the sake of the species. But why? What's wrong with loving life so much that one never wants to let go? Besides it is wasteful for life to start over each time, having to relearn old truths and unlearn old falsehoods. As for life winning, it may instead destroy itself, and even if it doesn't we will not survive as individuals. In the end nothing in Durant's portrait soothes our worries about the futility of an infinite repetition.

In 1930 Durant received a number of letters from persons declaring their intent to commit suicide. They asked Durant, by that time a popular public intellectual, for reasons to go on living. In his book *On the Meaning of Life* (1932) Durant tried to answer their queries by extending the theme found in Tennyson, Kazantzakis, and Maurois. He suggests that we cannot answer the question in any absolute sense, for our minds are too small to comprehend things in their entirety. Nonetheless he does believe we can say a few things about terrestrial meaning:

The meaning of life, then, must lie within itself ... it must be sought in life's own instinctive cravings and natural fulfillments. Why, for example, should we ask for an ulterior meaning to vitality and health? ... If you are sick beyond cure I will grant you viaticum, and let you die ... But if you are well—if you can stand on your legs and digest your food—forget your whining, and shout your gratitude to the sun.

The simplest meaning of life then is joy—the exhilaration of experience itself, of physical well-being; sheer satisfaction of muscle and sense, of palate and ear and eye. If the child is happier than the man it is because it has more body and less soul, and understands that nature comes before philosophy; it asks for no further meaning to its arms and legs than their abounding use ... Even if life had no meaning except for its moments of beauty ... that would be enough; this plodding thru the rain, or fighting the wind, or tramping the snow under sun, or watching the twilight turn into night, is reason a-plenty for loving life.[11]

We should be particularly thankful for our fellows; they are a primary reason for loving life.

> Do not be so ungrateful about love ... to the attachment of friends and mates who have gone hand in hand through much hell, some purgatory, and a little heaven, and have been soldered into unity by being burned together in the flame of life. I know such mates or comrades quarrel regularly, and get upon each other's nerves; but there is ample recompense for that in the unconscious consciousness that someone is interested in you, depends upon you, exaggerates you, and is waiting to meet you at the station. Solitude is worse than war.[12]

Love relates the individual to something more than itself, to some whole which gives it purpose.

> I note that those who are cooperating parts of a whole do not despond; the despised "yokel" playing ball with his fellows in the lot is happier than these isolated thinkers, who stand aside from the game of life and degenerate through the separation ... If we think of ourselves as part of a living ... group, we shall find life a little fuller ... For to give life a meaning one must have a purpose larger and more enduring than one's self.

> If ... a thing has significance only through its relation as part to a larger whole, then, though we cannot give a metaphysical and universal meaning to all life in general, we can say of any life in the particular that its meaning lies in its relation to something larger than itself ... ask the father of sons and daughters "What is the meaning of life?" and he will answer you very simply: "Feeding our family."[13]

Durant too finds meaning in love, connection, and activity. "The secret of significance and content is to have a task which consumes all one's energies, and makes human life a little richer than before."[14] Durant found the most happiness in his family and his work, in his home and his books. Although no one can be fully happy amidst poverty and suffering, one can be content and grateful finding the meaning in front of them. "Where, in the last resort, does my treasure lie?—in everything."[15]

7. The Purpose of Our Lives

After our survey of religious, philosophical, and scientific ideas about the meaning of life, here are our conclusions.

First *we affirm that religious solutions to the problem of meaning in life are deeply problematic and largely irrelevant.* As for religion's near universal appeal, evolutionary biology and cultural conditioning provide the best explanation—religious belief bestowed a survival advantage to our ancestors or to their genes, a fact only exacerbated by the proliferation of religious memes cleverly designed to repel the invasion of rivals. This mixture of genes and environment make religious beliefs and its comforts irresistible for most, especially in a world full of existential anguish. This explains the ubiquity of religious beliefs.

But the advance of science and technology, with the concomitant extension of lifespan and eventual elimination of death, will render religion passé. If humans no longer fear death—the wellspring of much religious belief—and if other physical and mental limitations have been largely overcome, the ancient stories will be forgotten. In a world of unlimited life spans, of mastery of atom and cell, of remarkably powerful machines, of augmented and artificial intelligence—and perhaps in a universe teeming with an unimaginable quantity and diversity of life forms—ancient myths and legends, as well as sophisticated arguments for invisible, godlike creatures, will lose their influence. Neither intelligent aliens nor our post-human descendents will believe that Jesus or Mohammed is the answer. To the extent that humans fail to put old myths behind them, they impede progress and delay an increase of meaning. *Thus humanity needs to outgrow religion and accept responsibility for creating, discovering, and increasing meaning in life.*

Second *we affirm that meaning emerges through the interaction of conscious subjects and the objective natural world.* This means that the subjectivist and objectivist are each partially correct. Subjects *create* meaning in the context of an objective reality which is amenable to such creation, and do this in different ways corresponding to their unique subjectivity. (Like a mosaic whose pieces can fit together differently and still be meaningful, two persons can live differently and both live meaningfully.) Subjects also can be said to *find* meaning because objective reality contains this possibility. Subjects find meaning in similar things because they share a human nature which exists in an objective reality. (Like a puzzle where the pieces fit together in only one way, individuals find meaning by uncovering objective values that are shared by beings like themselves.)

This means that people generally find happiness, joy, engagement, purpose, fulfillment, and meaning through subjective engagement with objectively good things such as: loving relationships, pleasurable activities, helping others, productive work, seeking knowledge, aesthetic enjoyment and so forth. Objective reality imposes limits on the ways subjects create meaning; yet, at the same time, subjects determine whether the potential for meaning in reality is actualized. Therefore m*eaning arises when conscious subjects bring forth the potential for meaning that exists in an objective reality.*

Third *we affirm that the possibility of more meaningful lives increases proportionate to the extent we overcome subjective and objective limitations in human life.* This implies a moral imperative to diminish and, if possible, ultimately abolish all constraints on our being—intellectual, emotional, psychological, physical, and moral—in order to render our lives as meaningful as possible. It also involves remaking the external world in ways conducive to the emergence of meaning. We should reconstruct both ourselves and the world. Thus we should embrace our role as protagonists of the evolutionary epic, working to increase the quantity and quality of knowledge, love, joy, beauty, goodness and meaning in the world, while diminishing their opposites. *This is the ultimate purpose of our lives.*

8. The Limits of Purpose

Nonetheless knowing the purpose of life does not ensure that life is meaningful, for we may collectively fail in our mission to give life more meaning; we may not achieve our purpose. Instead of remaking the world for the better, we could destroy ourselves, leaving behind a dark, cold, lonely universe to expand forever without the light of consciousness or joy or beauty—until *everything* finally passes away. Or, even worse, we might create and perpetuate a horrific future. All may be for naught or all may be for ill, and no amount of thinking changes that fact. We know what we should do, but we don't know if we will succeed. In other words, our lives could have a purpose, but not have a meaning.

Moreover, intellectual reflection never fully dispels our deepest existential concerns. For the movement of time spoils even those things that make us happy and which, for the moment, give our lives purpose. This passage of time haunts us; that perpetual perishing which diminishes our joy by its intrusion into the present. This radical impermanence, and our consciousness of it, reminds us that our own demise rushes toward us as the present recedes away. The awareness of our impending doom is a constant companion capable of poisoning our momentary happiness, leading in turn to the inevitable realization that it not just we who may die, but our children, and their children, and all children, and everything else. Knowing what we should do—fulfill our purpose—does not fully gratify.

9. Living More and Thinking Less

Reaching the limits of the intellect's power to dissuade our existential fears, we previously turned to hopes and wishes. They have their benefits; they beget thinking about better worlds and often incite action. Still, we found that our hopes rely on expectations our intellects cannot confirm, and dreams mostly bypass our intellects altogether. Such concerns led us to the emotive poetry and prose of Tennyson, Kazantzakis, Maurois, and Durant, who talked not of intellectual ideas or blind hopes and wishes, but of meaning found through the crucible of journeying, struggling, playing and loving. They each offered an exuberant affirmation of the meaning found *in* life's activities.

This insight is profound. As we review this work we are struck by the stark contrast between the somber tone of our philosophical musings and the joy we feel through our immersion in the world of the senses. In the mountains and oceans we see, in the walks we take and the meals we eat, in the joy we find in physical play and philosophical talk, and in the warmth we feel when surrounded by those that love us and whom we love, *there we don't so much find meaning as transcend the need for it.* At those times life is sufficient unto itself. When we laugh and play and love, all the misery of the world momentarily vanishes. We hardly give meaning a thought. And if thought brings existential anguish back again—perhaps we can and should think less. In short, we *live deeper than we can think.*

10. Can We Think Less? Should We Think Less?

But is living with less thinking a realistic antidote? *Can* we live this way after reflectivity has become interwoven into our natures? Can we live constantly in motion, so that troubling thoughts do not disturb? No, we cannot suppress our most important questions indefinitely. For after laughing and playing and loving, thought returns. What is happiness so fleeting? Why must we suffer and die? What if all is for naught? We cannot avoid our questions for long; eventually we drop our guard and they return.

But even if we could avoid our deepest questions, *should* we? We think not. Our questions bring forth the deep reservoir of our inner life that is often hidden from normal viewing. Moreover, our curiosity and inquisitiveness ennoble us, differentiating us from less conscious beings. Our thinking may not make us happy, but it gives us a deep and rich interior life. However much we love the world of body and sense, thought is our salient feature. We should not repress it. And, since we cannot and should not evade our questions, the prescription to find meaning in activity only partially satisfies. No matter what we think or do, our questions remain.

11. How Then Do We Live?

Nothing then completely silences all our doubts and soothes all our worries —not the limited meaning life offers us, not the knowledge of our purpose, not the promise of hope, not the engagement in activity—unless death silences us forever. How then do we proceed? We must accept something of our present life lest resentment cause us to curse it; yet, at the same time, we must reject the present or nothing will improve. This creative tension admits the limitations of reality as a starting point while rebelling against its shortcomings. It involves working to mold, create, and increase meaning. We don't know that reality will progress, but if we partially accept our present reality, if we dream of a future without limits and struggle to bring it about, we may increase meaning in the world.

Yet for now we are forced to live with uncertainty and angst, as a testimony to our intellectual honesty and emotional integrity. Unlike those who adopt blind faith or accept easy answers, we scorn the facile resolutions of the cowardly. And if we must die, we will die as free people who did not yield to the forces that sought to destroy them from the moment of their birth. Those are the forces we seek to defeat, but which have not yet been defeated. In the meantime, *we should relish the limited joy and meaning life offers, work to eliminate human limitations, and suppress negative thoughts as best we can.* This is no solution, only a way to live.

12. Is Life Ultimately Meaningful?

We know our purpose, and we know how best to live. But is life ultimately meaningful? Could it be fully meaningful?

If all good things come to be infinitely or are approached as limits, if individuals somehow participate in this being or becoming, and if this somehow makes up for all past evil, then we could say that life, seen from the eternal perspective was profoundly meaningful. However, if consciousness ceases to be, our lives were completely and utterly meaningless. And if life degenerates toward greater ignorance, ugliness, and suffering, then life was not only meaningless but evil. In that case it is better that life end quickly, and better still if it had never been at all. Thus we cannot yet know if our lives are ultimately meaningful, somewhat meaningful, utterly meaningless, or purely evil. Such answers will reveal themselves, if ever, only in the far distant future.

Thus the final answer to our initial question—is life ultimately meaningful—is that *we know how life could be ultimately meaningful, but we do not know if it is or will be ultimately meaningful.* It will become fully meaningful only if we fulfill our purpose by making it so. Therefore, despite our best efforts, we have not found all we were looking for. We cannot erase all our doubts; we cannot allay all our fears. In the end we have no assurances and the abyss, as much as we wish otherwise, always accompanies us. Between eternal light and infinite darkness we navigate on a razor's edge. We are adrift, and we must save ourselves.

13. Bertrand Russell: Afterword

We end with some words from Bertrand Russell, in our view the greatest philosopher of the twentieth-century. His last manuscript, which remained unpublished for more than twenty years after his death, was an untitled one-page essay that Russell annotated "1967." At that time it was written Russell was 95 years old, and rumored to be senile or at least no longer capable of coherent writing. The hand written page proved otherwise, displaying a lucidity of style that eludes most writers at their peak. It began: "The time has come to review my life as a whole, and to ask whether it has served any useful purpose or has been wholly concerned in futility. Unfortunately, no answer is possible for anyone who does not know the future." After so many years of study, an answer to the most important question we can ask was not forthcoming. Yet a glimmer of optimism remained. The final sentences ever written from the pen of one of Western civilizations great writers and philosophers looked—as we have—to the future.

> Consider for a moment what our planet is and what it might be. At present, for most, there is toil and hunger, constant danger, more hatred than love. There could be a happy world, where co-operation was more in evidence than competition, and monotonous work is done by machines, where what is lovely in nature is not destroyed to make room for hideous machines whose sole business is to kill, and where to promote joy is more respected than to produce mountains of corpses. Do not say this is impossible: it is not. It waits only for men to desire it more than the infliction of torture.
>
> There is an artist imprisoned in each one of us. Let him loose to spread joy everywhere.[16]

END NOTES

Chapter 1

[1] Albert Camus, "The Myth of Sisyphus," in The Meaning of Life, ed. E.D Klemke and Steven Cahn (Oxford : Oxford University Press, 2008), 72.

[2] Karl Jaspers, *Nietzsche* (Tucson: University of Arizona, 1965), 333.

[3] Victor Frankl, *Man's Search for Meaning* (New York: Beacon Press, 1963).

[4] Robert Solomon, *The Big Questions* (Boston: Wadsworth, 2010), 44.

[5] Aristotle made a similar point about the subject matter of ethics in the *Nicomachean Ethics,* Book I, Chapter III.

[6] Antonio Damasio, *Descartes' Error: Emotion, Reason, and the Human Brain* (New York: Harper Perennial, 1995).

[7] Joshua D. Greene, "The Secret Joke of Kant's soul," in *Moral Psychology, Vol. 3: The Neuroscience of Morality*, ed. W. Sinnott-Armstrong (Cambridge, MA: MIT Press, 2008).

[8] Sigmund Freud, *The Letters of Sigmund Freud* (New York: Basic Books, 1960), 436.

[9] Thaddeus Metz, "Happiness and Meaningfulness: Some Key Differences," in *Philosophy and Happiness*, ed. Lisa Bortolotti (New York: Palgrave Macmillan, 2009).

[10] James Baldwin, *The Fire Next Time* (New York: Vintage, 1992).

[11] I would argue that philosophy does not discover truth, science does. Philosophy should concern itself with values and meaning. For more see Jean Piaget's *The Insights and Illusions of Philosophy* (New York: Routledge & Kegan Paul, 1977).

[12] God may be a problem in astrophysics that will stand or fall on the empirical evidence. For more see E.O. Wilson's "The Biological Basis of Morality" in the Atlantic online April 1998.

[13] The phrase "god of the gaps" refers to the idea that the gods exist in the gaps of current scientific knowledge. The term is generally derogative; i.e., critical of the attempt to use gods to explain phenomena that as yet do not have naturalistic explanations.

[14] This claim is so easy to verify one could construct a separate biography of hundreds of works by experts to justify the claim. You could begin simply by consulting the multiple publications and statements at the website of the National Academy of Sciences. http://www.nationalacademies.org/evolution/Reports.html

[15] For an introduction to this idea see E.O. Wilson's *On Human Nature* (Cambridge: Harvard University Press, 1988), and *Consilience: The Unity of Knowledge* (New York: Vintage, 1999).

Chapter 2

[1] http://christianity.about.com/od/denominations/p/christiantoday.htm

[2] Leo Tolstoy, "My Confession," in *The Meaning of Life*, ed. E.D Klemke and Steven Cahn (Oxford: Oxford University Press, 2008), 9.

[3] Tolstoy, "My Confession," 10.

[4] Tolstoy, "My Confession," 12.

[5] Tolstoy, "My Confession," 13.

[6] Tolstoy, "My Confession," 14.

[7] David Swenson, "The Dignity of Human Life," in *The Meaning of Life*, ed. E.D Klemke and Steven Cahn (Oxford: Oxford University Press, 2008), 17.

[8] Swenson, "The Dignity of Human Life," 18.

[9] Swenson, "The Dignity of Human Life," 18.

[10] Swenson, "The Dignity of Human Life," 19.

[11] Swenson, "The Dignity of Human Life," 19.

[12] Swenson, "The Dignity of Human Life," 22.

[13] Swenson, "The Dignity of Human Life," 23.

[14] Louis Pojman, "Religion Gives Meaning to Life," in *The Meaning of Life*, ed. E.D Klemke and Steven Cahn (Oxford: Oxford University Press, 2008), 27.

[15] Pojman, "Religion Gives Meaning to Life," 28.

[16] Pojman, "Religion Gives Meaning to Life," 28.

[17] Pojman, "Religion Gives Meaning to Life," 28.

[18] Pojman, "Religion Gives Meaning to Life," 28.

[19] Pojman, "Religion Gives Meaning to Life," 29.

[20] Pojman, "Religion Gives Meaning to Life," 29.

[21] Pojman, "Religion Gives Meaning to Life," 29.

[22] Pojman, "Religion Gives Meaning to Life," 29.

[23] Pojman, "Religion Gives Meaning to Life," 30.

[24] Pojman, "Religion Gives Meaning to Life," 30.

[25] Reinhold Niebuhr, "The Self and Its Search for Ultimate Meaning," in *The Meaning of Life*, ed. E.D Klemke (Oxford: Oxford University Press, 1981), 41.

[26] Niebuhr, "The Self and Its Search for Ultimate Meaning," 43.

[27] Niebuhr, "The Self and Its Search for Ultimate Meaning," 50.

[28] Niebuhr, "The Self and Its Search for Ultimate Meaning," 51.

[29] Niebuhr, "The Self and Its Search for Ultimate Meaning," 51.

[30] Philip Quinn, "The Meaning of Life According to Christianity," in *The Meaning of Life*, ed. E.D Klemke and Steven Cahn (Oxford: Oxford University Press, 2008) 38.

[31] Quinn, "The Meaning of Life According to Christianity," 40.

[32] John Cottingham, *On the Meaning of Life* (London: Routledge, 2003).
[33] William Lane Craig, "The Absurdity of Life without God," in *The Meaning of Life*, ed. E.D Klemke (Oxford: Oxford University Press, 2000).
[34] Thomas V. Morris, *Making Sense of it All: Pascal and the Meaning of Life* (Grand Rapids: William E. Eardman's Publishing Company, 1992).
[35] Morris, Making Sense of it all: Pascal and the Meaning of Life, 56.
[36] Morris, Making Sense of it all: Pascal and the Meaning of Life, 59.
[37] Morris, Making Sense of it all: Pascal and the Meaning of Life, 212.
[38] William James, "Is Life Worth Living? in *The Search For Meaning In Life*, ed. Robert F. Davidson (New York: Holt, Rinehart, & Winston, 1962), 240.
[39] William James, "Is Life Worth Living? 241.
[40] William James, "Is Life Worth Living? 245.
[41] Huston Smith, "The Meaning of Life in the World's Religions," in T*he Meaning of Life in the World Religions*, eds. Joseph Runzo and Nancy Martin (Oxford: Oneworld Publications, 2000), 255.
[42] John Hick, "The Religious Meaning of Life," in *The Meaning of Life in the World Religions*, eds. Joseph Runzo and Nancy M. Martin, (Oxford: Oneworld Publications, 2000), 275.
[43] John Hick, "The Religious Meaning of Life," 285-86.
[44]

http://www.guardian.co.uk/commentisfree/belief/2009/dec/08/religion-society-gregory-paul
[45] http://www.telegraph.co.uk/news/worldnews/6261469/Britain-slips-out-of-top-20-best-countries-to-live-in.html
[46] http://www.adherents.com/largecom/com_atheist.html

Chapter 3

[1] Paul Edwards, "Why?" in *The Meaning of Life*, ed. E.D Klemke (Oxford: Oxford University Press, 1981), 227-240.
[2] Edwards, "Why?" 234.
[3] A. J. Ayer, "The Claims of Philosophy," in *The Meaning of Life*, ed. E.D Klemke and Steven Cahn (Oxford: Oxford University Press, 2008), 199.
[4] Ayer, "The Claims of Philosophy," 200.
[5] Ayer, "The Claims of Philosophy," 201.
[6] Kai Nielsen, "Linguistic" Philosophy and "The Meaning of Life," in *The Meaning of Life*, ed. E.D Klemke and Steven Cahn (Oxford: Oxford University Press, 2008), 211.

[7] John Wisdom, "The Meanings of the Questions of Life," in *The Meaning of Life*, ed. E.D Klemke and Steven Cahn (Oxford: Oxford University Press, 2008), 220-222.

[8] Antony Flew, "Tolstoi and the Meaning of Life," in *The Meaning of Life*, ed. E.D Klemke (Oxford : Oxford University Press, 2000), 209-218

[9] R. W. Hepburn, "Questions about the meaning of life," in *The Meaning of Life*, ed. E.D Klemke (Oxford: Oxford University Press, 2000), 266.

[10] Hepburn, "Questions about the meaning of life," 267.

[11] Hepburn, "Questions about the meaning of life," 267.

[12] Hepburn, "Questions about the meaning of life," 268.

[13] Robert Nozick, "Philosophy and the Meaning of Life," in *The Meaning of Life*, ed. E.D Klemke and Steven Cahn (Oxford: Oxford University Press, 2008), 224.

[14] Nozick, "Philosophy and the Meaning of Life," 225.

[15] Nozick, "Philosophy and the Meaning of Life," 227.

[16] Nozick, "Philosophy and the Meaning of Life," 230.

[17] W.D. Joske, "Philosophy and the Meaning of Life," in *The Meaning of Life*, ed. E.D Klemke (Oxford: Oxford University Press, 2000), 283.

[18] Joske, "Philosophy and the Meaning of Life," 284.

[19] An activity could be intrinsically worthwhile—drinking beer—but not worthwhile considering the end to which it might lead—alcoholism. An activity could be intrinsically worthless—running in circles around a track—but worthwhile considering the end to which it leads—cardiovascular fitness. We desire an activity which is intrinsically significant and significant considering the end toward which it leads—say loving our spouse which brings happiness.

[20] Joske, "Philosophy and the Meaning of Life," 286.

[21] Joske, "Philosophy and the Meaning of Life," 293-94.

[22] Joske, "Philosophy and the Meaning of Life," 294.

[23] Oswald Hanfling, *A Quest for Meaning* (Oxford: Basil Blackwell, 1987), 214.

[24] *Tractatus Logico-Philosophicus*, 1922, trans. C.K. Ogden (London: Routledge & Kegan Paul). Originally published as "Logisch-Philosophische Abhandlung", in Annalen der Naturphilosophische, XIV (3/4), 1921.

Chapter 4

[1] Michael Allen Gillespie, *Nihilism Before Nietzsche* (Chicago: University of Chicago Press, 1996).

[2] Arthur Schopenhauer, "On the Sufferings of the World," in *The Meaning of Life*, ed. E.D Klemke (Oxford: Oxford University Press, 1981), 45.

[3] Schopenhauer, "On the Sufferings of the World," 45.

[4] Schopenhauer, "On the Sufferings of the World," 45.

[5] Schopenhauer, "On the Sufferings of the World," 46.

[6] Schopenhauer, "On the Sufferings of the World," 47.

[7] Schopenhauer, "On the Sufferings of the World," 47.

[8] Schopenhauer, "On the Sufferings of the World," 50.

[9] Schopenhauer, "On the Sufferings of the World," 52.

[10] Schopenhauer, "On the Sufferings of the World," 53.

[11] Schopenhauer, "On the Sufferings of the World," 54.

[12] Arthur Schopenhauer, "On the Vanity of Existence," in *The Meaning of Life*, ed. E.D Klemke (Oxford: Oxford University Press, 2000), 67.

[13] Schopenhauer, "On the Vanity of Existence," 67.

[14] Schopenhauer, "On the Vanity of Existence," 68.

[15] Schopenhauer, "On the Vanity of Existence," 68.

[16] Schopenhauer, "On the Vanity of Existence," 69.

[17] Schopenhauer, "On the Vanity of Existence," 69-70.

[18] Schopenhauer, "On the Vanity of Existence," 70.

[19] Albert Camus, "The Myth of Sisyphus," in *The Meaning of Life*, ed. E.D Klemke (Oxford: Oxford University Press, 1981), 72.

[20] Camus, "The Myth of Sisyphus," 73.

[21] Camus, "The Myth of Sisyphus," 74.

[22] Camus, "The Myth of Sisyphus," 75.

[23] Camus, "The Myth of Sisyphus," 75.

[24] Camus, "The Myth of Sisyphus," 75.

[25] Camus, "The Myth of Sisyphus," 76-77.

[26] Camus, "The Myth of Sisyphus," 77.

[27] Camus, "The Myth of Sisyphus," 79.

[28] Camus, "The Myth of Sisyphus," 81.

[29] Thomas Nagel, "The Absurd," in *The Meaning of Life*, ed. E.D Klemke and Steven Cahn (Oxford: Oxford University Press, 2008)143.

[30] Nagel, "The Absurd," 144.

[31] Nagel, "The Absurd," 145.

[32] Nagel, "The Absurd," 146.

[33] Nagel, "The Absurd," 147.

[34] Nagel, "The Absurd," 147.

[35] Nagel, "The Absurd," 150.

[36] Nagel, "The Absurd," 151.

[37] Nagel, "The Absurd," 152.

38 Jonathan Westphal and Christopher Cherry, "Is Life Absurd?" Philosophy 65 (Cambridge: Cambridge University Press, 1990), 199-203.
39 Walter Stace, "Man Against Darkness," in *The Meaning of Life*, ed. E.D Klemke (Oxford: Oxford University Press, 2000) 86.
40 Stace, "Man Against Darkness," 86.
41 Stace, "Man Against Darkness," 87.
42 Stace, "Man Against Darkness," 90.
43 Stace, "Man Against Darkness," 91.
44 Stace, "Man Against Darkness," 92.
45 Stace, "Man Against Darkness," 92.
46 Stace, "Man Against Darkness," 93.
47 Joel Feinberg, "Absurd Self-Fulfillment," in *The Meaning of Life*, ed. E.D Klemke and Steven Cahn (Oxford: Oxford University Press, 2008), 164.
48 Feinberg, "Absurd Self-Fulfillment," 165.
49 Feinberg, "Absurd Self-Fulfillment," 175.
50 Feinberg, "Absurd Self-Fulfillment," 178.
51 Feinberg, "Absurd Self-Fulfillment," 179.
52 Feinberg, "Absurd Self-Fulfillment," 181.
53 Simon Critchley, *Very Little ... Almost Nothing* (New York: Routledge, 2004), 12-13.
54 Critchley, Very Little ... Almost Nothing, 31.
55 Critchley, Very Little ... Almost Nothing, 32.
56 Critchley, Very Little ... Almost Nothing, 32.
57 Critchley, Very Little ... Almost Nothing, 32.
58 Critchley, Very Little ... Almost Nothing, 118.
59 Thornton Wilder, *Our Town* (New York: Coward-McCann, Inc., 1938), 82.
60 Milan Kundera, *The Unbearable Lightness of Being* (New York: Harper Perennial Modern Classics, 1999), 3.
61 Milan Kundera, The Unbearable Lightness of Being, 5.
62 Milan Kundera, The Unbearable Lightness of Being, 5.

Chapter 5

1 Kurt Baier, "The Meaning of Life," in *The Meaning of Life*, ed. E. D. Klemke and Steven Cahn (Oxford University Press 2008), 83.
2 Baier, "The Meaning of Life," 110.
3 Baier, "The Meaning of Life," 101-102.
4 Baier, "The Meaning of Life," 103.
5 Baier, "The Meaning of Life," 109.

[6] Paul Edwards, "The Meaning and Value of Life," in *The Meaning of Life*, ed. E. D. Klemke and Steven Cahn (Oxford University Press 2008), 115.

[7] Edwards, "The Meaning and Value of Life," 117.

[8] Edwards, "The Meaning and Value of Life," 117.

[9] Edwards, "The Meaning and Value of Life," 117.

[10] Edwards, "The Meaning and Value of Life," 117.

[11] Edwards, "The Meaning and Value of Life," 118.

[12] Edwards, "The Meaning and Value of Life," 128.

[13] Edwards, "The Meaning and Value of Life," 130.

[14] Edwards, "The Meaning and Value of Life," 133.

[15] Kai Nielsen, "Death and the Meaning of Life," in *The Meaning of Life* ed. E.D. Klemke (Oxford University Press, 2000), 154.

[16] Nielsen, "Death and the Meaning of Life," 155.

[17] Nielsen, "Death and the Meaning of Life," 156.

[18] Nielsen, "Death and the Meaning of Life," 157.

[19] Nielsen, "Death and the Meaning of Life," 158.

[20] Hazel Barnes, "The Far Side of Despair," in *The Meaning of Life*, ed. E.D. Klemke (Oxford University Press, 2000), 162.

[21] Barnes, "The Far Side of Despair," 162.

[22] Barnes, "The Far Side of Despair," 162.

[23] Barnes, "The Far Side of Despair," 162.

[24] Barnes, "The Far Side of Despair," 165.

[25] Barnes, "The Far Side of Despair," 165.

[26] Barnes, "The Far Side of Despair," 166.

[27] Raymond Martin, "The Meaning of Life," in *Questioning Matters*, ed. Daniel Kolak (Belmont, CA: Mayfield Press, 2000), 711.

[28] Martin, "The Meaning of Life," 712.

[29] Martin, "The Meaning of Life," 714.

[30] Martin, "The Meaning of Life," 714.

[31] John Kekes, "The Meaning of Life," in *The Meaning of Life*, ed. E. D. Klemke and Steven Cahn (Oxford University Press, 2008), 239.

[32] Kekes, "The Meaning of Life," 239.

[33] Kekes, "The Meaning of Life," 241.

[34] Kekes, "The Meaning of Life," 244.

[35] Kekes, "The Meaning of Life," 250.

[36] Kekes, "The Meaning of Life," 250.

[37] David Schmidt, "The Meanings of Life" in *Life, death, and meaning*, ed. David Benatar (Lanham, MD: Rowman & Littlefield, 2004), 92.

[38] Robert Solomon, *The Big Questions* (Belmont, CA: Wadsworth, 2010), 44.

[39] David Lund, Making Sense Of It All: An Introduction to Philosophical Inquiry (Upper Saddle River, NJ: Prentice-Hall, 2003), 195.

[40] Lund, Making Sense Of It All: An Introduction to Philosophical Inquiry, 198.

[41] Lund, Making Sense Of It All: An Introduction to Philosophical Inquiry, 203.

[42] Lund, Making Sense Of It All: An Introduction to Philosophical Inquiry, 204.

[43] Lund, Making Sense Of It All: An Introduction to Philosophical Inquiry, 204.

[44] Julian Baggini, *What's It All About: Philosophy & The Meaning of Life* (Oxford: Oxford University Press, 2004), 174.

[45] Baggini, What's It All About: Philosophy & The Meaning of Life, 177-78.

[46] Baggini, What's It All About: Philosophy & The Meaning of Life, 184.

[47] Baggini, What's It All About: Philosophy & The Meaning of Life, 184.

[48] Baggini, What's It All About: Philosophy & The Meaning of Life, 188.

[49] Bertrand Russell, "A Free Man's Worship," in *The Meaning of Life*, ed. E.D Klemke and Steven Cahn (Oxford: Oxford University Press, 2008), 56.

[50] Russell, "A Free Man's Worship," 59.

[51] Russell, "A Free Man's Worship," 60.

[52] Russell, "A Free Man's Worship," 61.

[53] Richard Taylor, "The Meaning of Life," in *The Meaning of Life*, ed. E.D Klemke and Steven Cahn (Oxford: Oxford University Press, 2008), 136.

[54] Taylor, "The Meaning of Life," 136.

[55] Taylor, "The Meaning of Life," 139.

[56] Taylor, "The Meaning of Life," 140.

[57] Taylor, "The Meaning of Life," 141

[58] Taylor, "The Meaning of Life," 141

[59] Taylor, "The Meaning of Life," 141.

[60] Taylor, "The Meaning of Life," 141.

[61] Taylor, "The Meaning of Life," 142

[62] Taylor, "The Meaning of Life," 142

[63] R. M. Hare, "Nothing Matters," in *The Meaning of Life*, ed. E.D Klemke (Oxford: Oxford University Press, 2000), 43.

[64] Hare, "Nothing Matters," 45.

[65] Hare, "Nothing Matters," 47.

[66] Irving Singer, *Meaning in Life: The Creation of Value* (New York: Free Press, 1992), 73.

[67] Singer, Meaning in Life: The Creation of Value, 133.

[68] George Bernard Shaw, Man and Superman, 1903.

[69] Singer, Meaning in Life: The Creation of Value, 148.

[70] E. D. Klemke, "Living Without Appeal: An Affirmative Philosophy of Life," in *The Meaning of Life*, ed. E.D Klemke and Steven Cahn (Oxford: Oxford University Press, 2008), 184-195.

[71] Klemke, "Living Without Appeal: An Affirmative Philosophy of Life," 185.

[72] Klemke, "Living Without Appeal: An Affirmative Philosophy of Life," 185.

[73] Klemke, "Living Without Appeal: An Affirmative Philosophy of Life," 192

[74] Klemke, "Living Without Appeal: An Affirmative Philosophy of Life," 193.

[75] Klemke, "Living Without Appeal: An Affirmative Philosophy of Life," 193-4.

[76] Klemke, "Living Without Appeal: An Affirmative Philosophy of Life," 194.

[77] Klemke, "Living Without Appeal: An Affirmative Philosophy of Life," 194

Chapter 6

[1] Joseph Ellin, *Morality and the Meaning of Life* (New York: Harcourt Brace & Company, 1995), 325.

[2] Ellin, Morality and the Meaning of Life, 327.

[3] Garrett Thomson, *On the Meaning of Life* (Belmont CA: Wadsworth, 2003), 3.

[4] Thomson, On the Meaning of Life, 4.

[5] Thomson, On the Meaning of Life, 10.

[6] Thomson, On the Meaning of Life, 157.

[7] Karl William Britton, *Philosophy and the Meaning of Life* (Cambridge: Cambridge University Press, 1969), 16.

[8] Britton, Philosophy and the Meaning of Life, 192.

[9] Terence Francis Eagleton, *The Meaning of Life* (Oxford: Oxford University Press, 2007), 45.

[10] Eagleton, *The Meaning of Life*, 76-77.

[11] Eagleton, The Meaning of Life, 124.

[12] Eagleton, The Meaning of Life, 164.

[13] Eagleton, The Meaning of Life, 168.

[14] Eagleton, The Meaning of Life, 168.

[15] Mortiz Schlick, "On the Meaning of Life" in *The Meaning of Life*, ed. E.D. Klemke and Cahn (Oxford: Oxford University Press, 2008), 62.

[16] Mortiz Schlick, "On the Meaning of Life," 71.

[17] Susan Wolf, "Meaning in Life" in *The Meaning of Life*, ed. E.D. Klemke and Cahn (Oxford: Oxford University Press 2008), 232.

[18] Wolf, "Meaning in Life," 233.

[19] Wolf, "Meaning in Life" 234-35.

[20] Steven Cahn, "Meaningless Lives?" in *The Meaning of Life*, ed. E.D. Klemke and Cahn (Oxford: Oxford University Press 2008), 236.

[21] James Rachels, *Problems from Philosophy*, 3rd ed. (New York: McGraw-Hill, 2012), 169.

[22] Rachels, Problems from Philosophy, 174-75.

[23] Owen Flanagan, "What Makes Life Worth Living?" in *The Meaning of Life*, ed. E.D. Klemke (Oxford: Oxford University Press 2000), 198.

[24] Flanagan, "What Makes Life Worth Living?" 198.

[25] Flanagan, "What Makes Life Worth Living?" 199.

[26] Flanagan, "What Makes Life Worth Living?" 200.

[27] Flanagan, "What Makes Life Worth Living?" 206.

[28] Christopher Belshaw, *10 good questions about life and death* (Oxford: Blackwell, 2005), 128.

[29] Raymond Belliotti, What is the Meaning of Human Life? (Amsterdam: Rodopi, 2001), 29.

[30] Paul Thagard, *The Brain and the Meaning of* Life (Princeton: Princeton University Press, 2010), 165.

[31] Thaddeus Metz, "The Good, the True and the Beautiful: Toward a Unified Account of Great Meaning in Life." DOI: 10.1017/S0034412510000569. 1. Cambridge Online 2010, 1.

[32] Metz, "The Good, the True and the Beautiful: Toward a Unified Account of Great Meaning in Life." 2.

[33] Metz, "The Good, the True and the Beautiful: Toward a Unified Account of Great Meaning in Life." 3.

[34] Metz, "The Good, the True and the Beautiful: Toward a Unified Account of Great Meaning in Life." 13.

[35] Metz, "The Good, the True and the Beautiful: Toward a Unified Account of Great Meaning in Life." 19.

Chapter 7

[1] Leo Tolstoy, *The Death of Ivan Ilyich* (New York: Bantam Books, 1981), 37.

[2] Tolstoy, *The Death of Ivan Ilyich*, Chapter XI.

[3] Soren Kierkegaard, "Balance between Esthetic and Ethical," in *Either/Or*, vol. II, Walter Lowrie, trans., (Princeton, NJ: Princeton University Press, 1944).

[4] John Martin Fischer, ed., *The Metaphysics of Death* (Stanford: Stanford University Press, 1993), 15.

[5] Charles Neider, ed., *The Autobiography of Mark Twain* (New York: Perennial, 1990) ch. 49.

[6] Vincent Barry, *Philosophical Thinking About Death and Dying* (Belmont CA.: Thomson Wadsworth, 2007), 250.

[7] Stephen Rosenbaum, "How to Be Dead and Not Care: A Defense of Epicurus," American Philosophical Quarterly 23 no. 2 (April 1986).

[8] Oswald Hanfling, *The Quest for Meaning* (Oxford: Basil Blackwell, 1987), 63.

[9] Hanfling, The Quest for Meaning, 84.

[10] George Pitcher, "The Misfortunes of the Dead," *in Life, death, and meaning*, ed. David Benatar (Lanham MD.: Rowman & Littlefield, 2004), 192.

[11] Pitcher, "The Misfortunes of the Dead," 196.

[12] Pitcher, "The Misfortunes of the Dead," 197.

[13] Steven Luper, "Annihilation," The Philosophical Quarterly 37 (1985): 233-252.

[14] David Benatar, "Why It Is Better Never to Come into Existence" *in Life, death, and meaning*, ed. David Benatar (Lanham, Md.: Rowman and Littlefield, 2004), 155.

[15] Benatar, "Why It Is Better Never to Come into Existence," 167.

[16] John Leslie, "Why Not Let Life Become Extinct?" (1983) in *Life, death, and meaning*, ed. David Benatar (Lanham, MD.: Rowman & Littlefield, 2004), 128.

[17] Leslie, "Why Not Let Life Become Extinct?" 130.

[18] James Lenman, "Immortality: A Letter," Cogito 9 (1995): 169.

[19] Nick Bostrom, "The Fable of the Dragon-Tyrant," Journal of Medical Ethics (2005) Vol. 31, No. 5: 273.

[20] Bostrom, "The Fable of the Dragon-Tyrant," 277.

[21] Michaelis Michael & Peter Caldwell, "The Consolations of Optimism," (2004) *in Life, death, and meaning*, ed. David Benatar, (Lanham MD.: Rowman & Littlefield, 2004), 383.

[22] Michael & Caldwell, "The Consolations of Optimism," 386.

[23] Michael & Caldwell, "The Consolations of Optimism," 389.

[24] Michael & Caldwell, "The Consolations of Optimism," 390.

[25] William James, *Pragmatism and Other Writings* (New York: Penguin, 2000), x.

Chapter 8

[1] Aubrey de Grey, Ending Aging: The Rejuvenation Breakthroughs that Could Reverse Human Aging in Our Lifetime (New York: St. Martin's Press, 2007).
[2] Nick Bostrom, "The Simulation Argument," Philosophical Quarterly, 2003, Vol. 53, No. 211, pp. 243-255.
[3] Rodney Brooks, Flesh and Machines: How Robots Will Change Us (New York: Vintage, 2003).
[4] Ray Kurzweil, *The Age of Spiritual Machines* (New York: Penguin, 1999), 101-102
[5] Kurzweil, The Age of Spiritual Machines, 129.
[6] Kurzweil, The Age of Spiritual Machines, 141.
[7] Kurzweil, The Age of Spiritual Machines, 260.
[8] John Searle, "I Married A Computer," review of *The Age of Spiritual Machines*, by Ray Kurzweil, New York Review of Books, April 8, 1999.
[9] Daniel Dennett, *Darwin's Dangerous Idea: Evolution And The Meaning of Life* (New York: Simon & Schuster, 1995), 422-26.
[10] Hans Moravec, *Robot: Mere Machine to Transcendent Mind* (New York: Oxford University Press, 2000), 126.
[11] Moravec, Robot: Mere Machine to Transcendent, 131.
[12] Moravec, Robot: Mere Machine to Transcendent, 145.
[13] Moravec, Robot: Mere Machine to Transcendent, 162.
[14] Moravec, Robot: Mere Machine to Transcendent, 164.
[15] Moravec, Robot: Mere Machine to Transcendent, 164.
[16] Moravec, Robot: Mere Machine to Transcendent, 165.
[17] Moravec, Robot: Mere Machine to Transcendent, 167
[18] Charles T. Rubin, "Artificial Intelligence and Human Nature," The New Atlantis, No. 1, spring 2003.
[19] Marshall Brain, "The Day You Discard Your Body," http://marshallbrain.com/discard1.htm
[20] Michio Kaku, Visions: How Science Will Revolutionize the 21st Century (New York: Anchor, 1998).
[21] Jaron Lanier, "One Half A Manifesto," http://www.edge.org/3rd_culture/lanier/lanier_index.html
[22] Gregory Paul and Earl Cox, *Beyond Humanity: CyberEvolution and Future Minds* (Rockland, MA.: Charles River Media, 1996), 415.
[23] Bill Joy, "Why The Future Doesn't Need Us," Wired Magazine, April 2000.

[24] John G. Messerly, "I'm glad the future doesn't need us: a Critique of Joy's Pessimistic Futurism." ACM SIGCAS Computers and Society, Volume 33, Issue 2, (June 2003)
[25] Walt Whitman, "Song of Myself" in Leaves of Grass.
[26] Leon Kass, Life, Liberty, and the Defense of Dignity: The Challenge for Bioethics (San Francisco: Encounter Books, 2002).
[27] Francis Fukuyama, "Transhumanism," Foreign Policy (September-October 2004).
[28] Bill McKibbon, *Enough: Staying Human in an Engineered Age* (New York: Henry Hold & Company, 2003), 227.
[29] http://humanityplus.org/learn/transhumanist-faq/#answer_20
[30] http://humanityplus.org/learn/transhumanist-faq/#answer_40
[31] Charles Sanders Pierce, "The Fixation of Belief," Popular Science Monthly, 12, (November 1877).

Chapter 9

[1] Thaddeus Metz, The Stanford Encyclopedia of Philosophy, http://plato.stanford.edu/entries/life-meaning/
[2] Timothy Shanahan, "Evolutionary Progress from Darwin to Dawkins," http://biophilosophy.ca/Teaching/6740papers/shanahan.pdf
[3] Charles Darwin, On the Origin of Species by Means of Natural Se lection, or, the Preservation of Favoured races in the Struggle for Life (New York: Cosimo, Inc., 2007), 211.
[4] Barrett, P., Gautrey, P., Herbert, S., Kohn, D., and Smith, S., *Charles Darwin's Notebooks, 1836-1844* (Ithaca: Cornell University Press, 1987).
[5] Will Durant, "Ten Steps Up From the Jungle," The Rotarian, January 1941, 10.
[6] Durant, 56.
[7] For more see John G. Messerly, *Piaget's Conception of Evolution* (Lanham Md.: Rowman & Littlefield, 1996).
[8] Robert Wright, *Non-Zero: The Logic of Human Destiny* (New York: Vintage, 2001), 331
[9] http://www.slate.com/articles/arts/the_book_club/features/2000/nonzero/_2.html
[10] Steve Stewart-Williams, Darwin, God and the Meaning of Life: How Evolutionary Theory Undermines Everything You Thought You Knew (Cambridge: Cambridge University Press, 2010), 194.
[11] Stewart-Williams, Darwin, God and the Meaning of Life: How Evolutionary Theory Undermines Everything You Thought You Knew, 197.

[12] John Stewart, "The Meaning of Life In A Developing Universe," http://www.evolutionarymanifesto.com/meaning.pdf., 14.

[13] Teilhard de Chardin, Pierre, *The Phenomenon of Man* (New York: Harper Collins, 1975), 219.

[14] Teilhard de Chardin, *The Phenomenon of Man.* 227.

[15] Teilhard de Chardin, *The Phenomenon of Man*, 229.

[16] Teilhard de Chardin, *The Phenomenon of Man,* 231.

[17] Teilhard de Chardin, *The Phenomenon of Man*, 265.

[18] Jacques Monod, Chance and Necessity: An Essay on the Natural Philosophy of Modern Biology (New York: Vintage, 1972), 112.

[19] Monod, Chance and Necessity: An Essay on the Natural Philosophy of Modern Biology, 145.

[20] Monod, Chance and Necessity: An Essay on the Natural Philosophy of Modern Biology, 167.

[21] Monod, Chance and Necessity: An Essay on the Natural Philosophy of Modern Biology, 169.

[22] Monod, Chance and Necessity: An Essay on the Natural Philosophy of Modern Biology, 180.

[23] Julian Huxley, "The Creed of a Scientific Humanist" in *The Meaning of Life*, ed. E.D. Klemke (Oxford: Oxford University Press 2000, 81.

[24] Julian Huxley, *Religion without Revelation*, (London: Max Parrish, 1959), 236.

[25] Julian Huxley, New Bottles for New Wine (New York: Harper & Brothers, 1957), 13-14.

[26] Huxley, Religion without Revelation, 293.

[27] Huxley, Religion without Revelation, 304.

[28] Huxley, Religion without Revelation, 310-11.

[29] Edward O. Wilson, *On Human Nature* (Cambridge: Harvard University Press, 1979) 169.

[30] Wilson, *On Human Nature,* 170-71.

[31] Wilson, *On Human Nature*, 175.

[32] Wilson, *On Human Nature*, 192.

[33] Wilson, On Human Nature, 2.

[34] Wilson, *On Human Nature* 4-5.

[35] Wilson, *On Human Nature*, 201.

[36] Wilson, *On Human Nature*, 201.

[37] Wilson, On Human Nature, 209.

[38] Ludwig Wittgenstein, *Tractatus Logico-Philosophicus*, trans. D.F. Pears and B.F. McGuiness (London: Routledge & Paul Kegan, 1961), 25.

[39] Paul Davies, The Mind of God: The Scientific Basis for a Rational World (New York: Simon & Schuster, 1993), 232.

[40] Simon Conway Morris, *Life's Solution: Inevitable Humans in a Lonely* Universe (Cambridge: Cambridge University Press, 2003).
[41] Had the course of the asteroid 2005 YU55 that passed the earth on November 8, 2011 been slightly altered, millions might have died and this book not finished.
[42] Julian Huxley, 'Evolution: At the Mind's Cinema' (1922), in *The Captive Shrew and Other Poems of a Biologist* (London: Basil Blackwell, 1932), 55.

Chapter 10

[1] James Christian, *Philosophy: An Introduction to the Art of Wondering*, 11th ed. (Belmont CA.: Wadsworth, 2012), 653
[2] Christian, Philosophy: An Introduction to the Art of Wondering, 656.
[3] Christian, Philosophy: An Introduction to the Art of Wondering, 656.
[4] Nikos Kazantzakis, *Report to Greco* (New York: Touchstone, 1975), 23
[5] Will Durant, *On the meaning of life* (New York: Ray Long & Richard R. Smith, 1932), 52.
[6] Durant, On the meaning of life, 56.
[7] Albert Camus, *The Myth of Sisyphus and Other Essays* (New York: Alfred A. Knopf, 1955), 151.
[8] Will Durant, *The Mansions of Philosophy: A Survey of Human Life and* Destiny (New York: Simon and Schuster, 1929) 397
[9] Durant, The Mansions of Philosophy: A Survey of Human Life and Destiny, 407.
[10] Durant, The Mansions of Philosophy: A Survey of Human Life and Destiny, 407-08.
[11] Durant, On the meaning of life, 124-25.
[12] Durant, On the meaning of life, 125-26.
[13] Durant, On the meaning of life, 126-28.
[14] Durant, On the meaning of life, 129.
[15] Durant, On the meaning of life, 130.
[16] http://www.independent.co.uk/life-style/the-last-testament-of-bertrand-russell-published-for-the-first-time-his-final-word-on-the-state-of-the-world-and-his-own-achievements-and-failures-introduced-by-ray-monk-1506341.html

21494284R00199

Made in the USA
Middletown, DE
01 July 2015